JEWISH DOCTORS MEET THE GREAT PHYSICIAN

Ruth Rosen, Editor

Published by

Purple Pomegranate Productions
San Francisco, California

Cover Design and Illustration by Paige Saunders

Cover surgery image ©1995 PhotoDisc, Inc.
(Original image has been modified.)

First Edition. First Printing.
Revised 1998 Second Edition. Second Printing.

01 00 10 9 8 7 6 5 4 3 2

Rosen, Ruth 1956-
Jewish Doctors Meet the Great Physician/Ruth Rosen, Editor—
Rev. 2nd ed.

Library of Congress Cataloging-Publication Data
Jewish Doctors Meet the Great Physician

ISBN: 1-881022-36-6 (pbk.)
1. Jewish Christians—Religious life. 2. Christian life.

To Moishe Rosen
With love and appreciation for
everything, but most of all, for his
dedication to the Great Physician.
Thanks, Dad.

Contents

Part One

Jewish Doctors Who Prescribe Y'shua

JACK J. STERNBERG

If the condition spread to my left eye, I would be blind. My medical career would be over, and life as I knew it would cease. I was afraid—afraid and angry. I cursed God, figuring if he existed, he deserved it. I informed him—or was it the air?—that I would never believe in him until I understood his ways. "Who are you? What are you like? Why are you doing this when so many people you have allowed to have cancer depend on me? You must not exist!"

I never imagined that God would answer my angry questions. But then, I didn't realize that in my anger, I had actually uttered a prayer.

My parents were not "religious" although my mother spoke to God spontaneously, even personally. She spoke as though he heard regardless of where she was or whether she prayed from the *siddur* (prayer book). My father did not appear to believe in God and had little patience for religious institutions. In fact, he told me how much he disliked going to synagogue services when he was a boy.

Nevertheless, when the High Holy Days came around, we donned new suits and ties, put on new shoes and walked the mile or so to the local Conservative synagogue. We didn't go because we were religious; we went because we were Jews. Those September days in New York City were sunny and hot, and the new shoes pinched. I particularly remember the Yom Kippur services—by the time we arrived, my stomach was growling from the fast. I told myself that when I grew up, I would not suffer through these rituals.

My favorite tradition was our weekly family get-togethers. Every Sunday we gathered at a restaurant with the aunts, uncles and cousins from my mother's family. We'd spend the afternoon together and enjoy a big meal—usually Chinese, though occasionally it was Italian. I remember the laughter and how we loved being together, everyone telling the same stories over and over.

Regarding my Jewish identity, a couple of things happened when I was nine. I saw *The Ten Commandments,* starring Charlton Heston. Suddenly, I was impressed with my heritage. Moses was one of our guys, and he had an amazing relationship with God. I thought I'd try going to the synagogue to see what it was all about. However, as with the High Holy Days, most of the service was in Hebrew, and I could not understand what was said and done. That spark of excitement about God quickly died.

About that time my parents attempted to enroll me in Hebrew school. To their dismay, they could not afford the *bar mitzvah* training. We had been members of a congregation for three years. Yet when my parents disclosed their financial situation, all they received was a suggestion to defer my lessons until such time as they could pay. Incensed, my parents never sent me back to that synagogue, nor did we ever attend holiday services there again.

Religious or not, when I was twelve I began anticipating my bar mitzvah. My father's business was doing better, and my parents hired a tutor to help me memorize and learn to sing my *Haf Torah* portion. He arranged for me to be bar mitzvah at a Conservative synagogue that I had never been to before nor have I attended since. I did not know the rabbi. I could not translate Hebrew to English. But I knew how to pronounce the words well enough to sing in Hebrew for some forty minutes. Other than the cracking of my puberty-stricken voice, I sounded good. And because I sounded good, everyone congratulated me and told me how proud I'd made them.

I did not know how to respond to all the admiration that was heaped on me that day. I'd felt my performance was hollow. Didn't anyone care that I did not know the meaning of the words or the importance of the book from which I'd read? I didn't understand why people were proud of me. Yet I understood that I was Jewish, and I was proud of that.

As a teen, I began to question the existence of God. It wasn't a pressing question; it's just that I hadn't seen much (in my young estimation) to indicate he was real. When I was sixteen, my uncle was quite ill, and I asked God to let him live. Soon after, my uncle died. It struck me that the only time I spoke to God was to ask for something. I was embarrassed by my selfishness, but I didn't know how else to regard God. I didn't know who God was or even if God was. I reasoned that it was hypocritical to continue petitioning him and silly to expect an answer. So at the age of sixteen, I stopped communicating with a God I didn't know or trust.

I was seventeen when I left NYC to be a pre-med student at the State University of New York at Buffalo. I'd wanted to be a dentist from as early as I can remember and was accepted into dental school when I was a college junior. Yet when the door opened, I changed my mind.

Somewhere along the line, I decided what I really wanted was to save lives. To me, that meant being a doctor. I got work as a hospital orderly to make sure that I really wanted to enter the field—and I was hooked.

I lived in Buffalo for eight years. During college and medical school, I more or less floated in a sea of agnosticism. The more I saw, the less I believed in God. The question of suffering—specifically, why bad things happen to good people—distressed me. According to Reform Judaism, death (I was told) ended our existence. There was no heaven, no hell, no judgment. I began to wonder about the meaning of life in general, but I especially wondered why it was supposed to be such a blessing to be born Jewish. What could it mean if nothing awaited us beyond the pain and persecution we endured simply for being Jews?

"Religious" answers made no sense to me. Rabbis exhorted me to be proud of being Jewish but never gave concrete reasons or explanations of what that meant. I was told that we suffered persecution because the *goyim* (non-Jews) were jealous of us. They were jealous because we tended to strive more and achieve more, and (the rabbis hinted) we had higher standards. I found these answers unacceptable and flatly rejected the Jewish religion. Paradoxically, I was still proud to be a Jew and clung to my Jewish identity in a cultural sense.

After graduating from medical school, I went to Cleveland, Ohio for three years and completed my internship, residency and chief residency at Mt. Sinai Hospital. I also met and married Marilyn Meckler. Marilyn, also Jewish, was like me—we had similar values but were not religious.

Following my chief residency we moved to Houston, Texas,

where I did my medical oncology fellowship at M. D. Anderson Cancer Center. The two years in Houston affected me radically. I had seen enough suffering to wonder about God before, but specializing in cancer was even more intense. The hospital where I worked had 300 beds—every one of them occupied by a cancer patient.

At one point I decided to empty myself of as much emotion as possible—both professionally and personally. I joked about emulating Spock, a fictional character from the old Star Trek television series. Like him, I exalted logic and deemed emotions a hindrance to clear thinking. I resented feelings as an impediment to my ability to cope. I thought if I could feel only when and what I chose to feel, I would attain a sense of calmness—and control.

Ridiculous as that might sound, you must understand what was happening. The same skills that enabled me to help save lives forced me to watch other lives slip away. The work that enabled me to provide so well for my family was a constant reminder of those patients and families for whom I could do nothing. I did not want to be at the mercy of those painful feelings. I longed to feel in control—even if it was just an illusion.

I saw an opportunity to switch gears, to go into private practice, and I seized it. Soon after I gave notice at the hospital, the new job fell through. Before I even had a moment to despair, I ran into a doctor from Little Rock, Arkansas. He informed me that Little Rock needed a cancer specialist. Would I consider the move? After a quick trip to check things out, Marilyn and I decided that we would make Little Rock our home.

We decided we would take advantage of the move to purchase the kind of home we'd dreamed of having. It was little more than a skeleton of two-by-fours when we first saw it, but it was on a beautiful lot with more than seventy-five trees. We quickly bought the house and made changes to suit our taste (150 in all). When the house was done, it truly was our dream home. We would soon have a swimming pool in the backyard and two new cars in the garage. Our marriage was good, and we had two beautiful children—a girl and a boy.

Marilyn and I had our concerns about how we would fare in a city that probably only had 1,200 Jews at most. The answer turned out to be, "very well." We soon felt accepted and appreciated in our social circle. Our "success story" seemed complete. All the hard work had paid off, and we were as happy as any couple we knew. So why did we keep asking each other, "Is this all there is?" We could not explain why we were not completely happy, nor could we imagine what could possibly be missing. We only knew we would be forever restless without it, whatever "it" was.

We understood that material things alone would not satisfy us, so we involved ourselves in the social life of the medical community. We joined the Little Rock Medical Society and found friends who felt as we did: that despite every appearance of success, something was missing. For lack of a better word, we called it happiness. Our friends seemed to feel that they would "get happy" by having more fun. They invited us to join them drinking, disco dancing, and in pursuit of "kicks."

Marilyn and I (always eager to do well at whatever we tried!) took dancing lessons and jumped right into the world of disco along with its associated night life. Several months later we tired of the distraction—for that's all it was—and felt emptier than ever.

That's when it occurred to us to "try something spiritual." We decided to get back to our Jewish roots, reasoning that we might be missing a sense of identity, of belonging to our own people. Marilyn threw herself into volunteer work with the Jewish community, the preschool, the day school—wherever she was needed. She was very active in *Hadassah* (a Jewish women's organization).

We joined the Reform temple, but the plethora of organizations and activities had us bouncing back and forth between the Reform and the Conservative synagogue. There was the men's Sunday brunch, Hadassah, Ati Day Y'Isroel preschools, and many other activities.

These organizations were very cause oriented and seemed to do a lot of good, but frankly, I found they left me empty and unsatisfied. It bothered me that people I met considered themselves good Jews because of what they did. Somehow, I knew (and I don't know how I knew) that a good Jew ought to be defined by a relationship with the God of Judaism rather than a position in the Jewish community. It was certainly admirable to do good deeds. But one could do good deeds, *tzedacka,* without even believing in God.

Most of the activities fell to my wife as I was busy building the practice. Nevertheless, I attended all the fund-raising events, and Marilyn prevailed upon me to attend services at least twice a year. These were no more meaningful to me as an adult than they had been in my childhood. Marilyn had to nudge me occasionally, as I tended to fall asleep. To my annoyance, the only thing our rabbi communicated to me outside of the pulpit was how much I owed for either the building fund or monthly dues. This irritated me to the point that I eventually wrote a letter to the rabbi stating, "We hereby drop our temple membership because it has not met our spiritual needs."

In fairness to that rabbi, I did not really understand my own complaint. I did not know what my needs were, much less what he could or couldn't do about them. Frankly, he could not have made Jewish traditions meaningful to me because I felt hypocritical practicing the religion. I didn't know who or what God was—and could not even say with certainty that he existed. I don't know what kind of spiritual benefit I expected to receive when I doubted the very source of all things spiritual. My doubt occasionally gave way to resentment; that is, I couldn't say whether God existed, but if he did, I was angry with him.

I had seen too much pain, suffering and death. I felt elated over each life we helped save, but that elation quickly gave way to depression as I watched other patients suffer and die. I could do nothing to save them, and I had no comfort or hope to offer. I often worked twelve to fourteen hours a day, seven days a week. I was forever making life-changing decisions. Exhausted and drained, I was furious with God for allowing cancer to inflict so much pain, suffering and death.

I was about to take my subspecialty boards in medical oncology when I developed pain behind my right eye. I thought it was sinusitis and treated myself accordingly. Four days after the boards, I was walking down a hospital corridor when I realized the vision in my right eye was blurred. It turned out to be optic neuritis. I lost most of the vision in my right eye overnight. The pain persisted for months.

If the condition spread to my left eye, I would be blind. My medical career would be over, and life as I knew it would cease. I was afraid—afraid and angry. I cursed God, figuring if he existed, he deserved it. I informed him—or was it the air?—that I would never believe in him until I understood his ways. "Who are you? What are you like? Why are you doing this when so many people you have allowed to have cancer depend on me? You must not exist!"

I never imagined that God would answer my angry questions. But then, I didn't realize that in my anger I had actually uttered a prayer: Who are you?

Life and health stabilized. I did not regain the vision in my right eye, but my left eye remained sound.

As I continued my practice, several patients tried to tell me about Jesus Christ. I simply explained that I was Jewish and that Jews do not believe in Jesus. Most reluctantly accepted that as the end of the conversation. If they didn't, my immediate reaction was to take offense. I found that quite effective because most Christians seemed to think it was a sin to offend. However, in a few special cases, I felt I had to take out the hard artillery.

I once asked a well-meaning, persistent patient, "Let's see if I understand Christianity. Do you Christians believe that Jesus is the Son of God, and he is the Jewish Messiah?" The person replied in the affirmative and I continued, "Then if he was the Son of God, or God himself, and if he was the Jewish Messiah, why didn't he simply get off the cross and bring in the messianic Kingdom?" That person was unable to answer me. She was not accustomed to having to explain her faith—especially to someone whose tone was as hostile as mine.

The head nurse of the oncology unit in one of my major hospitals was also a Christian. I later learned that she had specifically taken that job because she felt that God wanted her to tell me, a Jew, about Jesus. I was surrounded!

I knew how to stop a conversation, and I intimidated more than one person into silence. No one knew it was just bluster. I didn't know anything about Jesus except that I wasn't supposed to believe in him. But although I could stop a conversation, I could not stop the love others had for Jesus. And that love seemed somehow to extend to me. I could see that their hearts were pure and that they wished only the best for me, no matter how I rejected their overtures. I couldn't ignore that love. Nor could I ignore the difference in the way that my Jesus-believing patients handled life's tragedies.

One woman with terminal breast cancer was in her early thirties—with a husband and a young child whom she would soon leave widowed and motherless. Yet she seemed more concerned about my spiritual welfare—in my knowing Jesus Christ—than the fact that she was dying. She saw my lostness, my separation from God as a greater tragedy than her own illness. She trusted this Jesus, then and for eternity. God had allowed illnesses to ravage her, yet she still loved, worshiped and followed him. She seemed confident about her future and genuinely concerned about mine. That overwhelmed me.

When she and others tried to tell me about Jesus, I told myself their beliefs were ridiculous. Yet, over time, I became envious of their faith. I shrugged off those feelings as irrelevant and told myself that Jesus is not for Jews and therefore he is not for me. Case closed.

I suppose a basic belief in God had survived my years of cynicism and grief. I was disappointed that the God my mother had prayed to during my childhood did not seem real to me, yet I truly wanted to believe in God. I never looked into any other religion because I knew that if there was a God, it was the God of Israel. I was open to knowing the truth about him but never supposed it was my responsibility to seek out that truth. I didn't see how it was possible to understand God. I desperately needed answers but didn't know the right questions to ask.

My wife was going through a similar process, but I was unaware of her struggle. Who ever talked about such things? Who even knew the words to frame a discussion of holy things? It was going to take something a little closer to home to jar us into action.

One Saturday evening, our eleven-year-old, Jennifer, mentioned that her friend Allison had begun attending church with her family. I knew Allison's father. He was a physician—and he was Jewish.

I was outraged. From my perspective, the man had turned his back on Judaism. (By this time my family and I had quit the temple and all Jewish organizations—still, I considered myself a loyal Jew.) I immediately called to confront Dr. Barg. I had no difficulty finding words for this discussion. Didn't he understand that as a Jew he was obligated to resist the Christians? Didn't he see that we Jews had no business going to churches where we would be swallowed up, assimilated . . . no longer Jews? Didn't he know that when you are in the minority, every family counts? Didn't he feel any kind of responsibility to our people?

Dr. Barg kindly told me that he had found his Jewish identity and the God of Israel at this church. He said that for the first time, he was truly proud and excited to be Jewish. I was shocked but intrigued. I happened to know that when Dr. Barg married, his gentile wife went through religious training, went through the *mikvah* (ritual immersion necessary for conversion to Orthodox Judaism), became an Orthodox Jew and did her best to keep a kosher home. After all that, he had to go to church to understand what being Jewish was all about?

My curiosity outweighed my anger and I asked if we could attend church with him the following day. He gladly extended an invitation for me to meet him at Fellowship Bible Church. "You better be there," I warned him. "Don't you dare get there late, because I do not intend for us to be the only Jews in that church." I remember that Sunday morning, October 19, 1980, vividly. I remember my discomfort as I walked into the worship service. It was a new church, and they were meeting in a school gymnasium, so it didn't seem as "churchy" as I expected. Charles Barg was as good as his word, and we quickly found each other. Still, I imagined that we would somehow stand out from the crowd— that people would identify us as Jews and would know we did not belong there. As impressed as I'd been with Christians I'd met at work, I suppose deep down I suspected that church somehow made Christians dislike Jews. I was surprised that those who noticed us were delighted that we were visiting.

The service began with a baby dedication. I was startled to hear the words, "Hear O Israel, the Lord our God, the Lord is One." What was the *Sh'ma,* the holiest of Jewish prayers, doing in a Christian church? When the minister began his sermon, I was even more startled. His text was Psalm 73, which posed the question of why evil seems to triumph over good—and if it does, why bother to keep God's laws and his ways? The minister explained that a pious Jew, Asaph, was asking God why righteous people suffer while the wicked prosper.

My heart was pounding. How did he know that I wrestled with those very questions? My attention was riveted as the pastor spoke about the seeming paradox. He said that God sees everything from an eternal perspective while we see everything from an immediate, finite viewpoint. He said that those who believe God and put their faith in him will enjoy him for eternity and that knowledge enables them to trust him and to endure present hardships. Those who do not care for God may enjoy whatever they amass for themselves now but will spend eternity without God.

I walked into that church an agnostic/atheist/skeptic and left knowing that God is real, good and worthy to be loved and worshiped. I cannot explain how that happened in the course of one church service. It had to be supernatural.

It was as though a light had been switched on. I knew that God was exactly what Marilyn and I had been missing. Not religion, but God. Marilyn knew it, too. We did not want to be without him any longer, in this life or in the life to come. There was no turning back. I had to discover who God was and what I needed to do to have him in my life.

I finally knew the right questions and could only hope that the answers would not lead to Jesus. I wanted to know God and was determined to follow him no matter where he took me. It would just be so much easier if I didn't have to become a Christian. I wanted desperately to discover that the God I now sought could somehow be found in mainstream Judaism.

After church we spent the next three hours with our Jewish Christian physician friend and his wife. They told us how the Jewish Bible and the "New Testament" fit together. They suggested that if Y'shua (Jesus) fulfilled the Hebrew prophecies concerning the Messiah, then Christians are worshiping the Jewish Messiah.

The Bargs also pointed out a concept we knew nothing about: sin. The only Judaism I knew had long since stopped teaching that sin separates people from God. After all, that's what Christians believe. The Bargs showed us that throughout the Jewish Bible, God was quite intolerant when it came to sin, yet merciful to the sinners who acknowledged that they had offended God's righteousness. They showed us from Scripture how God had provided explicit ways and means to cleanse our people from sin.

Separation from God caused a malignant sickness of the soul and the God-given means of atonement alone could reconcile us to God and make us whole. Judaism had survived the loss of the Temple by evolving into a basically humanistic religion. The emphasis on good deeds was noble, but not a solution to our separation from God. The Bargs believed that the Jewish Bible pointed beyond the sacrificial system to one who would personify God's plan of atonement. They believed that Jesus was that one.

The logic and scriptural basis of Dr. Barg's presentation astounded us. Marilyn and I continued to visit Fellowship Bible Church weekly for the next five weeks. We took an introductory course called "One to One" so that we could understand what Christianity was about.

It all seemed to make sense—so much sense that I spent three hours at an Orthodox synagogue one Saturday morning trying to counteract what I was learning. I hoped that with my newly acquired belief in God, my eyes would be opened and the service would shed light on my search. I would have been thrilled had that been the case. It was not.

Undaunted, I visited with rabbis, hoping that they could show me the fallacies of the case for Jesus. I went to two local rabbis, one Orthodox and one Reform. Marilyn and I met with each one for hours. Each effort we made to hear something to dissuade us seemed to strengthen the growing belief that Jesus truly was the answer.

I'm not sure if the rabbis we consulted had any particular belief about separation from God or how to be reconciled to him. They did not tell us what they believed. They felt duty bound to prevent us from believing in Jesus without interacting with those beliefs or offering others as superior. They mostly questioned our

motives and talked a great deal about Jews who had been persecuted by Christians.

One rabbi opened up a New Testament and poked a finger at
the pages, telling me that for every single word in that book there
was a Jew who was killed in the name of Christ. I did not doubt
the truth of that, but I asked what that had to do with the fact or
fallacy of Jesus Christ. I was not looking to minimize the
suffering of our people, but I didn't feel that bringing up those
sufferings was an appropriate answer to my questions. This so
infuriated the wife of one rabbi that she actually started hitting
me. Of course I was much bigger than she was, but I didn't feel
I could defend myself, and the rabbi had to pull her off. I was
stunned by this reaction and amazed that no one addressed the
issue of God's plan for the Jewish Messiah and whether it was
fulfilled in Jesus.

I knew that I was supposed to feel guilty, and I did feel
guilty—but not for the reasons the rabbis had in mind. I felt
guilty because I knew that I had sinned and I knew that God was
holy. I felt guilty for disappointing my God. I was not going to
allow anyone to make me feel guilty for seeking reconciliation. I
didn't want to be considered disloyal to my people—but if my
questions and determination to find answers made me appear
disloyal, then so be it.

When we heard that an ultra-Orthodox rabbi from Memphis,
Tennessee was coming to dissuade Dr. Barg from belief in Jesus,
Marilyn and I decided we ought to be there as well.

Dr. Barg had been a believer for two or three months when we
first started to believe in Jesus, but it had taken a while for him to
tell his father. His father's reaction was to send a chauffeured
limousine to pick up this rabbi in Memphis and drive him to
Little Rock, two and a half hours away.

All four of us (husbands and wives) met with him from 8 at
night till 2 in the morning. Most of his arguments centered
around guilt and why we should feel ashamed for betraying our
people, but we refused this approach. We kept bringing him back
to the Bible and asked him not only to dispute Jesus from there
but also to explain modern Judaism as it pertains to written
Scripture. He became very frustrated because these were not the

issues he had come to discuss. In response to some rather direct questions from me, he admitted that he found us all to be sane, intelligent people with good marriages, fine children, and success in business. He went on to add that we were different from other Jewish Christian converts he had met. The irony was that although Marilyn and I had argued the case for Christianity, neither of us had made up our minds yet about Jesus.

Meanwhile, we continued attending the five-week course where we spent many hours with a pastor going through the "Old" and "New" Testaments. We questioned him into the wee hours of the morning, and his answers were always based on what the Bible said.

The more we studied, the more we read and the more we spoke to Christians, the more we wanted the fellowship with God that they had. They told us that what we were seeking was only possible through Jesus Christ. They told us that God had taken the form of a man, Jesus, had lived a perfect life and was therefore able to offer his blood as an atonement for our sin. If we recognized the truth of that, we needed to ask Jesus to be the center of our lives. We needed to ask that he change us, by the power of his spirit, into the men and women he wanted us to be. It meant entrusting our lives to him—forever.

After much reading, prayer and internal turmoil, I finally came to believe in Jesus as my Jewish Messiah. I was unable to actually articulate my decision until a visit with a very sweet patient by the name of Mildred. Mildred was dying. As I was talking to her during her examination, she suddenly looked up at me and said, "Dr. Sternberg, there is something different about you over the last month. What is it?" Her simple observation brought me face to face with the fact that God had already begun to change me, and I found myself explaining to Mildred that I had become a believer in Jesus Christ as my Jewish Messiah, Lord, and Savior. She simply nodded and said, "I thought so."

In December 1980, Marilyn and I finally (and separately) made our personal decisions to follow Jesus.

News travels fast in the Jewish community of a small city like Little Rock. I won't minimize the pain of being rejected by the community and especially by my fellow Jewish physicians.

Nevertheless, I remembered my own outrage on first hearing of Dr. Barg's beliefs, and I understood how others felt. My anger was overcome by a profound desire to understand what he claimed to have discovered. I can only pray that the same might prove true for some of my colleagues.

Nevertheless, the Christian community has accepted us wholeheartedly, and has welcomed opportunities to learn more about the Jewish roots of their faith. Instead of losing my Jewishness in a sea of Christianity, I've met with respect and appreciation for my heritage and my identity as a Jew. Today, I feel more Jewish than ever.

Knowing Jesus has changed every area of our lives, not the least of which is my professional life. I am a full-time private practicing medical oncologist, board certified in both internal medicine and medical oncology. My average day begins at 5:15, which is when I wake up so that I can leave the house at 6:30 and start rounds at the hospital at 7. I arrive at my office at about 10 and see patients until 6 at night, diagnosing their problems and giving them different therapies, including chemotherapy.

When I tried to keep that kind of schedule before, I was continually exhausted—physically and emotionally—and felt I had less and less to give to my patients and my family. I had entered the field because I wanted to save lives and help people. The field had shown me my limitations. Knowing that life and death are not in my hands but in the hands of my God, who is entirely trustworthy, has changed everything. It has freed me to be more sensitive, loving and compassionate, which was not part of my basic personality. God is continuing to work on these areas of my life.

My relationship with the living God gives my life meaning and fulfillment. It brings contentment, despite the painful realities of life and death. Faith does not anesthetize me to the pain and suffering I encounter in my practice, but now I can pray for my patients—even as many prayed for me—that they will find peace and rest in Jesus.

I am grateful for opportunities to tell cancer patients the good news of Jesus Christ and his offer of eternal life. I can give patients who are willing to hear life-giving hope for eternity when there seems to be no hope for the present. Even my Christian patients have benefited, knowing that their physician believes as they do and can pray with them and for them.

Jesus filled the void that possessions, position and power never could and never would fill. Jesus was the answer, is the answer and always will be the answer to our deepest needs and desires. He is your answer, too. Please don't reject the answer before you ask God the question that he is waiting to hear.

Dr. Sternberg is a diplomat of the American Board of Internal Medicine and is board certified in Medical Oncology. He practices in Little Rock, Arkansas.

PETER GREENSPAN

When I was three years old, I asked my father if God had a first name. He paused then replied, "Rabbi."

"No," my sister protested, "his first name is Life." (We grew up in Brooklyn, where "lifeguard" sounds like "Life God.") It's one of those family stories we still laugh about—but perhaps my sister was closer to the truth than any of us realized.

My name is Peter Bogach Greenspan. I was born on September 12, 1954, in Brooklyn, New York.

My father, Reynold Solomon Greenspan, was also born in New York City. A family physician and hospital administrator, he died in 1983. My Brooklyn-born mother, Lenore Bogach Greenspan, taught social studies and was an artist as well as a homemaker. She died in 1975. My sister, Ellyn Rebecca Leverone, is two years older than I. She is a homemaker in Dobbs Ferry, New York, with a background in theater, languages, and psychology.

Ours was a typical New York, postimmigrant, liberal, egalitarian Jewish family. We expressed our Jewishness through involvement in social issues and a heartfelt concern for justice. These were integral to our lives. God was not. My parents did not believe in rituals, so we did not belong to a synagogue. I did not attend Hebrew school or become *bar mitzvah* at age thirteen.* Instead, my parents threw a big party at an Italian restaurant called Scarola's.

Jewish holidays were opportunities for family gatherings, and we celebrated accordingly. My mother's mother, Babba, cooked. I savored her chicken soup, matzoh balls, *kreplach* and *chaluptzahs,* and I often helped her prepare them. I recall the tantalizing smells of these delicacies with great pleasure.

I also recall with pleasure our summer cottage in Floradan Lodge, a bungalow colony in upstate New York. Many of our "Old Country" relatives lived nearby, so we used the cottage for big family get-togethers. What happy, noisy times those were!

---

* Eventually I chose to become bar mitzvah on my own.

My Great Aunt Sarah would say something in Yiddish to her sister, Ada (my Babba), who would respond in Russian. My mother would comment in English, my grandfather would answer in Russian again—and almost everyone spoke some Yiddish. The "new" Americans (those born in the United States) argued with great conviction about politics, philosophy, art and science against a background of great opera or classical music.

It was there in Putnam Valley, New York (near Peekskill) that I attended *Shabbat* services, mostly to be with friends and enjoy Yiddish goodies afterward. I also looked forward to the ritual and liturgy and loved to hear the cantor sing.

Back in the city, Papa (my mother's father) often brought me to the old Met (Metropolitan Opera House) in Manhattan to hear operas, many of which were performed by well-known local *chazans*. My love for music and liturgy drew me to high holiday services and Simchat Torah. I could always find friends to go with, or relatives like Aunt Marsha.

Aunt Marsha Bogach, my mother's sister-in-law, probably did more than anyone to develop my Jewish identity. She came from Luschki, Poland—the same town as Eliazar Ben Yehuda, the progenitor of modern Hebrew. Her family escaped certain death by coming to America just before Hitler annexed Poland. She kept a strict kosher home and observed the Sabbath—no homework on Saturday at Aunt Marsha's!

As I reflect on my childhood, one significant aspect was the fact that my mother had multiple sclerosis. She loved and cared for me, but her illness limited her. Our housekeeper, Ethel Rogers, was at times my surrogate mom. She was and is one of the finest people I know.

Ethel was from a southern black, Christian tradition. She never told me that I needed Jesus (she respected my parents' oversight) but Jesus was obviously important to her, a fact that did not escape my youthful notice.

Ethel was kind, compassionate, patient, long-suffering and possessed a kind of quiet pride that I now recognize as self-respect. Even as a boy, I could see that she was a knowing person, one who understood more about life than most people I knew. She took it upon herself to instill certain qualities in me, and to teach me about life. To this day, if I reflect on an important lesson I can usually trace the insight back to Ethel. She taught me quite a bit about self-defense—and I don't mean boxing lessons. She explained what causes adversity and how I could handle myself in such a way as to avoid violence. All this was during the great civil rights struggle of the early 1960's. I thank God for Ethel (now in her seventies) and for her family, with whom I am still good friends.

Zana Daniels was another important influence. She, too, was a Christian. "Aunt Zana" essentially raised my father. My paternal grandparents divorced when my father was about five years old. My grandfather, Gershon (George) Greenspan, got custody of his sons—something almost unheard of at that time. However, my grandfather was not a good parent. Zana lived in the same apartment building on Ocean Parkway and undertook to care for my father and my uncle Murray.

Murray was unmoved by her attentions, but my father, who was several years younger, became attached to Zana. She was like a mother to him. Even after he married, he maintained the relationship with Zana and her husband, Tom. My sister and I never really knew my father's natural parents, but we knew "Aunt Zana and Uncle Tom." As a teen, I discovered what Zana had been to my father and began referring to her as my grandmother. She and her family were very important to me.

It is hard to calculate Ethel's and Zana's spiritual influence on me, since neither ever suggested that I believe in Jesus. In hindsight, I believe their faith, their example, and probably their prayers affected me deeply.

If it is hard to calculate Ethel's and Zana's spiritual influence on me, it is even harder to calculate that of my parents. They emphasized that it did not matter if one was a Jew, a Mormon or a Catholic. What other people (especially gentiles) thought or did about God was nice but insignificant. Any belief was fine, so long as people realized that theirs was no better than the next person's. My parents taught me that God—if he existed at all—was not intimately involved with us or with world events. Despite all that, I have believed in God for as long as I can remember, knowing him to be a real Being who somehow influenced my life.

My earliest concept of God was that of a great, fear-provoking, transparent Being, much like the image Michelangelo produced on the ceiling of the Sistine Chapel. I continued to believe in God, even through a rebellious phase when I thought it was cool to be agnostic or even antagonistic toward God.

As for Jesus—who was he? I recall first discussing him when I was about thirteen years old. It was then that I read *The Passover Plot*, by Hugh Schoenfeld. To my young mind, Schoenfeld's book was serious scholarship and quite simply settled any questions regarding Jesus. I had no further interest in him for several years. I was, however, developing an interest in the field of medicine and began thinking about becoming a doctor.

I attended John Dewey High, an experimental school named for the famous humanist. We were indoctrinated with Dewey's philosophies, especially empiricism. I swallowed it hook, line and sinker. It fit well (I thought) with my interest in science and technology.

I attended high school at the time of the Vietnam protest/hippie era. I didn't really buy into the movement, yet I wanted to be part of "the scene." I dressed in bell-bottoms, let my hair grow down to my shoulders (but no longer—that's where I asserted my individuality!) and succeeded in impressing the Jewish mothers of girls I was dating, while still being outwardly "cool."

Being "cool" included participating in antiwar protests.

Those protests really heated up toward the end of my senior year (1972) when President Nixon admitted his campaign in Cambodia. Some of the widespread peace demonstrations were out of control and became violent, an irony that was not lost on me. It didn't help when special-interest groups like the Black Panthers and Young Americans for Freedom used the antiwar protests as a backdrop for staging their own demonstrations.

Ours was one of many NYC high schools whose student body decided to participate in the demonstrations. Well, we marched over to Brooklyn College just in time to see a group of Black Panthers overturn a car across the street from the world-famous Wolfie's Restaurant. That's when the trouble began. The Panthers were tame enough—they were merely flexing their muscles. The real threat seemed to be a group of basically white,

Protestant students (Young Americans for Freedom). I viewed them as some sort of offshoot of the Ku Klux Klan and presumed, without facts or knowledge, that they hated blacks and Jews. These guys lined up opposite us on the Brooklyn College quadrangle and seemed ready to riot. A shot (from where I don't know) was fired.

It turned out that one of "them" was a good friend of mine, a fellow ham radio operator named Ken Reisig. Ken saw me in the crowd and literally threw himself at me, leveling me and removing me from harm's way. He remained on top of me as the mini-riot got under way. After a few minutes—and thank God, very little violence—the episode ended. Ken got up, brushed us both off, arranged to contact me for a ham radio meeting, wished me well, then left with his *goyishe* pals.

After the fray, I managed to get into the administration building to occupy the dean's office with a number of the *machers* in this drama. Although not part of the leadership cadre, I was close in with that crowd and being somewhat of a "techno-nerd," I was useful. I could decipher telephone numbers for instruments that had no number written on them. I became hero for a day by restoring phone numbers and giving them to the leaders of our demonstration. Some of them spoke to organizers of the big-time protest effort in San Francisco on telephones I had worked on. Was I proud of myself! I even made it onto the local news, hanging out a window, flashing the peace sign as a camera panned by.

We occupied the office building for a couple of days, but I went home after dark to have dinner with my family and tell them the exciting things I was seeing and doing. They were qvelling. In their estimation, this showed that I was growing and developing as a free-thinking individual.

My actions, however, did not stem from deeply seated convictions. I experienced adrenal rushes from doing something remotely dangerous. I enjoyed the camaraderie of my friends and the thrill of "beating the establishment." In the long run, though, my heart was not in the antiwar movement. I felt Vietnam was probably morally wrong and a waste of precious life, but I really didn't understand it. Nor was I personally threatened by the draft. In fact, I received a medical deferment shortly after graduation.

The condition that led to that deferment might have contributed to my involvement in the antiwar protests. The Brooklyn College escapade enabled me to focus on problems outside myself and forget for a while that, with a greatly enlarged spleen, I faced a possible diagnosis of leukemia or Hodgkin lymphoma.

I was secretly worried—afraid in fact. My father, although he tried to hide it, was deeply alarmed. In July 1972, I underwent major surgery to diagnose and treat my problem.

While in the hospital, I pondered the questions of life, mortality and whether there was such a thing as eternal salvation. I refused to see a rabbi (with whom I felt, at the time, little in common). Instead, I befriended a cleric named John Valenzano, who came to my room and spoke with me about spiritual issues. I really don't recall the specifics of our conversation. I do remember that he visited me often and played cards with me while I recovered. I'll never forget the time that he took to be with me.

The surgery ultimately indicated a rare but benign condition. It seemed that my "life-God" was watching out for me. My condition kept me out of the war, which was good, because my days as a hippie were numbered and I doubt if I was capable of keeping up the facade.

It seemed to me that the whole flower child movement was destined to fail because of unrealistic goals and expectations. Even as a teenager, I saw that "free love," drugs, etc. had moral consequences that would lead to problems. The movement provided no satisfactory responses to any such consequences or problems. There was talk of peace, yet much of the ideology seemed like an excuse for immoral and irresponsible behavior. I was uncomfortable with the growing disapproval I felt toward such behavior.

Like my parents, I embraced every liberal cause and philosophy and was vehemently opposed to "closed-minded" people, i.e., those who accepted the Bible as true and morally binding. I agreed outwardly that abortion was not a moral issue, that homosexuality was no more or less than an acceptable lifestyle alternative, that premarital sex was healthy and all opinions to the contrary were unreasonably intolerant. Deep down I felt otherwise, and it caused me some anguish to be at odds with myself about these issues.

I managed to survive this era and set off for college on August 25, 1972. I landed in Kansas City, Missouri. Like Dorothy from *The Wizard of Oz* in reverse, I quickly realized that I was not in Brooklyn anymore!

I was in my dormitory room for all of two hours, still unpacking, when a fellow named Gary Henke entered my room with an open New Testament. I politely informed him (at least my tone of voice was polite) that I was not interested in anti-Semitic nonsense about some gentile in whose name countless Jews had suffered and died. I didn't even understand that Y'shua (Jesus) was Jewish. Gary, rather than pointing out my ignorance, was truly polite and respected my wishes.

New friends tried to tell me about Jesus. I had a crush on a beautiful young woman, Kathy Langkopf, who was a "born-again" Christian. She tried hard to get me to listen and gave me a Bible that included a New Testament. At the same time, the "Jesus Freaks" hit Kansas City. I considered them overbearing and obnoxious, yet I wanted to prove to them that reason and scholarship were on my side and that Jesus could not be the Messiah. Consequently, I had several loud "discussions" with them in the cafeteria. Needless to say, I was always right—at least in my own eyes.

My arguments depended on nonbiblical, mainly Jewish scholarship, with an occasional liberal non-Jewish scholar for support. I had virtually no knowledge of Scripture but was content to read and repeat other people's arguments that the Jewish Bible was not speaking of anyone like Jesus. Notwithstanding all the time and energy exerted in these extracurricular pursuits, I graduated from the University of Missouri-Kansas City with a B.A. in chemistry.

Next, I was off to the Chicago College of Osteopathic Medicine. There I met a professor of psychiatry named Dr. John C. Lee, and, for the first time, became interested in the gospel.

Dr. Lee's real name was Johannes Cecil Lehimski, and he was a real underground freedom fighter in World War II. The Nazis caught and tortured Dr. Lee, but by a phenomenal stroke of misidentification, they did not execute him. Instead, he spent a year in solitary confinement in Spandau. There, one of the guards made a show of mistreating him and other prisoners during the day. Then at night, the guard would sneak back into the cell blocks and give them food, blankets, and books. That guard was a Christian. The books he smuggled in were Bibles, which he managed to bring in various translations and languages. During that year, Dr. Lee studied the Bible (in several languages) and became a strong Christian and somewhat of a Bible scholar.

After being liberated by the United States, Dr. Lee joined the Army Intelligence Corps to interview Nazi war criminals and participated in the Nuremberg Trials. Remember, he was a psychiatrist.

Because Dr. Lee had involved himself in underground activities in World War II (like blowing up bridges and ammunition dumps), he was wanted by the Russians for war crimes. The United States granted him immunity and he eventually came to teach at my medical school in Chicago, where he remained for the rest of his life. He was such a respected scholar that, despite the fact that he was a gentile and a Christian, he was asked to be an examiner at an Orthodox rabbinical school in Chicago, where he reviewed doctoral theses, etc. He knew a great deal about Judaism and Jewish customs.

I was part of "the inner circle" of students who loved and respected Dr. Lee and spent time with him outside of the classroom. My admiration for him led me to believe that faith in Jesus must be worth more than I had previously thought. I told Dr. Lee that if Jesus was good enough for him, he was good enough for me. His response truly amazed me. He suggested that I look to Judaism for the answers. In retrospect, I believe he realized that my reasons for wanting to accept Jesus, while a tribute to him, were not a basis for real faith. Dr. Lee wanted me to find the truth for myself, which meant some exploring.

Dr. Lee died about four months later. My first response was to reach for a Jewish prayer book. Amidst my profound grief, I found comfort in reciting the *Kaddish*. At the same time I felt myself instantly captivated by the desire to explore aspects of my Jewishness about which I had been so ignorant: religious observance and the study of *Torah* and *Talmud*.

I began reading everything I could find regarding Judaism. I started attending services regularly, first at Sinai Congregation in Hyde Park. Sinai is an old, reform congregation, with neo-traditional leanings. Rabbi Phillip Kranz gave me access to the spare book room of the congregation's library, and I was able to choose from a hundred books or more on many aspects and issues in Judaism. Rabbi Kranz also taught me to read and speak basic biblical Hebrew, as I had decided I wanted a traditional bar mitzvah celebration. It wasn't until three years later that I actually went through with the ceremony, very simply and without fanfare. By then I was attending a conservative synagogue, Congregation Ohev Shalom in Prairie Village, Kansas. I was *davening,* laying *tefillin,* keeping kosher, and making all kinds of arrangements to avoid phone calls on the Sabbath.

Somehow I found time to fall in love and marry. Sara, a gentile, converted to Judaism after the birth of our first child, David. She practiced traditional Judaism with me.

All the while, I was trying to prove that Jesus was not the Jewish Messiah—only this time with Torah and Talmud. I felt compelled to do so, first, because people kept talking to me about Jesus, and second, because I needed to find reasons why I shouldn't believe what they were saying.

On my own, I gained far more religious training and involvement in Judaism than my parents ever dreamed of giving me. Yet instead of finding answers, I found that my efforts led to feelings of futility. I was doing the right things according to my religion, but none of the laws or the minutiae to which I had bound myself had brought me closer to God. I sensed that despite my best efforts, I was not pleasing him. As I grew more and more discouraged by the futility of all this striving . . . I began to cheat. I would sneak pork lo mein every chance I got, and I started to drive on the Sabbath again.

Then my marriage failed, and that was a terrible blow. I knew that our marriage was not ideal, and in fact we had decided to "separate for awhile, to get some space." After about 10 days or so, Sara sat me down and told me she wanted a divorce. Our separation, she said, was not going to "ignite the flame." Shortly thereafter, she developed a relationship with the man who became her second husband. He moved in with her and my children within a few weeks of our separation—another major blow for which I was unprepared.

After the divorce, I only saw my little children on weekends. All my observances fell by the wayside, along with any hope that these endeavors could make me righteous.

A year after the divorce I met Kim, a gentle, honest Christian woman who refused to argue with me about her beliefs. I tried hard to persuade her that she was wrong about Jesus. As our relationship grew, I began attending her church, mostly to be with her and to argue that the gospel was ridiculous. I remember listening carefully, waiting for the pastor to say something that I would consider anti-Semitic. He never did. I found I was actually stimulated by the preaching—and more motivated than ever to prove that Jesus was not the Messiah.

Kim and I dated for a year before becoming engaged, much to the dismay of her family. While they liked me, they were grieved that she had chosen someone who could not understand or appreciate the faith that had been such a very important part of her life.

We proceeded with a minimally Christian wedding. I continued searching for proof that Jesus was not the Messiah, the more so as we were expecting our first child together. We did not discuss how we would raise our children, but I think my concern about it added urgency to my need to resolve and dismiss the question of Jesus.

About that time, the movie, *The Last Temptation of Christ*, was released, along with the attendant flap. I read the book by Nikos Kazantzakis out of curiosity. I do not recommend that book (or the movie), yet God somehow used it to open my mind and heart to the fact that Jesus was more than I had been willing to admit. As I watched my daughter Lauren come into the world, I thanked Jesus. It was a spontaneous prayer that I uttered in the delivery room without even realizing it. Startled by what I had said, I asked myself, "Wow, what was that all about?!" I began thinking and praying intensely.

About a week later, I cried out to the Lord, "Jesus must really be who he says he is!" It was a realization most likely brought about by all my efforts to disprove him. I think I actually came to faith in Y'shua by reading what detractors wrote:

countermissionary material as well as philosophical works on concepts like existentialism that argued the differences between various theological views. The more I read, the less I was convinced by all the arguments against Jesus.

I realized that I needed pastoral help. The man who married us, Pastor Francis Lieb of Timothy Lutheran Church in Blue Springs, Missouri, gave me a folder of literature from Jews for Jesus, an organization I used to think was full of *mishuganners* who had lost their senses and deluded themselves into believing a falsehood of major proportions.

Years before, I had been ready to commit myself to Jesus, not because of who Jesus was, but because of who Dr. Lee was. Now that I knew who Jesus was, I had a basis for faith, but I needed the association of people who were like me—people who were Jews. Pastor Lieb understood that I had to reconcile my Jewishness with my need to accept Y'shua as my Lord and Messiah. With packet in hand, I went home and read everything he had collected from Jews for Jesus. There were a few tracts and several issues of the Jews for Jesus newsletter. I especially remember a Christmas issue with an article by Moishe Rosen reflecting on the announcement of the Messiah's birth. I was struck by the realization that those angels had appeared to Jewish shepherds—that the Good News had come first to my people.

Included in the Jews for Jesus literature was a prayer one could say to formally repent from sin and declare trust in Y'shua. I said that prayer quietly and privately. I suddenly felt a presence that was new to me, and yet very familiar. I now know that it was the *Ruach Ha Kodesh,* the Holy Spirit. I was excited, but not outwardly. I knew that I had much to learn.

I was baptized on Christmas Day, 1988, and in my declaration of faith before the congregation, I quoted from that Jews for Jesus newsletter, citing Luke 2 and observing that Jewish shepherds were the first to hear Y'shua's birth announced.

My life has changed considerably since coming to faith in Y'shua. One of the promises God makes to those who trust in Jesus is that we will undergo a personal transformation, and that transformation is a process. Caring for God, caring for others, becomes more and more central.

I have involved myself in many messianic and church activities. My love for *chazanut* led me to become an amateur (real amateur) cantor at a local messianic congregation. I am a messianic *moyl*. I speak often to gentile believers about the Jewish roots of their faith and the Jewishness of the gospel.

Slowly but surely, I am growing in the grace and knowledge of Messiah Y'shua, and that affects every area of my life. Faith in Y'shua has brought me closer to my wife and children. Putting God first (at least trying to) brings all else into perspective, and in that perspective, my love and sense of responsibility for my family has grown.

My faith also affects my medical practice. I am an obstetrician and gynecologist, and I practice the specialty as a generalist. I am firm (but sane) in my stand against abortion, and I peripherally assist at a shelter for unwed pregnant teens who intend to keep their babies. One thing my faith has done for me (and for some of my patients) is enable me to pray with them about their concerns. Years ago, I would have considered praying with patients nonsensical and inappropriate. Now, it is uplifting and helpful in managing their problems. Patients often ask me to pray for them, and the closeness I feel to God through the Messiah makes this a natural and normal part of my profession.

I am a traditional physician, but I do believe that God has occasionally intervened in my practice. I have seen the power of prayer affect the healing process in a number of medical situations. I have been confronted with surgical complications that seemed to resolve better than I expected, based on God's answer to prayer. At times I've been compelled to move quickly to deliver a baby when there was no apparent danger—only to discover later that expediting delivery had been necessary. One such patient had a ruptured uterus, which was not apparent until after the birth. That condition carries a mortality rate of 50% for the mother and 75% for the baby. Because of the "inexplicable" prompting (by God's Spirit, I believe) mother and baby were just fine.

In a sense, my sister was right those many years ago: the Lord is our "lifeguard." He is the God who saves, not only physically, but spiritually. He sent Jesus to dive headlong into this world to rescue humanity. If you call upon him, he will answer.

Peter B. Greenspan, DO, FACOG, is an obstetrician/gynecologist practicing in the Kansas City area. He is also a clinical assistant professor of obstetrics and gynecology at the UMKC School of Medicine and the University of Health Sciences-College of Osteopathic Medicine.

ARI-BETH COHEN

My major objections were not about truth; they were about consequences. I was fearful—afraid of changes I might have to make, because I knew there was sin in my life that could not continue if I were to take a relationship with God seriously. I was also afraid of what "religion" I would have to convert to if I believed in Jesus. Most of all, I was afraid of how my parents would react.

My name means "house of the lion" or, in my case, the lioness. I like my name. I think of a lioness as strong and quiet, yet aggressive and graceful. She is also protective, dedicated and loyal toward family, determined and highly motivated. It's a good name by which to measure oneself. This "lioness" was born October 7, 1962, in New Brunswick, New Jersey, the oldest of three children and the only daughter.

My dad, Solomon Cohen, is retired from the Postal Service but continues to work at Lockheed Space Center in Florida. He works out five days a week and attends temple regularly. My mom, Marilyn Cohen, passed away in December 1994, with complications from metastatic lung cancer.

My earliest memories about being Jewish are from Hebrew school on Wednesdays (I didn't have to go to swim practice!). I remember how strange it was to be in third grade, able to read and write, yet suddenly we were back to basics with a whole new alphabet. The reading was just like it had been in first grade, except instead of Dick, Jane, and Sally, we had David, Yosef, and Sarah. I enjoyed learning the Bible stories but wondered why God was so active in the lives of my ancestors yet had little, if anything, to say to us today.

We belonged to a Conservative synagogue, and my parents went out of their way to rearrange their schedules so that we could attend services and Hebrew school lessons. I loved singing *Adon Olom, Lechah Dodi, Aleynu,* and other Hebrew songs every Friday night. I appreciated the sense of order in the liturgy and particularly remember reading from Psalms 92 and 95. Most of all, I loved the way I felt after a Friday evening service—somehow closer to God.

We stayed home from school on *Rosh Hashanah* and *Yom Kippur.* I loved the crisp, tart apples dipped in smooth, sweet honey at Rosh Hashanah, and even tried this treat at other times of the year, but somehow it never seemed to taste the same. I remember the long, long hours of services on Yom Kippur, and fasting to cleanse myself from sin and to ensure that my name was written in God's Book of Life. I felt special during the holidays, singled out, and happy to be one of God's chosen people.

My favorite holiday was Passover, and I'll never forget my excitement over being the one to chant the four questions in Hebrew. As the oldest, I only did so once; after that my brothers, as the youngest members of the family, were chosen. I also remember delicious breakfasts of fried matzoh. It's the only thing I'll ever admit that Dad could cook better than Mom!

We celebrated the other holidays at the synagogue. At Purim I loved making and eating *hamantashen* (three-cornered pastries filled with cherries, blueberries or lemon), but it was even more fun making noise at the mention of Haman's name as the *megilah* (the Book of Esther) was read. For *Sukkot* I remember building the *sukkah* outside the synagogue, decorating it with palm leaves, and waving the various plants to symbolize that God was everywhere.

Yet I didn't really think of God as being everywhere. I knew God was powerful, caring and all-knowing. He protected his chosen people from danger—when we obeyed him. God was described as being everywhere, yet he seemed far away, somewhere high and quite removed from anything having to do with me. It did not occur to me that the Almighty had time to listen to my insignificant complaints and requests. In fact, I never thought of God "hearing" or "listening" to anything outside of the synagogue.

There were brief occasions when I was not happy to be Jewish. When I was six years old, a classmate told me that I had killed Jesus. I didn't know who Jesus was, but was very hurt and confused by the accusation. Years later (seventh grade), we had a class on world religions. During the Judaism section, a classmate wrote "Moses Saves" on the back of my jacket. Whereas I had normally enjoyed the special feeling of being Jewish, these experiences made me feel isolated and lonely.

Becoming *bat mitzvah* at age 13 remains the highlight of my religious upbringing. I studied the various prayers for months—and, of course, the *Haftorah* reading. I'd marked my little red paperback with all the scriptic notations for how to pronounce and sing the words of my portion. I studied for months and finally, when I was ready, I put on a *tallis* (not a fashionable thing for a female to do at our synagogue) and led the congregation in the Friday night service. As I performed my solo Haftorah, I somehow became an adult in the eyes of the people and in the eyes of God.

After I was bat mitzvah, there were no more Sunday school classes. The point of Hebrew school seemed to be preparation for "the big event," so that also ceased.

When I entered high school, the all-important Friday night football games took precedence over Friday night services. I reasoned that it was okay, since my dad went to the games with me. I still went to services on High Holy Days, but rarely attended outside of that. This pattern continued when I went off to college. I did not feel any "farther" from God by my lack of regular temple attendance. He remained all-powerful and all-knowing and still very far removed from the little details of my life. I never thought that God could be personally involved with me—why would he want to be?

Despite my lack of synagogue involvement, I still had an unwavering faith in an unseen God. I didn't think I could prove that God existed—as I was asked to do in several courses in college—I just knew that he did.

The first time that I listened seriously to anything concerning Jesus was during my junior year of college (1982–83). I was taking a heavy load of science courses and, at the same time, studying in preparation for the Medical College Admissions Test (MCAT). I was severely depressed and felt I was beginning to fold under the heavy burden.

Close friends noticed my struggles and began gently suggesting that I consider Jesus. Their gentle presentation (which I call "tip-toeing around the gospel") was no surprise, as they were part of a group at Huntingdon College known affectionately as "The God Squad." They knew I was Jewish and tried not to offend me in any way. I listened tolerantly and later eagerly, as they spent months building up a case for Jesus Christ as Lord and Savior. Nevertheless, when they made their actual evangelical "pitch," asking me to accept him, I backed away and told them that I was not ready to make such a commitment. They backed off, but (I later discovered) never stopped praying for me or caring for my spiritual welfare.

It wasn't that the things they said didn't make sense. My major objections were not about truth; they were about consequences. I was fearful—afraid of changes I might have to make, because I knew there was sin in my life that could not continue if I were to take a relationship with God seriously. I was also afraid of what "religion" I would have to convert to if I believed in Jesus. Most of all, I was afraid of how my parents would react. I finished my senior year without any more "badgering" from Christian friends, then spent the next four years in medical school, far removed from any Christian influence.

After medical school, I took an internship in Georgia, which turned out to be in fairly close proximity to some of my "God Squad" friends. During my very stressful internship year, I once again felt that I was nearing the limit of what I could endure. Again, my friends told me that Jesus had made it possible for me to have a real, everyday relationship with God. They gave me a Bible for my birthday, and I began reading, especially in the New Testament. I also began attending a large Bible study in Atlanta.

The first time that I set foot into the Bible study, I felt so out of place that I almost walked out. Something made me stay—and the teaching intrigued me so much that I found myself returning week after week. The other interns with whom I worked all had their own means of reducing stress, so we covered for each other to allow each of us time to engage in whatever activity would best help us cope with the tremendous pressure. The Bible study I attended was held on Tuesday nights. Since a friend of mine in residency attended church every Wednesday night, we agreed that he would cover any Tuesdays that I was on call, and I would cover any Wednesdays that he was on call.

I found myself reading my Bible every night and eagerly anticipating Tuesday evenings. I looked forward to the Bible study, not only as a way to break up the stresses of residency, but also because the teaching was so unique, so real and seemed so surprisingly true. As I involved myself more and more with daily Bible reading and weekly study, I found (and others noticed) that I was better able to handle my residency. The change was not immediate, but it was definitely apparent.

After approximately six months of listening to these studies and reading the Bible for myself, I believed that what I was hearing and reading about Jesus was true. The accounts of his miracles, his wisdom, and his simple plan for salvation were real, consistent and practical, with application for modern daily living. One single and final atonement for sin made so much more sense to me than annual atonement for sin (*Yom Kippur*), which cannot even be done today as commanded in Scripture since the Temple no longer exists.

I was still afraid to admit what I believed to my friends—even to myself. However, there were a few things at work to help me overcome fear. First, there was prayer—and not only the prayers of faithful friends. I had learned that I could talk to God directly, and I was praying, asking him to help me make the right decision. Second, in some unspoken way, I believe that God was talking to me, reassuring me of his reality. Third, God ultimately gave me the strength I needed to face whatever confrontations would result from my belief in Jesus.

During a visit with my parents, I showed my mother what I thought was a fascinating passage from the New Testament. She read the passage and asked me if I believed that Jesus was the Messiah. To my own surprise and without hesitation, I replied, "Yes." I'd had no idea that our conversation that morning would lead to my first outward declaration of my belief in Jesus as my Messiah. I think it was also my first inward realization that I truly believed and was no longer fearful about the possible consequences of my profession of faith.

I was so excited by this first-time "confession," that I found myself wanting to tell others. Still, at twenty-seven years of age,

I was fearful of how my father, who had been raised Orthodox, would react. I put off telling him for as long as possible—eight, perhaps nine months.

One evening on another visit to my parents, my father and I were watching the news when a story came on about a rabbi in New York who believed that Jesus was the Messiah. Dad immediately commented that one could not believe in Jesus Christ and be Jewish. I told him that one could, and that I was speaking from firsthand experience. When I told my father that I believed in Jesus, he tore his sleeve and told me to leave the house.

That was the beginning of an extremely difficult eight-month period of silence between my parents and me. It hurt to be estranged from my parents, but at the same time, I knew that I had done the right thing in telling them the truth. God helped me deal with the pain, and gave me inexplicable joy and peace.

Thankfully, my parents and I were eventually reconciled to one another. One Sunday, I was visiting a local Baptist church in Atlanta. The guest Sunday school speaker, also a Jewish believer in Jesus, was teaching a lesson on anger, bitterness, and forgiveness. He spoke of asking for forgiveness for our part in whatever argument or dilemma might exist. I realized then that I had sinned by not honoring my mother and father. After church, as soon as I got home, I called my parents and apologized. I asked for their forgiveness for not honoring them, but also told them that I was not asking for forgiveness for my faith and belief in Jesus as the Messiah. We cried and spoke openly and freely from our hearts. I found out the very next day that my mother had mailed three cards asking for forgiveness, and more than anything, she wanted to reconcile and talk. Although my parents do not agree with my beliefs, we love and respect one another—for which I am thankful.

My life immediately changed when I admitted that I believed and trusted in Jesus as my Lord and Savior. The first area was an ungodly relationship, which immediately stopped. I also had a problem with binge drinking; that, too, ceased. Professionally, I have been able to handle the stresses that go along with being a doctor, which have thus far included finishing residency as well as finding and keeping a job in the world of private practice medicine.

I am grateful to God for the strength and courage he gives to stand for certain principles in the ever-changing and challenging practice of medicine. When faced with medical problems that have more than one solution (i.e., a secular solution vs. a spiritual solution), I will opt for the godly solution, though it might cost me a patient. For example, unwed females who wish to be sexually active have found they must look for another doctor to prescribe birth control. Likewise, drug-seeking patients who wish to escape from pain rather than deal with their problems are also disappointed. I care for my patients and will do my utmost to help them within the boundaries of what God permits. I pray for my patients before I see them, and I end each patient session with prayer. This has become one of the greatest joys in my life.

On the shingle hanging outside my office, I have the Scripture reference Matthew 25:35–40. The last statement in this speech that Jesus made summarizes how I see each and every patient who comes through my office "inasmuch as you did it to one of the least of these My brethren, you did it to Me."

I am currently in private practice as a solo practitioner in the field of family medicine in Griffin, Georgia. I try to see to it that patients' health problems are dealt with from a "wholly" medical standpoint, which I believe includes their physical, mental and spiritual health. This focus has been a source of joy, not only for me, but also for many of my patients.

One of the biggest effects of my faith on my practice is the realization that God is ultimately in control of our health and the length of our days (Psalm 139:16). It is tremendously helpful to realize that I am not the one in control of the length of a person's days, that I am NOT God! Yet I do believe that the all-powerful God, who is everywhere, is with me as I care for people.

Ari-Beth Cohen, M.D., is a board certified family physician in a solo practice in Griffin, Georgia.

ROBERT ROSETT

One woman came with an ovarian growth and a firm faith that God would heal it. As we prayed, I was worrying about which medicine to choose for this woman, when I sensed God telling me, "Don't worry, I've got this one." The follow-up ultrasound showed a normal ovary.

I did not grow up with aspirations of becoming a doctor, though my family certainly has a scientific bent. My father was an optical engineer as well as an optometrist. My mother began as a chemist; later she taught high school chemistry.

I was born October 15, 1953, in Queens, New York, the youngest of three children. My brother is two years older and my sister is four years older than I. As far back as I can remember, my world was strongly (culturally) Jewish. My grandparents (who were a regular and important part of our family life) spoke mostly Yiddish, and my parents spoke it when the subject matter was not for children's ears. We had grand feasts for Chanukah, with hundreds of relatives gathered in a rented rumpus room of an apartment building. And what a rumpus we made with *dreidels,* dozens of *"latke* stations," and proud cooks who all tried to prove the superiority of their recipes by the number of people who would stand in line for their latkes. Passover was a smaller circle of extended family, with a formidable feast and an abbreviated *Haggadah.*

We had a smaller feast on *Yom Kippur.* Why, you ask, should we feast on a day of fasting? My family knew exactly what the Day of Atonement stood for, but they had no reason to afflict their souls (which they didn't believe they had) in obedience to a God who they didn't believe existed. You see, despite strong cultural and ethnic Jewish identification, our family—at least as far back as my great grandparents—was atheistic. My father was the most militantly so, in the name of "science, rationalism and humanism."

Yet from a very young age I had a sure sense that God was watching me. I don't remember ever talking to him or asking for anything. I do remember lying in bed wondering if I would be more disrespectful to God by sleeping on my back, in which case my genitals would be facing heavenward, or on my belly in which case my derriere would be toward him. What a dilemma for a child of four or five! I think the silent and fearful tenor of my childish concern in some way reflected my relationship with my father. Somehow I received reassurance from the Almighty that I need not worry about such things, but it didn't develop into a relationship.

I must have asked my father about God; I don't recall the question, but I can well remember the extensive orientation that he gave me to his atheistic viewpoint. He stated categorically that there simply is no God; it is a primitive idea fabricated by weak people who need a crutch; the rational man stands on his own by the superiority of his reason, etc., etc. By the age of seven or eight, I could argue the atheist position vociferously and with great certainty. I teamed up with a like-minded buddy, and together we took on other kids in lengthy and heated battles of the wits. We knew we had won whenever a believing young soul burst into tears as confusion filled his mind and doubt assaulted his tender heart. (God forgive me!)

My denial of God had no effect on my ethnic sense of Jewishness. Our daily struggle was to remain unnoticed and unmolested by a certain group of Catholic schoolboys who poured out of school with what seemed like a lot of pent-up hostility. We Jews tended to aggress one another with mental challenges (as stated above) and, compared to others our age, it seemed we were physically meek. I learned, from my parents, of all people, the instructions of Jesus to "turn the other cheek." The only problem was, when I turned my cheek, my nose would also turn—not merely to the side, but a little up in the air! I felt decidedly superior—"above" the impulse to fight—which also served to disguise my abject fear.

Beginning at the age of eight, I attended a progressive *Yiddishe shul* on Saturdays. We learned Yiddish language and literature, Jewish history, songs and dances—all within the context of a leftist political stance. There was always some activity relating to the civil rights movement, workers solidarity or the antiwar movement. I graduated to the *mitlshule* and attended until graduating from high school. There was always a high percentage of scoffers at mitlshule—kids who only came because their parents forced them. I *wanted* to be there, even when I arrived bleary-eyed after a night of smoking pot with my rock-and-roll band.

Every week as we walked from the subway to the mitlshule on 14th Street and Broadway, we passed an intense, unkempt black man who continually waved his Bible and shouted, "Trust in Christ Jesus and remember to pray." As New Yorkers, we were inured to every kind of *mishegoss* imaginable (we barely noticed the lady who hollered angrily at invisible adversaries in phone booths), but this man and his message were somehow different. I found myself defending him to my jeering friends.

As a teenager I had begun to recognize a spiritual emptiness which I sought to fill in typical 1960's and 1970's form, through yoga, Zen, drugs and the occult. One Saturday in mitlshule, my literature professor told me that he perceived a mystical bent in me, then assigned me to write a paper on false messianic movements. The research I did for that assignment was my first introduction to religious concepts of Judaism, such as our need for redemption and a messiah.

I graduated high school at age sixteen, having taken accelerated classes, which in effect enabled me to skip a grade. I enrolled at Queens College and became a music major, while my hunger for spiritual truth continued to grow. With no one to guide me toward faith, I delved further into Eastern religion and drug experiences in order to "scratch the itch." At one point, I even went to a Billy Graham crusade at Madison Square Garden. There I sat, all alone in the midst of this huge crowd. I felt something like embarrassment over the simplicity of faith these folks had, yet I felt stung by Graham's words about sin and pride. I knew he was talking about me, and I had to restrain myself from going forward for the altar call. Whatever the truth was, I felt it had to be more complex than the plain spoken message I had heard.

At age eighteen, I bicycled across the continental United States, sleeping in fields, campsites, parks or wherever—and if there was no appropriate place to lay our sleeping bags, we'd ask for permission to sleep in the county jail. (Actually the "we" was

for the first half of the trip only. Halfway through, my companion and I had a parting of the ways.) The eight to ten hours of
daily pedaling seemed to help me discharge years of anger over
unnamed fears and unexplained emptiness. I seemed to gain
some peace of soul, plus I was drug-free during the trip, and that
felt great.

The following year I traveled in East Africa: Egypt, Sudan
and Ethiopia. I had a real wanderlust and a hope that I might find
some real meaning in more "primitive" cultures. I did not find
what I was looking for and did not experience the same benefits
I had on the cross-country trip. In fact, after six months, the high-
est goal that I could imagine for myself was to return home to the
woman I was then dating and become a heroin addict (I didn't
know what that would entail, and in fact I did not become an
addict, but it seemed about right for me at the time)! After a bout
with malaria, I returned to Queens College, where I was a music
major, but gradually petered out in those studies. I remember
noting that I felt really old, more like forty than nineteen.

While at Queens, I met and fell in love with Diana. When she
graduated in 1975, we decided to move to Berkeley, California
with other musician friends and try to "make it" as a jazz band.
We played wild, frenetic music and actually had a small following for about a year.

One summer, Diana and I traveled through Oregon and went
to a jam session. The bass player was David Friesen (a well-
known recording artist with some Jewish background). He
preached the gospel with a power I had never heard before! He
asked if I wanted to be baptized, and I said, "Sure." I don't think
his explanation of baptism fully registered with me, and, though
I was moved once again by the gospel message, I figured this was
just another religious ritual. (I'll try anything once, I thought).
That night, after being baptized from a tea cup, Diana and I could
sense a presence, but we also felt a sense of conviction regarding
our lifestyle which we weren't yet ready to handle.

For the next two years I went headlong in the opposite direc-
tion, trying to develop my own righteousness through intense
meditation, a strict vegetarian diet, kundalini yoga and the like.
Despite the intense energy I expended to improve myself, I found

myself caught up in the things I despised: adultery, lies, drugs and tobacco addiction.

The pain in my soul seemed to press every spark of joy out of my life. One day while I was *kvetching* to my girlfriend, she threw the New Testament at me (the bass player had given it to us) saying, "Read this!" And I did. It was like being hit with a brick. The righteousness I was trying so desperately (yet unsuccessfully) to produce had been offered to me as a free gift! As I continued to read, I fell in love with Jesus—but my journey was far from over. At that time I was in the sway of a small-time guru. My ignorance of God's true character, combined with my insatiable need to be spiritually acceptable, kept me devoted to this fellow who, unknown to me, was undermining my relationship with Diana.

Finally, in order to preserve her own sanity, Diana left without telling anyone. I was devastated. To make a long story short, she ended up 3,000 miles away receiving Jesus through her sister's prayer group. Back in Berkeley, I cried out to Jesus for help. He opened my eyes and I saw this guru for what he was. God gave me a new confidence, enabling me to sever the relationship and make a long overdue commitment to the Lord, and to Diana, who became my wife. My decision to follow Jesus was a stepwise process over several years, which culminated on October 18, 1977.

We had just finished apple picking in Washington State. The Lord was gradually building faith into our lives, but I was still holding on to some strange beliefs such as reincarnation, the unity of all religious paths and other such notions.

As we traveled back through Oregon, we met up again with David, who had baptized me three years earlier. I began telling him my various beliefs and also ran on about the failings of the church—the Crusades, the Spanish Inquisition—I even scorned the popularity of bingo in so many churches. David was quiet for a moment (praying, I later discovered) and then he said, "You know what I hear? You want to be knowledgeable, but you can't humble yourself before God!"

His words struck me to the heart. I felt as though I was made entirely of glass, with cracks swiftly spreading throughout my whole being. All my arguments, all my pride fell to pieces as that note of truth rang through me. It seemed like all my barriers to faith were lying shattered on the ground in a worthless heap of rubble. I was dazed, but ready for what God wanted me to do. David said, "You come to my house. Let my wife tell you about her life, then you can tell me if it's bingo or Jesus!" I accepted his invitation.

The next morning we came to a simple, gracious breakfast with Kim Friesen. She spoke to us briefly, then asked if she could pray for us. As she laid hands on us and prayed, I felt a tremendous overwhelming presence. For the first time, I knew that Jesus had completely forgiven all my sins. (It was also the first time I could admit to God and myself that I was a sinner.) I wept for what seemed to be hours. I knew that the love that was overwhelming me was only the millionth part of the full love that Jesus has for us, but it was all I could do to handle even that much.

After my decision, I still needed to be delivered from some of the dark spiritual forces that I'd unknowingly opened myself up to during my spiritual journey. Diana and I eventually moved into a Christian retreat center in Oakland, California. During this period, I had some one-on-one Bible instruction with some people from Jews for Jesus.

Certain things changed rapidly once Jesus was the central person in my life. I brought my fears before him and found that I could let go of them. I was no longer subject to the tailspin into destructive expressions of anger or depression that had previously been a pattern. Other issues seemed to require much time and healing.

For several years I still was intent on escaping from the world and its responsibilities. I was working as a woodwind instrument repair man—that job tucked me away in the back of a shop, and the "retreat" setting exemplified my desire not to be involved in society. Then, one day, it was as if the Lord spoke these simple words to my heart: "What are you saving it all for?" After all, God had literally saved me from incredible pitfalls into which I had seen others fall, never to be restored. Suddenly I realized that the blessings God had given me—a good education, good health, a sound mind—all these were meant to be used to serve him. The next words I heard astounded me: "Become a doctor!"

I said, "Lord, how can this be? I have no money, I have two small children to support, I'm older than the usual medical school applicant, and I don't believe much of the mind-set they'd be teaching me!" Yet the thought would not leave me. Beginning that very day, various "coincidences" began to present themselves and seemed to confirm what I thought God was telling me. But I still had doubts. Finally, after I had prayed about it for nearly a year, a wise and very blunt pastor heard my story and said, "Well, you'd better hurry up and get started—you're not getting any younger!" The doors opened and the Lord provided for all our needs throughout the whole process of pre-med courses, med school, and family practice residency, spanning a period of ten years.

Presently I work in a rural clinic in Soledad, focusing on pre-natal and obstetrical care for predominantly Mexican and Mexican-American migrant workers. Many patients, although they believe in God, have not thought to take their particular problem to him. They are often surprised that their doctor wants to pray with them. I also have a practice in Salinas where more than 90% of the patients believe in Jesus, and we regularly pray during the visits. Sometimes I learn about faith from these patients. One woman came with an ovarian growth and a firm faith that God would heal it. As we prayed, I was worrying about which medicine to choose for this woman, when I sensed the Spirit of God assuring me, "Don't worry, I've got this one." The follow-up ultrasound showed a normal ovary!

I've become a member of the board of directors of our local Crisis Pregnancy Center. We are hoping to become a clinic soon and perhaps expand to provide other services to the community. I am still somewhat active in music in our church. Our family now consists of four children (for the price of three—twins born in 1989), and Diana and I took our first honeymoon, after seventeen years of marriage.

My heart echoes the words of Psalm 116:12, 13 (NIV): "How can I repay the LORD for all his goodness to me? I will lift up the cup of salvation and call upon the name of the LORD." I also understand just what one of Jesus' disciples meant when Jesus asked the Twelve. "Do you also want to go away?" Simon Peter answered him, "Lord, to whom shall we go? You have the words of eternal life" (John 6:67b, 68b).

Robert Rosett, MD, is a family physician practicing in Soledad and Salinas, California.

STEPHEN A. SCHACHER

When I was a child in the 1940's, I heard the rabbis talk about whether we should support the founding of Israel or wait for the Messiah to lead us there. As I grew older and learned more about the history of my people, I learned just how long we have yearned for the Messiah to come. Never in all my musings did it occur to me that he had already come, or that he would enter my life.

I was born in New York City in 1941 to a Conservative Jewish family. My father was a dentist; my mother was a homemaker with a love for clothing design. Eventually (after I went off to college) she became a buyer of high-fashion clothes for various stores. I had a wonderful secular and Jewish education. I went to an Orthodox summer camp and also received religious training at my temple's school until I was *bar mitzvah.*

At camp, I mingled with Jewish kids who mostly came from homes that were more Orthodox than my own. There were prayer services each morning and abbreviated Orthodox services on Friday nights and Saturday mornings. In addition, we said grace before and after each meal, and the food was strictly kosher! I enjoyed the Jewish community atmosphere of this camp but have no memory of missing it when, at summer's end, I returned to the less observant environment of my home and school. In retrospect, however, it must have made a deep impression on me, because a few years later I began to long for the presence of God in my life.

One experience that did much to stimulate appreciation for my heritage was a summer grand tour of Europe I took with my parents when I was eleven. It was 1952. With Europe just recovering from the ravages of the Second World War, Americans were still heroes and friends to Europeans—American tourists had not yet worn out their welcome. I remember being greeted with smiles, especially in smaller towns throughout the continent. Occasionally, we would meet Jewish families. At the time, I was not aware of how great a miracle it was that they had survived the war. What impressed me the most was that my father could speak to them in Yiddish.

Because of this common language, we weren't strangers to each other. There was camaraderie and community. Whenever we joined these families for a meal, I discovered that we also shared common traditional foods. The warm, connected feeling of belonging with people we'd never met has remained with me to this day. Even though I didn't speak Yiddish, I had learned to say grace in Hebrew at my summer camp, so I could participate in this feeling of common culture.

The European grand tour provided me with a second, very different religious experience as well, and that was the experience of art.

Included in our tour of every city were the requisite visits to the great museums and cathedrals of that city. I saw thousands of paintings in England, France, and Italy, and hundreds of frescoes, stained glass windows, and sculptures. Many of the early paintings and sculptures depicted royalty, nobility and conquering heroes, and many of the later paintings were landscapes and portraits of ordinary people—but the overwhelming majority of art was about Jesus Christ. I received a pictorial presentation of the life of Jesus—his birth, life, death and resurrection—but I didn't know what any of it meant. I had no idea who Jesus was or what he might mean to me as a Jew. I only knew that Jesus was an important person to other people.

Following this trip, my parents became emboldened to travel to more distant lands. In 1957, when I was sixteen, we embarked on a grand tour of Asia. I remember most vividly taking a motor launch up a river in Vietnam, which at that time was enjoying a brief period of peace after the war with France and before the war with itself and with America. I can still picture us on the launch, dressed in vacation clothes and preparing to eat a luxurious lunch, while the people on the river were selling food from their boats. Many turned to avoid our cameras. This dissonance produced a feeling within me that I find difficult to describe.

I remember seeing a child with a swollen belly on a tattered vessel. He looked devastatingly undernourished. I tried to imagine his life, what he could possibly hope for himself. A natural inclination to help arose in me, but I had no idea what to do or how to go about it. I found myself wondering, *How is it that I am here in this launch, enjoying this life, while he is there suffering? Could an accident of fate suddenly transpose our souls, and he would sail off to live the rest of my life, and I would be left on the boat to live his?*

The Far East seems to generate questions like that. Buddha himself, while still a pampered prince, was tormented by such questions. Although I did not realize it at the time, that experience was the seed of a Buddhist phase in my own life, a phase that would come much later.

Meanwhile, I graduated high school and entered Yale University in 1957. I was drawn to philosophy and psychology, but my parents did not want me to lose myself in internalizing disciplines; they had always hoped and planned for me to follow after my father and become a doctor. Accordingly, they continued to encourage me toward biology and medical school. I was confused, partly because I was uncertain as to how much I should look inward for guidance and how much I should look outside myself to well-meaning people in authority over me.

Nevertheless, the issues of education and career were not the real source of the confusion I experienced. Although I could not have articulated it then, I was concerned with something deeper and higher than that. I needed to understand who God was, and to understand who I was and what relationship there was or should be between us. These concerns, however, were somewhat buried beneath the more apparent confusion that most college students experience in transition from the protection of childhood and adolescence to the uncharted waters of adulthood. I leaned toward medical school under my parents' guidance, not realizing that a crucial, unanswered question lay at the source of my ambivalence.

Despite the apparent, outward acceptance of my parents' wishes, I was not entirely convinced. With no one else whom I would consider a mentor available, I instinctively went directly to God for a second opinion. I began taking long walks around the Yale campus in my senior year, asking for his opinion on my future, simultaneously wondering if I was going about such a conversation in the right way.

Despite dozens of hours walking around the campus, I did not receive anything that could be called an answer, nor even the slightest hint that God was there. Finally, with no "second opinion" offered, I accepted the plan my parents felt was best for me.

During medical school, also at Yale, I forgot about God, but after I finished my specialty training in internal medicine, I began to seek him again.

In the early 1970s, I took a research position in medical education at the University of Vermont. My interest was how to keep physicians broadly knowledgeable about intersecting issues from all specialties, while they trained narrowly and deeply in their own specialty. This led me to explore the idea of stress as a common source of illness. I began attending holistic health conferences and delving into the New Age philosophies that they presented. This in turn led me to examine Eastern medicine, and finally, Eastern philosophy—disciplines that were gaining quite a following in the Western world at that time.

Between 1971 and 1981, I immersed myself in Asian thought. Though my original intent was to learn how to apply it to stress reduction (which I did), the religious aspects eventually pervaded my personal life. I moved to New Mexico to become part of a New Age community. Together with friends from this community, I lived for a while in Findhorn, Scotland. Findhorn had become internationally famous for its mystical origins, its Druid practices, and its open communication with "Nature spirits." I traveled to the French Alps one summer to be a student at the Sufi community's summer retreat and engaged in Sufi dancing and chanting.

At that time, I was of the opinion (seemingly shared by my entire generation and encouraged by our spiritual teachers) that all spiritual paths led to the same goal. That goal was the discovery of one's Self. The choice of spiritual "method" (a.k.a. religion) was simply a matter of deciding which path was most compatible with one's own personality or stage of spiritual development. The outcome of any path, however, was the same—the discovery of one's Self. Anyone who succeeded in reaching this goal became a Master, an awakened or enlightened Being, regardless of the tradition by which he or she arrived. No tradition offered any more or less than any other.

Oddly enough, to be consistent with this point of view, the teachers and trainers expounding Eastern philosophies felt a need to tell Western students that what they were teaching was no different from what Jesus taught. Sometimes they said this to underscore their philosophy: that all teachers ultimately taught the same message. Sometimes they said it because they assumed that all of us Western students were Christians and would find it easier to accept Eastern metaphysical teachings if we found them in harmony with the memories of our childhood biblical lessons. They often ended with a quote from Jesus to reinforce the idea that there was universal agreement among various spiritual masters. As a result, I heard quite a bit of the gospel preached, albeit with an Eastern interpretation of "oneness," a teaching that Christians would call gnosticism.

Throughout this period, I did have one central, unifying spiritual practice—Zen Buddhism. I began practicing early in 1971, after reading Philip Kapleau's autobiography and Zen text, *The Three Pillars of Zen*. I read this book dozens of times, actively sat in Zen Buddhist halls (called *zendos*), and took part in Zen retreats. I liked the meditation, I loved the teachings, I found the teachers (*roshis*) to be wonderful people and I became increasingly certain that this was the way of life for me. This kept me focused while I tried to digest the rest of the spiritual smorgasbord. I sampled many movements such as EST, Silva Mind Control and others but always returned to Zen.

By 1975, I had left both the research and practice of medicine to devote all my time to spiritual pursuits, supporting myself with part-time medical positions. I felt that what I was learning would ultimately make me a more effective physician as I still desired to teach patients how to deal with stress. I considered becoming a full-time Zen roshi, a goal that would take many years of single-minded meditation under one or more teachers. Many other Westerners, including many Jews like myself, were following an identical path.

All of these plans, however, came to a dramatic and complete halt on June 4, 1981, even as I was meditating in a zendo in Seattle and preparing to deepen my study of Buddhism. I shall attempt to present what went on inside my mind in an orderly and understandable way, even though the reality happened very quickly.

I had moved to Seattle in 1980 to become a flight surgeon with the Federal Aviation Administration. At that time, air traffic controllers were famous for their problems with on-the-job stress, and I felt that I was ready for a full-time position handling stress-ridden individuals and their medical problems. I had always planned to reenter the medical field when I reached this point.

I joined the local Zen community and soon was sitting with them regularly in meditation. This community had been fortunate to obtain the services of a Japanese Zen master, who had left Japan expressly to lead their meditations and training.

The series of events to which I referred began while I was sitting in this zendo in Seattle. I was deeply immersed in my Zen *koan*, which, as many people know, is a complex question which can be solved only by looking at the world through Buddha's point of view, the point of view of enlightenment. Attempting to solve the problem from the point of view of dualism—the natural belief that each of us is a separate being, distinct from everything and everyone else—is considered a fruitless exercise. One is instructed to abandon that point of view in favor of the enlightened perspective of oneness. Success in achieving the Buddhist perspective provides an immediate and satisfying answer to the koan's conundrum. The answer appears with lightning speed, once the perceptual shift is achieved, much as three-dimensional pictures spring from the pages of a flat book when the eyes are correctly relaxed. Subsequent koans are chosen by a teacher to deepen the student's insight, the ultimate goal being to achieve the identical frame of mind that Buddha achieved at his great enlightenment.

As my understanding of Buddha's teachings deepened, I found my meditation practice wonderfully relaxing and intellectually exciting. My life simplified. I now had only one spiritual practice and was not constantly seeking others. I was employed in a full-time position at the FAA, with no part-time work. In Zen fashion, I reduced my possessions to the bare minimum (a few clothes, books, skis, and cooking spices). My furniture was minimal and orderly. My desire to understand more about "my path" accelerated. I was ready to discuss with the roshi the issue of taking vows to become a formal Zen student.

However, there was one point on which I was not completely satisfied. The more I heard various teachers state that Jesus and Buddha were saying the same thing, the more I wondered about the contrast between Jesus' agony on the cross and Buddha's beatific and totally relaxed enlightenment. I began to think that if I could understand how these expressions of spiritual completeness could be identical while appearing to be completely opposite, my understanding of both of these paths would grow. I would experience a leap in my spiritual understanding. I felt with increasing certainty that my next focus should be to understand what Jesus was saying—just to be certain that it was as I had been told. After all, I had pursued every other major religious teacher on earth; why shouldn't I examine Jesus Christ before making a final decision?

But how should I go about understanding what Jesus said?

As a good Zen student, I knew that the way to discover what an apple tastes like is to bite the apple, chew it, and swallow it. Therefore, I reasoned that the way to discover what Jesus taught was to identify with him, to become a Christian. But how does one become a Christian? Well, I knew the answer to that: One simply believes and confesses that he or she accepts Jesus as the Messiah. Being a Jew, I knew—or thought I knew—what that meant. It meant that one accepted Jesus as the Promised One of Israel, the one who would bring peace forever and forever.

Having convinced myself that I definitely needed to undertake this thought experiment, I said loudly in my mind and with complete conviction, *Jesus, I accept you as the Messiah of Israel.* In my mind I heard the words *The Passover Lamb who takes away the sin of the world.* Without warning or preparation, following a series of mentally visualized images—to my utter astonishment—I suddenly saw that it was true!

The thoughts and images that flooded my mind in the next few seconds were so vast, so all-encompassing of my years of religious/spiritual experiences, that I couldn't contain them. Bins of stored information, previously unconnected in my mind, suddenly flooded together in a manner that produced insight after insight and connection after connection.

I remember visualizing Jesus on the cross in my mind, seeing him as the Passover lamb with his blood on a transparent door, with the blood itself covering the door frame. I identified him as the Passover lamb in Exodus. At the same time, the words *who takes away the sin of the world* activated the thought, *but sin is removed by the Yom Kippur atonement, not the Passover lamb.*

I realized that this phrase was stating that the Passover blood was similar to, maybe even identical with, the blood of the Yom Kippur sacrifice. This was a completely novel thought for me. I had always assumed that Passover was a ritual celebrating the exodus from bondage in Egypt and that Yom Kippur was a ritual that God provided in the wilderness for taking care of subsequent sins. Now I reasoned that if Jesus' death fulfilled both ritual sacrifices—Passover and Yom Kippur—this meant that his death on the cross simultaneously fulfilled escape from bondage *and* atonement for sins. I had a sudden sense that this meant that he was the Messiah.

My mind was now in high gear. If Jesus' death represented the two most significant sacrifices in the Jewish liturgy, which heretofore I had assumed were different and unrelated, clearly his death was extremely meaningful. It could not be merely an accidental and random occurrence.

I remembered being in synagogue on Yom Kippur and praying to have my name written in the Book of Life for the following year. I knew enough about Christianity to realize that this atonement sacrifice was what Christians meant when they said that Jesus had died for our sins and that we now had eternal life.

I had the strange thought that perhaps the purpose of the Old Testament Temple had been to provide a stage and a meaning for Jesus' death. I recalled a New Testament passage of Jesus telling his listeners that someone "greater than the Temple" was standing in their midst. The phrase had always struck me as very odd and I could attach no meaning to it. Suddenly I saw it. The purpose of an arena is to provide the spectacle. Without the spectacle, an arena has no meaning.

All this was whetting my appetite to read more of the Bible as soon as the Zen meditation session ended. But what was truly odd was that at the same moment I had begun to realize the meaning of Jesus as the Passover lamb, I experienced a second insight that produced tremendous inner peace. I realized that I no longer needed to become a Zen roshi. To explain this, I need to explain what is meant by the doctrine of "karma."

Buddhism, like most Eastern philosophies, teaches that after death we are physically reincarnated. In each subsequent lifetime we experience the benefits or punishments for our deeds from the previous lifetime. Good deeds produce beneficial circumstances in rebirth, and evil deeds lead to punishments or discouraging circumstances. Since the Buddhist universe is interconnected, we must experience the fruits of each action we perform, either in this lifetime or in a subsequent one. For example, in Buddhist thought, if you bring about an abortion, sooner or later you will have to be aborted yourself.

By engaging in Buddhist meditation—a remarkably neutral activity—an individual is thought to cease generating new karma while simultaneously becoming strong enough to face his or her past karma as it slowly unfolds over many lifetimes. Eventually, if one creates no new karma (by sitting in meditation as much as possible and bearing all circumstances with equanimity), one runs out of past karma to face. At this point one is a *bodhisattva,* a being with no remaining karma to pay back. Subsequently, one gives up being even this and passes into the nonexistence of Buddhahood, presumably a highly desirable state.

Now here is why all my plans to continue in Buddhism ceased as soon as I realized the truth about Jesus.

If Buddha's point of view about life were really the Truth, and I had been sidetracked from pursuing it because of what Jesus Christ had said about himself, then to a certain extent, Jesus Christ would be responsible for having distracted me from the benefits of the Zen path. If this then led to more karma and suffering for me, Jesus would have to take at least some of the blame for my predicament. In other words, it would be Jesus' "karma" to take at least part of the punishment for some of my past and possibly future sins.

It hit me with great force that Jesus had no "karma" of his own, yet he was willing to take the punishment for all my sins, past, present, and future. That fact slowly sank in. Why was I sitting in a zendo? There was no need to go through thousands of lifetimes hoping to pay back all my karma without creating any new karma when Jesus was willing to do it all for me right now, forever, for free!

I was done.

I had been on the spiritual path for ten years, and the farthest I had come was simply to know why I was on the path. It was to pay back the old karma so that I could be free. Every single religion, philosophy, growth seminar and spiritual practice I had ever studied made that the first step. Goal number one was pay back your karma, get over your unconscious guilt, and free yourself from unconscious fears, needs, and desires. Yet here was Jesus offering to do it all at once, with no special training program or years of arduous study and self-denial required.

In an instant I had gone further than my own Zen teacher, who, however advanced he was, nevertheless was still paying back *his* karma. He would continue attempting to do so until he reached Buddhahood, which, according to his religion, could be thousands or even millions of lifetimes away!

I sat in stunned silence. I'd had my first understanding of what it meant to say that Jesus is the Messiah. Why had I never seen it before? He is the Temple itself, the bridge linking us to the Father. He is the sacrificial system, wiping away the separation from God that exists even inside the Temple. For me, the veil had torn. I had access to the Holy of Holies, even as the New Testament book of Hebrews says. Many famous Bible phrases became clearer. A key had fit perfectly into a lock that I hadn't even known was there. When it turned, my heart had opened.

None of this was what I had expected or imagined would happen. I had simply engaged in a thought experiment to find out if Buddha and Jesus were saying the same thing. My reason for embracing Christianity was merely to help me decide whether or not to commit myself more strongly to Zen. Now I was sitting in a zendo with the answer to a question I hadn't asked. My spiritual journey had not been extended; rather it had ended abruptly in a totally unexpected way. I knew I had found what I had been looking for from the very beginning. It was such an unexpected switch from my ongoing inner dialogue about Zen that I was flabbergasted.

The zendo bell rang. Time to go to *dokusan* (face-to-face meeting with the roshi). I ran to be at the head of the line. Two people were ahead of me. I rehearsed how firmly I was going to hit the bell. (The roshi can determine the state of your mind by how firmly and focused or weakly and distractedly you hit the bell before entering his room.) When my time came, I hit it with everything I had. (Sometimes when you hit it too hard, it clanks instead of ringing.) To my satisfaction, the bell resounded through the zendo.

The roshi smiled when I entered. I told him that I had experienced a great insight and that I wanted to become a Christian. I told him I felt as though my heart had opened. While this was being translated into Japanese, and his answer back into English, I imagined that he was going to tell me that this was a *makyo* (illusion). Everything short of enlightenment is an illusion. Instead he said (through translation), "When your heart opens, you have found what you are looking for."

I laughed. In Zen talk, this is code for enlightenment. The "heart" means the spot in the belly toward which you direct your meditation. When it opens you experience the "Nothingness" of enlightenment, which was not my experience. I hadn't been emptied, I'd been somehow filled. Yet at the same time, I took his remark as meaning, "Good-bye and good luck. It sounds as though you know what you're doing."

I slept very well that night and was still enjoying thinking about this experience the next day in my office, when I casually mentioned to a patient that he appeared to be very stress-free. He said, "That's because of my faith in Jesus!" Apparently I looked as though I had just been shot, because he began telling me about his faith with great energy, as though he had only seconds to get it all out. Suddenly, without warning, all my prejudice—which I hadn't known was inside me—came roaring to the surface. Regardless of whatever I had experienced the previous day, I was not ready to be what I considered a traitor to my people. "What about all the Christians who persecuted us Jews? What about the Holocaust? What about the Jewish expulsions of the Middle Ages, the badges, the ghettoes and all created by Christians?" and on and on.

Now it was his turn to look shot.

"You're Jewish?"

"Yes."

"I can't answer your questions," he said, "but I know people who can. You need to call Jews for Jesus." He told me that Jews for Jesus had no staff in the Seattle area, but that a couple, Dick and Polly Perkins, volunteered some of their time with the organization.

I called Dick and Polly, and they invited me for dinner that night. I asked them many questions about Jewish history and how they could explain God's seeming abandonment of the Jews. I asked them how Christians could justify their historical support of anti-Semitism and how they felt about being part of a religious group that had so persecuted the Jews. Dick listened carefully to my questions, but instead of giving me the kind of answer I was expecting him to give—a personal answer—he turned to the Bible. He responded to each of my questions by saying, "Let's see what God has to say about that."

"God?" I said to myself silently. "What does he have to do with this?" I was looking for an explanation of why people who professed to follow Jesus could be so un-Christ-like. Yet Dick kept showing me passages in the Old Testament where God revealed how *he* would honor obedience and punish disobedience, how *he* would scatter us and bring us back. He then shared passages with me about God making a new covenant. This was now familiar ground to me. I was already aware of many messianic passages.

What kept striking me was the tone Dick had taken. He was telling me what God said. He regarded the Bible as though it had come from a real God, not merely from people. Out of a deep corner of my mind, I remembered reading the Bible in Hebrew school. How often I had heard, "And then God said to Moses. . . ." This God was still around? The God who had parted the Red Sea was still alive?

I remembered thinking about God when I was a child. Some artist had attempted a picture of him in a children's Bible I once had. There was another picture on the ceiling of the Sistine

Chapel in Rome, attempting to portray God conveying the Spirit of life to Adam. This God they attempted to portray was real?

Some inner resistance relaxed. Of course this God was real. This is the God we had prayed to at camp, the one I had talked to at college, the one I was looking for. Nothing Dick Perkins said to me that night impacted me quite as much as the manner in which he conveyed to me that this personal God was real. My understanding of Jesus and atonement for sin had all been about what a person had done for other people. Now I realized what God had done for me. Christianity was not just freedom from bondage to "karma" (which I now realized was sin) and it was not just eternal life—it was a relationship with God, the Creator I had learned about as a Jew.

My questions ceased. I realized that none of them were really my questions anyway. I was asking them because I thought they were questions that a Jewish person ought to ask. In fact, I really didn't have any questions, at least none for people. I did have a question for God, a real question that only he could answer in the way that I wanted it answered. "Why did you set up the universe so that the Jews would end up suffering at the hands of people who also claimed to love you?" I didn't think a human being could answer that question to my satisfaction, so I decided that I would wait and ask God at an appropriate moment. If we are going to spend eternity together, I reasoned, there will undoubtedly be a right time for that kind of question.

I was oddly at peace. Even as I experienced this peace, I recalled asking my bar mitzvah teacher why we Jews did not accept Jesus as the Messiah. He said that it was because when the Messiah came, there would be peace—and was there peace?

I had been searching for that peace for a long time. I tried to find it in zendos, New Age conferences, and pop psychology cults; I'd gone to Sufi camps and to New Age communities. And finally, I had found that peace. The Messiah had come. It was Jesus whom I had been seeking all those years. Of course, in a way it was really Jesus who had been looking for me, biding his time, waiting for the right moment. When that moment came, he revealed the truth, and it was clear and obvious.

I became an avid Bible reader. I met my wife-to-be, Roberta

Kern. We married and now have two children. I went into the private practice of internal medicine with a newfound interest—for though I am still interested in helping to relieve people's stress, I do so from a completely different perspective. We found a church in Seattle where we feel very much at home and where I teach classes on understanding Judaism (for Christians) and on the Old Testament.

When I was a child in the 1940's, I heard the rabbis talk about the Messiah, because they were debating whether we Jews should support the founding of Israel or wait until the Messiah came to lead us there. As I grew older and learned more about the history of the Jews, I learned just how long we have all yearned for the

Messiah to come. Never in all my musings, did it ever occur to me that I could know him in my lifetime.

While I was looking in a faraway place among Eastern idols, trying to become one with everything and with "Nothingness," the Messiah came for me. How amazing! I pray, dear reader, that he has come for you as well. Blessed is he that comes in the name of the Lord.

Stephen Schacher, MD, practices Occupational Medicine in Seattle, Washington.

You've read how people who deal with the physical maladies of others sought answers for their own spiritual maladies. The next five chapters give a brief change of perspective, telling how a few Jewish believers in Jesus found spiritual strength to deal with physical crises. These people have had their faith tested through chronic pain, an uncertain future after a heart transplant, the birth of a child whose Down syndrome came as a total shock, the death of a loved one, and finally, you'll meet a doctor who knew he would lose his life if he told the truth. Their experiences each attest in their own way to the power of the Great Physician.

Part Two

Where Is Jesus in a Personal Crisis?

SCOTT RUBIN

The invitation came from my father, a physician with privileges at Cedars Sinai. I was eager to attend the lecture because the speaker, Dr. Michael Fowler, was from Stanford University Hospital. His topic was "Transplantation in 1987," a topic of utmost interest to me. I sat in the back with my father and watched the room fill with doctors and nurses who also had an interest in this high-tech, life-saving medicine. The first case history presented was referred to as Patient Number One. To me he was John.

Back in 1987, I arrived at the coronary care unit at Stanford the day before John. I got the room with an outside door—though I was hooked up to far too many tubes with IV drips to get anywhere close to the exit. When one suitable heart for transplant became available, it was either John or me (they haven't figured out a way to clone donor hearts just yet). I got the call. John made it to the next available heart, and we recovered together.

Along with Jim, a 50-ish cardiologist who received a transplant a week or so before we did, we formed an odd sort of tontine. A year later, the three of us gathered for a reunion in Los Angeles. We had a great meal, a trip to Olvera Street and a glass of wine at John's Palos Verde home overlooking the Pacific Ocean. Two months later John awoke in the middle of the night and stirred his wife awake with the question, "Can you feel my heart beat?" The next thing she knew, he was gone.

As I sat listening to John's medical history, it sounded distant and cold. I wanted to interject, to tell them something about John the person, John the inventor, John the father, John the husband. But this was a hospital and the lecture was purely scientific. Then came Patient Number Two.

He was a 28-year-old male admitted in June 1985 with tachycardia. Biopsy revealed necrosis. There was talk of Shwann-Gans catheterization and lots of numbers that meant nothing to me. Then a readmit. Then another. Then more numbers. Those last numbers must have been bad because there were some gasps in the room.

Then an older, distinguished-looking gentleman approached me and introduced himself. He said that it was not often that the subject of the case study is present. He wondered if I might be willing to answer questions from the medical staff. Might as well, I thought, so I (a.k.a. Patient Number Two) responded, "I'd be happy to."

Some of the questions were trivial, such as what did I think of the difference between the hospitals? They were merely "warm-ups" for the not-so-trivial. What was life like living as a transplant patient? What did I think of all this? What helped me get through? For many of these personal questions, I found myself strangely unprepared.

I had gotten through the waiting and the surgery with a great deal of confidence. In fact, I think my confidence was somewhat unnerving to my parents. I am from a close-knit Jewish family but, unlike my parents, I had come to believe that Jesus is the Jewish Messiah. I had tremendous confidence in him and in the prayers that friends across the country were offering on my behalf. I just knew that I would survive.

Life takes on a different perspective after surgery. I had tried to be there for John, but he was a rock and seemed not to need the extra encouragement. Jim was another story. I spent a lot of time talking to Jim about God, about life, about making the most of the time we had been given. Yet I hadn't sorted out some of the tough questions for myself. I knew that I was thankful to be alive, and to have time with my wife, and especially the added time with my twins, but I still had a lot to process. How was I ever going to process *this*?

As I spoke to Jim I made some comments about coming to terms with what a friend euphemistically called, "an abbreviated life," one which Allstate simply referred to as "uninsurable." I mentioned that I was in seminary and still seeking answers to some of the tougher questions that are unique to heart transplant patients. It seemed that my faith would provide some help, at least that's what I was counting on when I rejected offers of psychiatric care and antianxiety drugs on which many people in my position lean. When those semisleepless nights hit, I sometimes questioned if I had made the right choice. But I knew that even if some mind-numbing drugs could help me through the night, there would be too many nights and I didn't want to start down that road. I needed answers, and I wanted a clear head when I got them.

Jim was a bit more angry than I. He was upset and he was scared. He knew all the risks to all the procedures we had yet to undergo. He would come over to my house with his medical papers showing me how brief our lives would be. He was filled with fear. I would pull down the Bible and show him that with faith in Jesus the Messiah, we would live for eternity. I was filled with confidence. When he left, he would go with Scriptures and peace. I would be left with his medical papers and fear. Where could I find answers for myself?

Then came a class in systematic theology. This course was taught by a world-renowned scholar. I was going to get some answers to some big questions. The first day of class began with 100 or so eager students crammed into the "classroom"— a church basement. The professor walked slowly to the front of the room and gave an overview of the class. Then he began in earnest.

How could Christ be both God and man? He summarized how this question has been answered through the ages, and explained why each answer was inadequate. After hours of questions and answers and detailed analyses, he was ready to tell us *his* answer. He certainly had my attention. And then this world-class scholar with impeccable credentials had the audacity to say it: "I don't know." *He did not know.* Furthermore, he added, that didn't bother him. Didn't bother him? Isn't this what it's all about? And he didn't know? And it didn't bother him that he didn't know?

Then he explained why it didn't bother him. He was only human. There were some things that humans haven't been made privy to by God. He knew he didn't have all the answers, and he had learned to live with uncertainty.

There was my answer. Actually, it was a non-answer, but more powerful and more truthful than all the trite attempts to sweep my questions away. I am not God. I do not have all the answers. God does not want me to have all the answers. I could live with a certain amount of uncertainty. In fact, I needed to live with certain amounts of uncertainty. Furthermore, we all—transplant patients, nurses, doctors, indeed everyone—need to live with uncertainty. From then on, life took on a certain amount of urgency. I wanted to make the most of the time God had granted me.

There were talks to be had with my wife. There were relationships that needed mending. There were people to whom I should reach out. There were two children who bore my name, and I needed to instill them with values and help build their character.

There were many things I could not do. There were games I could not play with my boys. There were jobs that I could not perform because of the debilitating effects of the medicines. Rather than lament the losses, however, I could rejoice in the gains. Each time I watched the news or read the paper, I was reminded of tragedies I had escaped, the life that I had, the grace of God that sustained me and permitted me to reach this day.

There would be calls to visit others who were deathly ill. The medicine men and women could only do so much. Would I be so kind as to bring a word or two of comfort or encouragement? There was another Jewish believer in Jesus who had a heart transplant and then developed pneumonia. The treatment for the pneumonia severely damaged her liver, so she was being evaluated for a liver transplant. When I met her, she was yellowed with jaundice. She asked not to be touched because she itched from the inside out, but she wanted my prayers. The liver transplant was not to be.

There was the call from the Midwest, from a pastor asking me to stop in on one of his congregants who had received an emergency retransplant but did not want to live. The father of the young girl was grateful, the mother's anger was hid behind a gritted smile, and the daughter herself was silent. The wall was too great, the determination too strong. She had simply had enough. Nothing could or would change her attitude, and she would soon have her wish.

Then there were others. There was the middle-aged man who wondered, would he get a heart? How long could he live without one? How long could he live with one? What kind of life could he and his wife expect? To them, and to others, I could repeat the words of my professor. Some say this and some say that, but they don't know and neither do I, for I am not God. God has seen fit to withhold certain information, but I believe he does so in his mercy and grace. And while he does not give us all the answers, he has given us ways of living with uncertainty so that we can make the most of our lives. Somehow God, who is in the business of redeeming us from ourselves, allows us to find redemption in the short time we have here.

That is where God's questions to us enter in. When the gifts of healing (which come from God) have been exhausted, or even when those gifts have worked mira-cles, God still questions us. Healing is not an end in itself. God wants to know: What will we do with the time he has given us? How will we treat others whom he also created? How will we relate to the One who gave himself for us? Will we accept the gift of life by faith in the One who was the universal donor?

LAURA BARRON

"Is my baby okay?"

Two hours after Rafael's birth, the obstetrician had taken him to the neonatal unit because he "wasn't happy with his color."

"I think they're just concerned about his temperature," the nurse replied. Yet something in her eyes and in the timbre of her voice told me that she knew more than she was saying. Maybe I was just sensitive after giving birth, but I thought the midwife and nurses seemed quiet—almost somber—for such a joyous occasion. My baby boy entered the world with a healthy cry, but when I put him to my breast, the midwife told me too quickly, too emphatically, that she didn't think he would suck right away.

Three hours after Rafi was born, the pediatrician informed my husband Andrew and me that he believed our baby had Down's syndrome.

"Are you sure?" I gasped. My heart was pounding and my mind was plummeting into disbelief. I wanted to make the doctor's words disappear! I had waited until I was thirty-one to have my first child and suddenly all my dreams for him had shifted in a moment. I looked at Andrew's tear-filled eyes and wondered if he could see that I was cold and shaking. The doctor's eyes were compassionate as he met each of our gazes, but he was very direct.

"I won't be able to tell for certain until the chromosome tests come back in a couple of days, but I do think that Rafael has Down's syndrome. I've asked the cardiologist to examine him. If his heart is sound, there is no reason why you can't take him home. If you have any questions, I'm available."

"If I have questions?" I thought. I felt dizzy and confused. My every thought was a question and I didn't know what to ask first. What could I expect from this little person who had just entered my world with a completely unexpected set of troubles?

Andrew had already phoned our family and friends to announce our joy at Rafi's birth. Now he had to phone them again to inform them that our son probably had Down's syndrome. Was there any right way of saying this? Would we forever have to add a caveat to our son's existence? We had fallen in love with Rafael instantaneously and were still thrilled by the gift of his life. We wanted to inform our loved ones of this unexpected turn of events, yet we still wanted them to rejoice with us over the birth of our beautiful boy.

Rafael was the first grandchild to be born in Andrew's family. His mother had been so excited about my pregnancy; for the first six years of our marriage, I had always felt the question hanging in the air—whether spoken or unspoken—in every conversation: "So when are you planning to have children?!" I felt that there would be high expectations accompanying Rafael's birth, and to a degree, I feared that I had disappointed them by producing a genetically "mixed up" child.

They had already faced deep disappointment when Andrew changed careers. He was working as an aerospace engineer when he came to believe that Jesus is the Messiah of Israel. I think they wondered "where they went wrong." After all, they had brought him up in a kosher home, sent him to *cheder*, and brought him to *shul* regularly. It must have been quite a shock when he decided to work on a master's degree at a Christian seminary instead of continuing with his master's degree in physics. Ultimately, I think their realization that they had a son whom they loved, and who loved them, took precedence over any other disagreements or disappointments.

I was grateful that their attitude toward Rafi was just as loving. He hadn't turned out quite as we had expected, but they were ready to accept him wholeheartedly. The first words my mother-in-law said to me after the birth were, "I just wish I was there to hug you right now."

I felt upheld by the enveloping love and understanding from all of our family and friends. They gave me the much-needed freedom to talk. My mother gave me literature on Down syndrome. After I spoke with my brother, he commented, "Now I can see how deep your faith really is, just by hearing you talk about Rafi." My father was away for the holidays and sent us a card a few days after Rafi's birth saying: "It's *Rosh Hashanah* and I just wanted to tell you both how good it made me feel to talk on the phone yesterday. Little Rafi may not go to Oxford but he will return our love in so many wonderful ways. I can't wait

WHERE IS JESUS IN A PERSONAL CRISIS?

to hold him. And Laura, I'm so proud of you. You're a woman who meets life head-on and has surpassed her old man in the guts department. I admire the way you did pregnancy, labor, work and marriage. You'll be a wonderful mom, too. See you soon. All my love, Dad."

The way my father responded to Andrew, Rafi and me has formed a solid foundation of warm family memories—it has strengthened me. My father and I had our differences in the past. When I decided to marry Andrew, my father—a Jew who does not believe in Jesus—was upset and angry because I was marrying a missionary. Even worse in his estimation was the fact that I wanted to make it my life's work to tell people about Jesus, too. My faith was nothing new to my dad—I have believed in Jesus since I was twelve years old. But the career change caused him pain. From the time of the wedding in 1989 until 1991, we hardly spoke to one another. When we began communicating again, we realized how much we valued our mutual love and respect. Our responses to Rafi's birth in 1996 cemented our relationship and helped us to focus on what we had in common rather than what separated us.

For the next few days in the hospital, Andrew and I alternated between crying and cooing over our newborn. How could we have anticipated the mixture of pure joy and profound pain that accompanies the birth of a handicapped child? The "unknown" had hit us in the face with full force. The worst part about not knowing is not being in control.

Yet in a way, we were prepared. Before our son was born, I'd begun keeping a journal for him. Without knowing what was ahead, I'd written, "Whoever you are, you'll be yourself and I'll love you just the way you are—you'll be my special adorable baby!" I had chosen the name Rafael Reuben (if my baby was a boy) when I was eight weeks pregnant. In Hebrew, Rafael means "God is my healer" and Reuben (in honor of my late maternal grandfather) means "Behold, a son." Our son's name was more appropriate than I could have imagined. God had already granted us the gift of acceptance—to be able to accept our son exactly the way he had been given to us.

Part of that acceptance came from knowing that our God, the Creator of the Universe, is in control. Nothing comes as a surprise to God. He knew the prophet Jeremiah even before "he formed him in the womb" (see Jeremiah 1:5). That same God knew that Rafi would have an extra chromosome. For reasons beyond our understanding, God allowed this to happen.

Andrew and I could not know what the future will hold for Rafi, but we could trust that God would be with us as we faced the future—and we knew that he who is supremely trustworthy was in control. His certain presence provided peace that prevailed amidst the uncertainty of those first few shocking and interminable days after Rafi's birth.

The "preacher" wrote in Ecclesiastes 11:5, "As you do not know what is the way of the wind, or how the bones grow in the womb of her who is with child, so you do not know the works of God who makes all things." God understands why he allowed Rafael to have Down syndrome even if I cannot. Throughout the Scriptures, I read that God takes full responsibility for forming each one of us in our mother's womb. This knowledge comforted me when I needed a reminder of God's power.

I was also comforted in the knowledge that God's values differ from the values of this world. In his kingdom, something that seems foolish to the world is actually wisdom, and sometimes what the world considers weakness is actually strength. I knew my son would be different—not as clever or as cute as most "normal" children—but I also knew that God would love and value him more than I can imagine.

The greatest comfort of all is this: I believe that God has a son, who was born as a child on this earth. When he was grown, people rejected him because he wasn't what they thought he should be. His name is Y'shua, which means salvation, because he was sent to earth to save people from their sins. God knew what would happen to his son before the beginning of time, yet he still saw fit to carry out his plan. Y'shua's life was a paradox of pure joy and profound pain, exultation and suffering and finally victory. Because of Y'shua and all that he endured, I know that God understands my feelings in the most intimate way possible.

Andrew and I see Rafi as our reward from the Lord. That doesn't mean we haven't had hard times or that we won't have to face even harder times up the road. Sometimes the simplest scene has wrenched my heart. I'd be waiting in line at the grocery store, watching as the six-month-old baby sitting in the cart ahead of me babbled noisily while grabbing at the candy by the cash register. The mother, worn out by trying to keep up with the active tot, was obviously annoyed. My eyes filled with tears as I smiled at my nine-month-old baby lying silently, smiling in his stroller because he could not sit up on his own yet. How I yearned to see him sit in the cart laughing and grabbing at items beyond his reach. Those moments, I knew, would arrive eventually through loving, attentive parenting and many physiotherapy, occupational therapy, and speech therapy sessions.

My relationship with God brought me through the shock of Rafi's birth and I trust God to take me through each day of my son's development. I will continue to trust in the Lord for him through every potential illness and every learning disability. At Rafi's *bris,* our congregation read together the words of King David from Psalm 139:13–16: "For You formed my inward parts; You covered me in my mother's womb. I will praise You, for I am fearfully and wonderfully made; Marvelous are Your works, and *that* my soul knows very well. My frame was not hidden from You, when I was made in secret, *and* skillfully wrought in the lowest parts of the earth. Your eyes saw my substance, being yet unformed. And in Your book they all were written, the days fashioned for me, when *as yet there were* none of them."

King David trusted God in all kinds of circumstances, whether facing a giant, the wrath of a jealous king, the awesome responsibility of ruling a nation, or the death of a newborn son—he even trusted God when he had to face his own sin.

God is worthy to be trusted. Will you turn to him before you hit another circumstance that brings you face to face with the reality that you are not in control of your life or the lives of those you love?

AVI SNYDER

The ceiling didn't open and the walls didn't collapse. No sea of relief engulfed my soul, as far as I could tell. No burdensome weight dropped from my heart. From the vantage point of my couch, I could see and feel no change.

Yet a miracle had occurred. My sins had been forgiven, and my reconciliation with God had begun a relationship that would last forever. Soon that relationship would break into my consciousness as the confidence of God's present help and the guarantee of his eternal presence.

It was March 1977, and I had finally made the decision I had been putting off for four months. That's how long it had been since I'd concluded that the Bible was what it claimed to be—an inspired communication from God to the human race. I'd also concluded that if my own Jewish Bible were true, Y'shua had to be the Messiah who was promised to us in the Law, the Writings and the Prophets. I'd reached these conclusions in December, but it took four months to grapple with the truth. Understanding it wasn't enough. I needed to take a step of faith and act upon what I'd discovered to be true.

So, in March I sat in my apartment and said a simple prayer, making a commitment to follow Y'shua in an open way.

A little over a year later, in June 1978, I was diagnosed with a chronic illness called Crohn's disease. It's also called regional enteritis and terminal ileitis (because it affects the terminal section of the ileum). I'd been ill from time to time throughout my life, so the onset of this new condition simply seemed like a new circumstance with which I'd have to cope. It didn't send me into a tailspin nor did I think it would require me to reorient the way I lived my entire life. I would simply have to make some accommodations, particularly regarding what I ate—or so I thought.

I didn't know that pain was to become my regular companion. So was the frustration of pre-empted plans. Eight years and eleven hospitalizations later, my wife, Ruth, and I concluded that something had to change. The doctors were reluctant to operate because—as they explained it—one operation often needed to be followed in time by others. It was better not to introduce surgery if the situation could be managed somewhat with medication.

It wasn't a promising scenario, but there was something the doctors had not factored in: the confidence of God's present help and the guarantee of his eternal presence. Ruth and I prayed for something that would alter a course that was getting progressively worse, and God performed another miracle.

Suddenly, complications changed my condition from chronic to life-threatening. Surgery was the only option. And so I underwent what is called a resectioning, in which the doctor attempts to remove all the diseased portion of the intestinal tract and re-attach one clean end to the other. My doctor warned me not to be too hopeful; the operation, he said, was a management tool—not a cure. There are no cures for Crohn's disease, he reminded me. That's why it's called "chronic."

Despite the warning, I felt God would accomplish more than the doctor expected through this surgery. So, after the surgery I was very pleased but not surprised to hear that follow-up tests indicated no further presence of the disease in my body. Apparently, the doctor explained, the condition had been much more localized than anyone could have imagined. They were able to remove every part of the diseased intestine. Some might think that was a lucky break. I think it was an answer to prayer. It was certainly not what the doctor expected . . . another miracle, as far as I'm concerned.

Shortly before my release from the hospital, I spoke with a man in an adjacent room. He also was scheduled to go home, but our situations were completely different. Whereas my surgery had been for Crohn's disease, his had been for cancer. I was going home to recuperate; he was going home to die. I believed in Y'shua; he believed only in himself. I wanted to offer him something before our paths parted. The nurse who attended both of us had told me that despite our differing points of view, the man next door would be happy to chat with me before each of us went our separate ways. I stopped into his room, and we had a pleasant conversation.

"Do you believe in miracles?" he asked me at one point.

"Yes," I said, "I do."

"Miracles would be nice," he admitted.

"Miracles are all right," I parried.

He was discernably surprised. "Just all right?"

"Well, there's a problem with miracles," I told him.

"What could be wrong with a miracle?" he wanted to know.

"Actually, the problem isn't with the miracle," I explained. "The problem is with the kind of miracle that we want. We usually ask God for smaller miracles, which he may or may not grant. But we overlook the most important miracle of all—the one he's always willing to perform."

"What's that?" he wanted to know.

I asked if I could show him a passage from the Bible to give an example of what I meant, and he shrugged in a noncommittal fashion to let me know that he wasn't opposed to seeing what the Scriptures had to say. I opened to the Gospel of Mark, Chapter 2, verses 1–12. The narrative records an event particularly relevant to the situation. A paralyzed man had some friends who brought him to Y'shua on a stretcher. Actually they lowered him into a crowded room from a rooftop. The people watched to see what Y'shua would do. They were hoping that he would heal the man—but they were hoping for less than what God was ready to give. On that particular day, the Messiah startled some people, angered others, and made at least one person happier than he'd ever been before.

The paralyzed man wanted a miracle, a healing. But what did he receive? A greater miracle—a pardon. "My son," Jesus said to him, "your sins are forgiven."

Some of the religious leaders in the crowd responded with anger. They knew what the Scriptures said: All of us are guilty of sin and deserve God's judgment, and any of us can receive forgiveness if we repent. But only God can bestow that forgiveness.

So, who did this Jewish carpenter from Nazareth think he was? God? As a matter of fact, yes. What did Y'shua think he could do—pardon sins and give men and women the gift of an eternal, personal relationship with God? Yes, he did. That's why, when Jesus saw the faith in the paralytic's face, he said, "My son, your sins are forgiven." The religious leaders considered the statement blasphemous—and if Jesus had not the power to forgive sins, indeed it would have been blasphemous.

To prove that he had just performed this greater miracle that no one could see, Jesus condescended to perform a lesser miracle that could be seen by all. "Arise," he said, "take up your pallet, and go home." When that man stood up and walked, everyone knew that Y'shua was who he claimed to be, and that he had the power to forgive sins. God's power would not be so displayed through a blasphemer.

"There's one miracle that God wants to perform in every person's life," I told my acquaintance in the hospital room. "He wants to forgive our sins and give us an eternal relationship with him. That's a miracle he'll always perform."

My new friend rubbed his palm down the length of his face, then dropped his head back against his pillow. He was tired, and it was difficult for him to concentrate. In a polite way, he let me know that he really wasn't so interested in miracles after all. We shook hands, said good-bye, and I left. I never saw him again.

After a month-long convalescence at home, I was well. After all those years, it was such a pleasure not to be ill. I was glad to be to be free from the burden and the inconvenience of the disease. I was glad to be rid of the medication. I remember the night I awoke with the realization that I wasn't in any pain. I remember the day that I ate my first piece of cantaloupe.

Three years after the surgery, I returned to the same hospital, but not as a patient. A friend had asked me to visit her daughter, Leslie. She was young, and she was dying. The doctors had "opened her up" only to discover that there was nothing they could do for her.

When I knocked on the door and entered the room, Leslie was propped up on a pillow, reading the financial page of the *L.A. Times*. I introduced myself as a friend of her mother's and a minister with Jews for Jesus. She gave me a knowing smile, and we talked about inconsequential things for a minute or so.

Then I asked, "So, how can I pray for you?"

Suddenly, she started to cry. Actually, it was a sob. Her tears were falling on the financial page lying across her lap, blurring words and figures that had once been a source of great interest.

"Can Jesus make me well?" she asked.

I didn't hesitate to answer. "If he wants to," I said. "But he can do something even better."

"What's better?" she wanted to know.

"You and I are strangers. Do you mind if I speak very personally to you?"

She managed a smile. "I'm dressed in a hospital gown, you're sitting at the foot of my bed, and I'm dying. How much more personal can you get?" She wiped her eyes, and sat up a bit straighter, as though she were pretending to be an attentive second-grader. "What do you want to tell me?" she asked.

I told her about Y'shua. I told her that he died as a payment for her sins and then rose from the dead. I explained that if she believed this message and asked for his forgiveness, she'd be spared the judgment that our sins deserved. "Is that personal enough?" I asked.

"That's pretty personal," she agreed. "What else?"

I explained that God wanted to help her through this time. He didn't want her to feel alone.

"Will he make me well?" she asked again.

"I don't know. If he does, and if you live another ninety years, you'll have all that time to enjoy a close relationship with him in whatever other hardships and joys you face. But if you die next month, well, then to tell you the truth, I'll be a little jealous."

Her eyebrows shot up in a tacit question, so I explained. "You'll get to see him before me." Now it was my turn to smile. "That's pretty personal, too." Neither of us said anything for a moment. Neither of us objected to the silence. It was very comfortable. Then I asked, "So would you like to pray with me?"

"All right," she said.

I prayed, she echoed my words, and it was a miracle.

A month later, she died.

I suppose someone might say, "It's easy for you to talk. It's easy for you to say that the most important miracle in a person's life is the miracle of God's salvation. It's easy for you to talk," someone might say, "because you're well. But maybe you wouldn't talk that way if you were still ill."

Yes, I would.

Yes, I do.

In March 1996, nearly ten years after my surgery, I returned to the hospital—as a patient. The doctors told me that surgery wouldn't be necessary this time. They said they could handle the recurrence with steroids.

The pain returned. The medication was once again necessary, and the side effects had to be endured again. As I write, I hope I won't need any future hospitalizations, but we'll see. In the meantime, I'm not eating cantaloupe.

So what happened? Did God change his mind? Did God play a joke? Was there something deficient in the miracle that God performed through the surgery in 1986? No. I believe that miracle was just as complete as the miracle that God performed for the paralyzed man described in the Gospel of Mark.

I think about that man from time to time. I also think about the blind beggar who received sight from the hand of the Lord (John 4). And I think of Lazarus, who died and who was raised from the dead (John 11). I'm looking forward to speaking with them when we meet in the Kingdom. Did the healed paralytic feel betrayed when his legs ultimately began to fail with the onslaught of age? Did the healed blind beggar resent it when his vision ultimately blurred as the years piled up? Did Lazarus feel that Jesus failed him when his body grew old and died a second time? I wonder if they felt disappointment for the impermanence of God's physical miracles, or whether they felt gratitude for the only miracle that really counts in the long run: the forgiveness of sins and the gift of eternal life.

Actually, I don't really wonder at all. I'm confident that neither the healed paralytic nor the beggar with new eyes nor Lazarus are disappointed right now. I don't think Leslie is disappointed, either. I know I'm not.

I can always eat cantaloupe in heaven.

MILT KOHUT

My first encounter with the death of a loved one occurred just before my ninth birthday when my mother died after a terrible two-year struggle with tuberculosis. I was old enough to understand the finality of death, yet too young to feel anything beyond my own sense of loss.

I will never forget the long and silent ride to the cemetery. I sat in the back seat of the big black limousine next to my grown-up cousin Irma. At one point, in an attempt to comfort me, she reached her arm around my shoulder and drew me close. "You know what they say; God always takes the best ones first."

I didn't respond, but I remember thinking, "If my mother was so good, why did God make her die?" I imagined that God must be pretty selfish to take my mom when I needed her most. The silence would have been preferable to hearing such terrible things about a God I did not know.

A year later, I returned to the cemetery for the headstone unveiling. I had been instructed to pick up a stone and place it on the flat surface of the headstone as a mark of respect for my mother's memory. I carried out those instructions with a sense of awe, but more than anything, I felt a terrible ache that my mother was still in the grave and not with me.

Fast-forward twenty-eight years. I was an Air Force officer serving in Germany, totally self-sufficient in my career, my abilities and my life. I had married a wonderful woman who was a perfect mother to our three sons. At age thirty-eight I felt in control of all the things that mattered most—but of course, that control was an illusion.

I remember the early morning telephone call from the States. It was my older sister Cynthia. "Our father had a stroke," she said. "He's in a coma. Please come to San Diego."

Thirty-six hours later, I arrived, exhausted after an overnight flight from Frankfurt and a shuttle flight from Los Angeles. I'd come as quickly as possible, but it wasn't quickly enough—my father died during the flight. When l heard the news, all I could think of at that moment was that he never got to see his newest grandson, Chris, our two-year-old, who'd been born in Germany.

My sister and I arranged for our father's funeral. We contacted a local rabbi whose congregation Dad had been attending and saw to the myriad of details associated with dying in America.

It seemed to me that the rabbi intoned the burial portion of the *siddur* in a detached and perfunctory manner. As we chanted the *kaddish* I was mildly surprised to discover that I still recalled the Hebrew words. It had been almost thirty years since that same prayer had formed on my lips at the Pride of Judea Children's Home in Brooklyn. That's where my sister and I were placed following our mother's illness. After she died, I joined the other children who had lost their parents in chanting the *Kaddish* at our Saturday morning services.

As I mumbled the words at my father's funeral, I recalled what my cousin Irma had said so many years before, "God always takes the best ones first." Oh? My mother died at thirty-nine, my father at seventy-one. Did that mean that one was better than the other?

That cynical, unspoken and purely rhetorical question reflected my worldly and secular view of life—and death. All I really knew was that both my father and mother were gone, and that was that. Death was sad but inevitable. Lucky ones outlived unlucky ones. All one could do was live life to the fullest for as long as possible because once you're dead, you're dead forever, or so I believed.

After my father's funeral I decided I would never chant the Kaddish again. It was a relic of my childhood and my Orthodox upbringing at the Pride of Judea many years and many experiences ago. It no longer held meaning for me.

My wife Shirley and I rarely talked of death or dying. It was an uncomfortable subject. We had both endured the death of parents. She was sixteen when her father died. And, although she had been active in her family's church as a young girl, her commitment had long since faded. I considered myself a secular Jew, and as far as I knew, we were both content in our unbelief.

Following our European assignment with the Air Force, we moved to Riverside, California. It was then that Shirley began to awaken late at night in cold sweats. It didn't happen often, but when it did, she would pace the floor for hours, trying to settle what she perceived to be mounting panic and a rapid heartbeat.

Many years later she was able to verbalize to me what was behind those panic attacks. It was, she told me, her great fear of the unknown . . . of what lay beyond this life.

We continued our self-sufficient lives, dealing as best we could with our oldest son who was born profoundly deaf, charting our own course by wits, intelligence and instinct.

Significantly missing from our lives was God . . . until 1974. I was forty-one and Shirley, thirty-nine. We entered into fellowship with the God of Abraham, Isaac and Jacob through his son, our Messiah, Jesus. We began our long and sometimes difficult walk with God, learning to trust him, learning of his promises that offered hope for the present, as well as the future and into eternity.

When we learned on November 7, 1989 that cancer had invaded Shirley's body, we leaned heavily on God. We sensed his strength through those first few months following surgery and chemotherapy. We never lost faith in his promises throughout all the nausea, hair loss, fatigue and weakness.

And God was faithful to answer our prayers! Shirley beat the cancer! She underwent "second look" surgery in April 1990 and was completely cancer free! How we rejoiced and praised our God. He gave Shirley three wonderful years of health. Three years of joy, of travel, of seeing Dustin, our first grandchild, born.

They were the best years of our lives.

On April 17, 1993, Shirley and my sons prepared the most incredible surprise birthday party for my sixtieth birthday. It was truly a magnificent night! A night to remember, to savor, to cherish. Added to our joy was the anticipated arrival of our second grandchild. Our whole family was so full of life.

Exactly one month later, Shirley was in the hospital for surgery to remove the cancer that had suddenly returned. I felt as if all the joy of our special evening, of the three wonderful years that preceded it, had been shattered into a million pieces.

If ever my faith in God's promises was tested, it was then. I believed God was in control. I knew that Shirley and I had been reconciled to him through Jesus and the atonement provided by his death and resurrection. Yet there were other promises—unfulfilled hopes. Would Shirley survive this time to see our second grandchild. It was a hope we clung to through those dark days as we held onto the promise of God's spirit to comfort us through any hardship.

Yet at that moment, the hardships were so profound, the disappointment so great, those promises were hard to believe.

As chemo protocol followed, nausea and hair loss returned, and Shirley grew ever weaker and subject to blood clots, frequent visits to the emergency room and brief hospitalizations. The realization that the end was near became an ever present and unwelcome intruder in our lives.

However, our faithful God is not in the business of crushing hopes. As his plan unfolded and his precious daughter Shirley would be going home to him, a new daughter would be born. She would be the first girl in the Kohut family in sixty-three years! Ashley Christine was born on September 2, 1993, as her Grandma Shirley lay home in bed, hooked to an IV machine.

A few weeks later, Shirley held Ashley in her arms for the first time. A soft golden light bathed the room as I grabbed my camera to record the miracle.

Shirley was admitted to the hospital for the last time on December 20. I watched as the woman I loved and with whom I had shared thirty-seven years of my life lay dying, sustained through her unremitting pain by a constant infusion of pure heroin.

Visitors streamed into her room—friends, family, church workers. Many prayed; all wept. In retrospect, that was the point at which my pain was the most profound. While I trusted God to deal with that pain and bring me his promised peace, it had not yet come. Still I waited and hoped.

One day, the nurse called me away from Shirley's room to take a phone call. It was Moishe Rosen, the founder—and at that time executive director—of the Jews for Jesus ministry. Moishe was calling from his office in San Francisco. He was using a speaker phone so that I could hear from the many other friends who were standing with him. They had known and loved Shirley for years, had been praying for her, and were there to support me with wonderful words of encouragement and hope.

When I told them that Shirley's time was very near, Moishe said something that at first struck me as ludicrous. "Go back and sit at her side," he said. "Take her hand in yours and start singing her favorite hymns."

A hymn sing? As she lay dying? To what avail?

Nevertheless, I went back to her room and did as he suggested. I started to sing softly the words of faith in our God, and almost immediately I could feel the tension in her body ease. Her pulse slowed. Her breathing, so labored only moments before, became less so. A gentleness seemed to pervade her body. The words of praise and thanksgiving to God that both of us had sung so many times before truly made a difference.

As I sang, I sensed the power and presence of God ministering his comfort through the words that formed on my lips and were received by Shirley's spirit. Years before she had been subject to panic attacks because she feared death, though it was nowhere in sight. Now, as death hovered in the room, Shirley was relaxed and content to listen to hymns of our faith. And as I saw that contentment and comfort envelop her, I too was comforted.

In fact, the peace was so tangible as to be almost overwhelming. It was made even more so when Sally Klein O'Conner and her husband, Michael, came into the room. Both gifted musicians and composers, both fellow believers in our Messiah, Jesus, they came to cover Shirley with their gift of music. Sally had brought her portable keyboard and began to sing one of Shirley's favorite songs, "I am eternally grateful to Jesus." While she was still singing, Jeanne Kimmel (one of the Jews for Jesus staff) and her mother entered the room.

Without hesitation or preplanning Jeanne joined Sally in song. Their voices blended in sweet tenderness and the music soared through the room and into the hallway.

Shirley lay motionless throughout the song, giving no outward sign of having heard. But her breathing was steady, her body relaxed. Sally leaned down close to Shirley after the song and whispered, "Shall we stop now?"

We didn't know if she had heard or understood. Then her tongue darted across her parched lips. "No. One more," she murmured.

Before I left my wife that day, I bent to cover her face with kisses, telling her over and over again how much I loved her. It was the last time I saw her alive.

When it was time to let go, to bury my Shirley, I was amazed to feel the incredible grace of God sweep over me, dissipating my apprehension, bringing tears of triumph to my eyes. Shirley was alive! I knew without a doubt that she was in God's presence and would be for eternity.

The sustaining power of God's love and assurance was my shield against the pain of parting. I cannot fully express the joy I felt in the midst of profound personal grief. It's not that the grief disappeared, or that the pain dissolved . . . but they could not overcome the deep and abiding assurance I had that all was well.

In the time since, I have tried as best I could to tell others, especially my unbelieving family, of God's tenderness and assurances—and how he alone, through his son, Jesus, transformed sorrow into joy, despair into hope, death into life.

I tell them that they, too, could have that precious promise, that blessed assurance, that all-encompassing peace, and have their tears dried forever.

Shirley claimed the promise. She never complained. She won the crown of righteousness.

Our pastor, Reverend Jon Imme of Peace Lutheran Church, posed a question to Shirley shortly before she died. He asked her to think about everything she ever wanted, everything she ever dreamed of having or achieving in life, and then make a two-column list. On the first column, he asked her to list those desires and hopes she had seen fulfilled, and on the second, to list anything left undone.

Shirley pondered that challenge for a few days. Later, during her final hospital stay, Pastor Imme asked her if she had come up with her list.

"Oh," she told him, "I have received everything I ever wanted, and then some." She paused briefly, then said, "But I sure wish that I cleaned my garage. And I'd love to see my grandson married."

My precious Shirley, the garage is clean. And Dustin is just a little boy. . . but I'm sure you'll be watching, beaming with love, when he marries.

A RUSSIAN DOCTOR

No reporters have visited the prison camps of Soviet Russia, unless they have gone as prisoners. So to this day we have little information about the millions who have lived, suffered, and died there, especially during Stalin's reign of terror. Most will remain nameless for all time, remembered only in the hearts of those who knew and loved them. But from time to time, scraps of information have filtered out about a few. One of those few was Boris Nicholayevich Kornfeld.

Kornfeld was a medical doctor. From this we can guess a little about his background, for in post-revolutionary Russia such education never went to families tied in any way to czarist Russia. Probably his parents were socialists who had fastened their hopes on the Revolution. They were also Jews, but almost certainly not Jews still hoping for the Messiah, for the name Boris and the patronymic Nicholayevich indicate they had taken Russian names in some past generation. Probably Kornfeld's forebears were Haskalah, so-called "enlightened Jews," who accepted the philosophy of rationalism, cultivated a knowledge of the natural sciences, and devoted themselves to the arts. In language, dress, and social habits they tried to make themselves as much like their Russian neighbors as possible.

It was natural for such Jews to support Lenin's revolution, for the czars' vicious anti-Semitism had made life almost unendurable for the prior two hundred years. Socialism promised something much better for them than "Christian" Russia. "Christian" Russia had slaughtered Jews; perhaps atheistic Russia would save them.

Obviously Kornfeld had followed in his parents' footsteps believing in Communism as the path of historical necessity, for political prisoners at that time were not citizens opposed to Communism or wanting the Czar's return. Such people were simply shot. Political prisoners were believers in the Revolution, socialists or communists who had, nevertheless, not kept their allegiance to Stalin's leadership pure.

We do not know what crime Dr. Kornfeld committed, only

that it was a political crime. Perhaps he dared one day to suggest to a friend that their leader, Stalin, was fallible; or maybe he was simply accused of harboring such thoughts. It took no more than that to become a prisoner in the Russia of the early 1950s; many died for less. At any rate, Kornfeld was imprisoned in a concentration camp for political subversives at Ekibastuz.

Ironically, a few years behind barbed wire was a good cure for Communism. The senseless brutality, the waste of lives, the trivialities called criminal charges made men like Kornfeld doubt the glories of the system. Stripped of all past associations, of all that had kept them busy and secure, behind the wire prisoners had time to think. In such a place, thoughtful men like Boris Kornfeld found themselves reevaluating beliefs they had held since childhood.

So it was that this Russian doctor abandoned all his socialistic ideals. In fact, he went further than that. He did something that would have horrified his forebears.

Boris Kornfeld became a Christian.

While few Jews anywhere in the world find it easy to accept Jesus Christ as the true Messiah, a Russian Jew would find it even more difficult. For two centuries these Jews had known implacable hatred from the people who, they were told, were the most Christian of all. Each move the Jews made to reconcile themselves or accommodate themselves to the Russians was met by new inventions of hatred and persecution, as when the head of the governing body of the Russian Orthodox Church said he hoped that, as a result of the Russian pogroms, "one-third of the Jews will convert, one-third will die, and one-third will flee the country."

Yet following the Revolution a strange alignment occurred. Joseph Stalin demanded undivided, unquestioning loyalty to his government; but both Jews and Christians knew their ultimate loyalty was to God. Consequently, people of both faiths suffered for their beliefs and frequently in the same camps.

Thus it was that Boris Kornfeld came in contact with a devout Christian, a well-educated and kind fellow prisoner who spoke of a Jewish Messiah who had come to keep the promises the Lord had made to Israel. This Christian—whose name we do not know—pointed out that Jesus had spoken almost solely to Jewish people and proclaimed that he came to the Jews first. That was consistent with God's special concern for the Jews, the chosen ones; and, he explained, the Bible promised that a new kingdom of peace would come. This man often recited aloud the Lord's Prayer, and Kornfeld heard in those simple words a strange ring of truth.

The camp had stripped Kornfeld of everything, including his belief in salvation through socialism. Now this man offered him hope—but in what a form!

To accept Jesus Christ—to become one of those who had always persecuted his people—seemed a betrayal of his family, of all who had been before him. Kornfeld knew the Jews had suffered innocently. Jews were innocent in the days of the Cossacks! Innocent in the days of the czars! And he himself was innocent of betraying Stalin; he had been imprisoned unjustly.

But Kornfeld pondered what the Christian prisoner had told him. In one commodity, time, the doctor was rich.

Unexpectedly, he began to see the powerful parallels between the Jews and this Jesus. It had always been a scandal that God should entrust himself in a unique way to one people, the Jews. Despite centuries of persecution, their very existence in the midst of those who sought to destroy them was a sign of a Power greater than that of their oppressors. It was the same with Jesus—that God would present himself in the form of a man had always confounded the wisdom of the world. To the proud and powerful, Jesus stood as a Sign, exposing their own limitations and sin. So they had to kill him, just as those in power had to kill the Jews, in order to maintain their delusions of omnipotence. Thus, Stalin, the new god-head of the brave new world of the Revolution, had to persecute both Jew and Christian. Each stood as living proof of his blasphemous pretensions to power.

Only in the gulag could Boris Kornfeld begin to see such a truth. And the more he reflected upon it, the more it began to change him within.

Though a prisoner, Kornfeld lived in better conditions than most behind the wire. Other prisoners were expendable, but doctors were scarce in the remote, isolated camps. The authorities could not afford to lose a physician, for guards as well as prisoners needed medical attention. And no prison officer wanted to end up in the hands of a doctor he had cruelly abused.

Kornfeld's resistance to the Christian message might have begun to weaken while he was in surgery, perhaps while working on one of those guards he had learned to loathe. The man had been knifed and an artery cut. While suturing the blood vessel, the doctor thought of tying the thread in such a way that it would reopen shortly after surgery. The guard would die quickly and no one would be the wiser.

The process of taking this particular form of vengeance gave rein to the burning hatred Kornfeld had for the guard and all like him. How he despised his persecutors! He could gladly slaughter them all!

And at that point, Boris Kornfeld became appalled by the hatred and violence he saw in his own heart. Yes, he was a victim of hatred as his ancestors had been. But that hatred had spawned an insatiable hatred of his own. What a deadly predicament! He was trapped by the very evil he despised. What freedom could he ever know with his soul imprisoned by this murderous hate? It made the whole world a concentration camp.

As Kornfeld began to retie the sutures properly, he found himself, almost unconsciously, repeating the words he had heard from his fellow prisoner. "Forgive us our trespasses, as we forgive those who trespass against us." Strange words in the mouth of a Jew. Yet he could not help praying them. Having seen his own evil heart, he had to pray for cleansing. And he had to pray to a God who had suffered, as he had: Jesus.

For some time, Boris Kornfeld simply continued praying the Lord's Prayer while he carried out his backbreaking, hopeless tasks as a camp doctor. Backbreaking because there were always far too many patients. Hopeless because the camp was designed to kill men. He stood ineffectively against the tide of death gaining on each prisoner: disease, cold, overwork, beatings, malnutrition.

Doctors in the camp's medical section were also asked to sign decrees for imprisonment in the punishment block. Any prisoner whom the authorities did not like or wanted out of the way was sent to this block—solitary confinement in a tiny, dark, cold, torture chamber of a cell. A doctor's signature on the forms certified that a prisoner was strong and healthy enough to withstand the punishment. This was, of course, a lie. Few emerged alive.

Like all the other doctors, Kornfeld had signed his share of forms. What was the difference? The authorities did not need the signatures anyway: they had many other ways of "legalizing" punishment. And a doctor who did not cooperate would not last long, even though doctors were scarce. But shortly after he began to pray for forgiveness, Dr. Kornfeld stopped authorizing the punishment; he refused to sign the forms. Though he had signed hundreds of them, now he couldn't. Whatever had happened inside him would not permit him to do it.

This rebellion was bad enough, but Kornfeld did not stop there. He turned in an orderly.

The orderlies were drawn from a group of prisoners who cooperated with the authorities. As a reward for their cooperation, they were given jobs within the camp which were less than a death sentence. They became the cooks, bakers, clerks, and hospital orderlies. The other prisoners hated them almost more than they hated the guards. for these prisoners were traitors: they could never be trusted. They stole food from the other prisoners and would gladly kill anyone who tried to report them or give them trouble. Besides, the guards turned a blind eye to their abuses of power. People died in the camps every day; the authorities needed these quislings to keep the system running smoothly.

While making his rounds one day, Kornfeld came to one of his many patients suffering from pellagra, an all-too-common disease in the camps. Malnutrition induced pellagra, which, perversely, made digestion nearly impossible. Victims literally starved to death.

This man's body showed the ravages of the disease. His face had become dark, one deep bruise. The skin was peeling off his hands; they had to be bandaged to staunch the incessant bleeding. Kornfeld had been giving the patient chalk, good white bread, and herring to stop the diarrhea and get nutrients into his blood, but the man was too far gone. When the doctor asked the dying patient his name, the man could not even remember it.

Just after leaving this patient, Kornfeld came upon a hulking orderly bent over the remains of a loaf of white bread meant for the pellagra patients. The man looked up shamelessly, his cheeks stuffed with food. Kornfeld had known about the stealing, had known it was one reason his patients did not recover, but his vivid memory of the dying man pierced him now. He could not shrug his shoulders and go on.

Of course he could not blame the deaths simply on the theft of food. There were countless other reasons why his patients did not recover. The hospital stank of excrement and lacked proper facilities and supplies. He had to perform surgery under conditions so primitive that often operations were little more than mercy killings. It was preposterous to stand on principle in the situation, particularly when he knew what the orderly might do to him in return. But the doctor had to be obedient to what he now believed. Once again the change in his life was making a difference.

When Kornfeld reported the orderly to the commandant, the officer found his complaint very curious. There had been a recent rash of murders in the camp; each victim had been a "stoolie." It was foolish—dangerously so at this time—to complain about anyone. But the commandant put the orderly in the punishment block for three days, taking the complaint with a perverse satisfaction. Kornfeld's refusal to sign the punishment forms was becoming a nuisance; this would save the commandant some trouble. The doctor had arranged his own execution.

Boris Kornfeld was not an especially brave man. He knew his life would be in danger as soon as the orderly was released from the cell block. Sleeping in the barracks, controlled at night by the camp-chosen prisoners, would mean certain death. So the doctor began staying in the hospital, catching sleep when and where he could, living in a strange twilight world where any moment might be his last.

But, paradoxically, along with this anxiety came tremendous freedom. Having accepted the possibility of death, Boris Kornfeld was now free to live. He signed no more papers or documents sending men to their deaths. He no longer turned his eyes from cruelty or shrugged his shoulders when he saw injustice. He said what he wanted and did what he could. And soon he realized that the anger and hatred and violence in his own soul had vanished. He wondered whether there lived another man in Russia who knew such freedom!

Now Boris Kornfeld wanted to tell someone about his discovery, about this new life of obedience and freedom. The Christian who had talked to him about Jesus had been transferred to another camp, so the doctor waited for the right person and the right moment.

One gray afternoon he examined a patient who had just been operated on for cancer of the intestines. This young man with a melon-shaped head and a hurt, little-boy expression touched the soul of the doctor. The man's eyes were sorrowful and suspicious and his face deeply etched by the years he had already spent in the camps, reflecting a depth of spiritual misery and emptiness Kornfeld had rarely seen.

So the doctor began to talk to the patient, describing what had happened to him. Once the tale began to spill out, Kornfeld could not stop.

The patient missed the first part of the story, for he was drifting in and out of the anesthesia's influence, but the doctor's ardor caught his concentration and held it, though he was shaking with fever. All through the afternoon and late into the night, the doctor talked, describing his conversion to Christ and his new-found freedom.

Very late, with the perimeter lights in the camp glazing the windowpanes. Kornfeld confessed to the patient: "On the whole, you know, I have become convinced that there is no punishment that comes to us in this life on earth which is undeserved. Superficially, it can have nothing to do with what we are guilty of in actual fact. but if you go over your life with a fine-tooth comb and ponder it deeply, you will always be able to hunt down that transgression of yours for which you have now received this blow."

Imagine! The persecuted Jew who once believed himself totally innocent now saying that every man deserved his suffering, whatever it was.

The patient knew he was listening to an incredible confession. Though the pain from his operation was severe, his stomach a heavy, expansive agony of molten lead, he hung on the doctor's words until he fell asleep.

The young patient awoke early the next morning to the sound of running feet and a commotion in the area of the operating room. His first thought was of the doctor, but his new friend did not come. Then the whispers of a fellow patient told him of Kornfeld's fate.

During the night, while the doctor slept, someone had crept up beside him and dealt him eight blows on the head with a plasterer's mallet. And though his fellow doctors worked valiantly to save him, in the morning the orderlies carried him out, a still, broken form.

But Kornfeld's testimony did not die.

The patient pondered the doctor's last. impassioned words. As a result, he, too, became a Christian. He survived that prison camp and went on to tell the world what he had learned there.

The patient's name was Alexander Solzhenitsyn.

This story is true. Background details have been researched as thoroughly as possible, although at times inferences were drawn from the limited facts available. Where that is the case, it is made evident in the text.

Part Three

More Jewish Doctors Who Prescribe Y'shua

J. VERA SCHLAMM

Some say, "It is a disgrace for a Jew to believe in Jesus after what the Christians did to our people in the Holocaust." I lived through that nightmare, I and my family. We experienced all the hatred and prejudice that Hitler dredged up from the darkest shadows of the human heart. When I hear people, even Christians, use the memory of the Holocaust to prevent others from telling Jews about Jesus, it grieves me terribly. How can anyone equate sharing the message of love and reconciliation Jesus brought with what the Nazi did? That lie gives Hitler the power to reach beyond the grave and destroy Jews in a way that even his evil mind could not imagine—by keeping us from our own Messiah.

I was born in Berlin in 1923—a healthy baby of average size—but a severe attack of eczema nearly ended my life when I was a year old. The allergy-related disease resulted in a very restricted diet, as my parents feared a recurrence of illness, and the doctors warned of many foods that might cause a reaction.

The nurse my parents hired to help care for me remained with us for two years and taught me a bedtime prayer when I was about three years old. It rhymes in German, though not in English: "I'm small, my heart is clean, no one should live in it but God alone." She prayed it aloud each night as she made me ready for bed. The words "I'm small" made me feel that it really was my own prayer because I was, after all, a little girl. I listened carefully and agreed in my heart as my nurse spoke the words. Actually, the original prayer says, "No one should live in it but Jesus alone." She had taught me to say "God" instead of "Jesus" because we were Jews.

Ours was a Conservative Jewish home. My sister and I learned the meaning of the Jewish holidays, which our family observed. We often had twenty to thirty relatives gather for Passover and other such occasions. Of my immediate family, I was the most religious. My childhood prayer gave way to the *Sh'ma* (Deuteronomy 6:4–9), which I learned to recite in

Hebrew. Recited prayers eventually gave way to regular conversations with God concerning specific needs—and those needs were urgent once Hitler came to power. No matter what the circumstance, I always felt that God was someone I could trust and ought to obey.

I often spoke to God about my height, because it soon became apparent that I was not growing at the same rate as others my age. This made me conspicuously different and caused me much grief. I was painfully reminded of how small I was by students and teachers alike, who often laughed at me. When teams were chosen, I was always the last one. It was assumed that because I was small, I could not do as much as someone of "normal" height. How I wished God would make me bigger!

When I was eleven or twelve years old I thought less about what I wanted from God and more about what God might want from me. I noticed various degrees of observance in Judaism and wondered how these varying degrees could be equally pleasing to God. I admired the Orthodox for keeping the Sabbath and dietary laws, and assumed their stricter observance of these and other things showed greater devotion to God.

Yet mingled with that admiration I began to question how many of the rules they obeyed were really God-given. I wondered how many of the rules they kept were imposed by human standards and subjective interpretations of God's commandments. Even within the Orthodox community some were more serious than others about keeping the law. I found this troubling. From childhood I believed that if God provided instructions for us to come to him, there could be no variations.

Meanwhile, it was becoming dangerous to be a Jew in Germany. How vividly I remember the tenth of November, 1938, when organized mobs burned all our synagogues and demolished all the Jewish-owned stores! It became known as "Kristalnacht" because of all the glass from the shattered windows. Shortly after that my parents, older sister and I fled to Holland. We were caught during our first attempt. We'd waited in the dark for two hours—I was praying almost constantly the entire time. In the midst of prayer, I made many promises to God of what I would do (or not do) if only he would let us escape. One such promise was that I would stop asking God to make me taller. My small stature was still a source of misery, so this was quite a sacrifice for me.

Finally, instead of our contact, the German border guard came and marched us off to the Gestapo. I reassured my father, "Don't worry, God will get us out of this." He did. Our second try proved successful.

Shortly after we arrived in Amsterdam my sister Marga and I joined a Zionist youth group. I also took some private lessons in business and learned to do bookkeeping, which came in handy in my father's wholesale business.

In October 1939 my parents insisted I go to the hospital to see if there was any way to prompt my growth. I felt a little uneasy, remembering my promise not to ask God to make me taller. As a teenager, I stood only about four feet high. I remember kids chasing me, calling me "Lilliput." It was frightening and humiliating! Therefore, I did not really mind being in the hospital, away from those who tormented me.

The hospital staff was kind to me, and I remained there until March 1940. I missed participating in the Zionist group while in the hospital, but my sister Marga and my friend Lore would visit and tell me about their meetings and activities. Finally, I left the hospital—with no more hope of growing tall than I'd had when I was admitted. The doctor felt that my growth had been retarded as a result of malnutrition after my bout with eczema. The absence of foods to prevent a recurrence of the eczema probably also prevented my growth. We did not know so much about nutrition then, and there were no food substitutes such as we have today. The doctor felt that a diet rich in nutrients could promote some growth and indeed it did, but slowly. (I never grew beyond 4 feet 9 inches and didn't attain that stature until I was well into my adult years!)

We were in Holland less than a year and a half when Germany attacked. Within days, they had occupied the country. By 1942, the Third Reich was taking over all Jewish businesses, forcing Jews to wear the yellow star. That was also the year that Marga and her fiancee, Eric, were married. Two months later, Eric received a summons to report for transport to a concentration camp. Shortly after, Marga and I received a similar summons. The day before we were slated to leave, I got a reprieve for medical reasons. My size had come in handy for a change!

Marga and Eric were slated for Auschwitz. Thank God, they were never taken. Between delays and bribery, we managed to avoid being transported despite three separate summonses. In June 1943, the fourth summons came and we could stall no longer. We were all shipped to Westerbork.

Westerbork was more of a transit camp than a concentration camp. The worst part about it was that for most, it was only a "waiting room." People were continually loaded up and shipped out like cattle to real concentration camps—the kind you probably have read about. My parents and I were released two weeks later—only the Germans really knew why—but Marga and Eric were shipped to Vught. We were terrified for them because as soon as people became too ill or weary to work in Vught, we were told, they were shipped to Auschwitz and rarely was there any news of them after that.

A month later, my parents and I were picked up and taken back to Westerbork. Then it happened. My parents were taken to Vught and I was left alone. Still I trusted God and prayed hard that we would be reunited. As minuscule as the odds seemed of that happening, I felt confident that God had heard my prayer. Somehow I knew that we would be together by Hanukkah—my God was big enough to overcome the greatest odds.

Meanwhile, I did what I could to help others. I cared for a three-year-old boy whose mother had polio. And I began hoarding hard-boiled eggs so when my family arrived from Vught we could all have a "feast" for our reunion. The eggs would not last past the holiday, I knew.

We were separated for about three months, but my parents, sister and brother-in-law arrived shortly before Hanukkah—the only four people on the transport! I had never heard of the Nazis, so concerned with efficiency, using a transport for one family of Jews. God miraculously answered my prayers.

Shortly after this, in February 1944, the five of us were shipped off to Bergen-Belsen. Whatever you read or hear from camp survivors, whatever you see in the museums and film clips, it is impossible to exaggerate the nightmarish suffering of the Nazi camps. It is simply impossible. Nothing you read, hear or see can convey the horror of it.

Through it all, I knew that God is a real and good and loving God, although there are many things we cannot understand about him. Sometimes he protects people, sometimes he doesn't and we don't understand why. When people ask, "Where was God when six million Jews were killed?" I say, "Where he always was, in heaven, grieving over what was happening to his people." The Bible says the Jewish people are the apple of God's eye— that he is concerned about what happens to us—and I believe it.

Each member of my family, except for my brother-in-law Eric, was gravely ill at some point. I used to give away two-thirds of my meager portion of bread: one-third to my father and one-third to my brother-in-law. I also exchanged most of my soup for a cup of milk for as long as I could (for a while mothers received a cup of milk for their children. Because we were literally starving, some exchanged it for a moldy triangle of cheese, which they ate themselves.) I gave the milk to my mother and father on alternate days because they were sick.

I count it a miracle that we all survived—but survive we did; after a year in Bergen-Belsen, a large group of us was released in an exchange of Americans and Germans. Even the release was an ordeal. The Nazis questioned us, and we wondered if it was really possible that they would set us free. It could have been a ruse to send us quietly to the gas chambers.

But it was true. In January 1945 we were free at last!

I was exhilarated by the freedom but I also felt a sense of destiny in having been spared from death in the camps; I believed God must have something special for me to do. I only hoped that somehow I could make something out of my life. After a few months in an UNRRA camp in North Africa, my parents and I returned to Amsterdam; my sister and brother-in-law went to the United States.

In November 1947, my parents and I finally arrived in the United States. The relief of being in America! We headed for the Detroit area, where Eric had family. It was time to build a new life.

I was only fifteen years old when we fled Germany, so I

arrived in the United States in my twenties with no high school diploma. We had lived our lives from one day to the next, hoping merely to survive, and surely not thinking so far ahead as to wonder about vocations. I hoped that I would be able to work and go to school at the same time.

All I knew was that I wanted to work with children. Yet I also knew that God must have a plan for my life. It was that sense of destiny; I must have survived for a reason. I wondered anew how I could please God, and what I might do to help people. I thought perhaps I could be a practical nurse—I had so appreciated the nurses I met in the hospital in Amsterdam. Later, in the camps, I found it natural to care for others.

I visited an orphanage that offered training for nursing. While there, I observed the kindergarten teachers and that vocation appealed to me even more.

I went down to Wayne University, now Wayne State University, at the suggestion of Eric's family in Detroit. Had they not encouraged me to speak to the people there, I would not ever have realized that attending a university was an option. If anything, I expected to finish high school in America.

The school administrators explained the requirements for becoming a kindergarten teacher. To my surprise, the admissions officer didn't tell me to come back when I had my high school diploma. He said, "I'd like you to take our entrance examination for guidance only, just so I can advise you." After I'd taken the test, I was amazed to hear him say, "We'll take you on a trial basis." I think they called it "special student" status. I had to maintain a "B-plus" average in order to receive credit for my classes. I did well in my studies and spent a year and a half preparing for a career as a kindergarten teacher.

Then, to my dismay, I heard a rumor that there was a height requirement for that position. At twenty-five years of age, I was all of four foot eight. To this day I don't know if there was any truth to the rumor or if someone was playing a cruel joke, but as I had been told so often that my small stature would prevent me from amounting to much, that seemed plausible. When I questioned one of the faculty about it, he suggested dryly that if I had to ask, perhaps I should look into another field.

I'd shown more aptitude and interest in science than anything else, so I chose medical technology. I would process blood and urine tests, that sort of thing. Perhaps eventually I would branch out into some sort of research. When I asked my own physician his opinion about my choice, he said, "It will be a good stepping stone for you." He obviously believed I could do more, and I was grateful for his confidence.

My parents had moved down to San Antonio, Texas, and my father wrote and suggested I join them there. Reuniting with my family sounded good, and I was ready for change. In 1951, I transferred to Trinity University.

Many of my courses at Trinity were also required for the pre-med students, so I spent time with people who were on that track. A girlfriend with whom I studied began suggesting that I consider changing my major. She'd say, "I wish you could go to medical school with me so we could keep studying together." It never occurred to me that becoming a physician was an option—so much schooling—so expensive!

She persisted in her suggestions until finally I blurted out, "Please stop! I cannot afford medical school." Soon after, she invited me to her home for dinner. Her husband, a dentist, explained about scholarships and school loans. My friend and I spoke to our biology professor the next day, and he was very enthusiastic about my switching to pre-med. I remembered the confidence my physician had expressed in my potential to do more than I had aspired to. Everything seemed to point to medical school. I decided to try—the worst that could happen is I would not be accepted.

My conviction that God had a plan for my life had remained as strong as it was the day we were freed from the concentration camp. I wanted to obey God by doing whatever he had preserved me to do!

My chances of getting into medical school seemed small indeed. In those days, there was a quota for Jewish students as well as for women, meaning that schools had to be "encouraged" to take us (times have changed!)—so as a Jewish woman, I faced double discrimination. In addition, I had not taken the medical aptitude test that was required the year before applying, because

I was late. Last but not least, the only school I could hope to afford was a state-sponsored school and I was not yet a resident of Texas. Nevertheless, I knew that no chances are "too small" where God is involved, and I suspected that chance actually had very little to do with it.

I remember telling my sister, who was not particularly religious, "If God wants me to go to medical school I'll be accepted and if not, that's fine, too." As a doctor, I could certainly help people and I began to think perhaps that was what God had in mind for me. It was! I was accepted into both of the Texas medical schools to which I applied.

I had been in the United States a little over four years when I began to study medicine. English was not my first, nor even my second, language. The medical vocabulary was difficult to keep up with, and the professors went so fast that I had a hard time trying to understand what they were saying and take notes at the same time. I could concentrate on understanding the lecture and try to reconstruct it later on in my notes, or I could try to write down as much as possible without really understanding what I was writing. Somehow I managed to grasp enough to do well—but what a difference a tape recorder would have made!

1953 was a landmark year for me—I became a citizen of the United States.

I spent the summers of my second and third year of medical school as an "extern" at a private hospital. I was in charge of the emergency room during the day and even some evenings. On weekends, I was responsible for intravenous feedings and other such procedures. An obstetrician there was very kind and allowed me to assist her with quite a few deliveries.

I applied for internship during my last year and was accepted at UCLA for pediatrics. I would work with children after all! I graduated from medical school in 1956, packed my belongings and moved to Los Angeles.

Two months after I came to L.A., my parents joined me there. (My mother's brother also lived in the area.) A year later I finished my internship and began residency at Children's Hospital. I moved into the housing there and to my surprise, ended up with an old friend from Trinity as my roommate!

I began seriously investigating my faith during residency. I'd come through medical school, survived my internship—the dust was settling, the end was in sight! I could foresee having my own life, my own schedule, my own decisions. I knew that an important part of that life, that schedule and those decisions should be God. I pondered how I could be a good Jew, and I prayed a great deal about it.

I also talked about "religion" with gentile friends, all of whom I assumed were Christians. In my thinking, I was Jewish because I was born that way; they were Christians because *they* were born that way. I didn't realize that gentiles have to believe in the Jewish Messiah in order to be "Christians."

My roommate, Le Claire, was a faithful Catholic. She asked me many questions about Judaism and I didn't always know the answers. As we compared our religions, I explained to her that I didn't need to confess my sins to a priest as she did. I did that once a year on Yom Kippur, by reading a list of sins and asking God's forgiveness. I "felt" forgiven. After I had explained it to her, I began to question it myself. How could I feel forgiven when I knew I would be committing the same sins again, many of which had to do with being observant? The two issues that troubled me the most were the dietary laws and the Sabbath. I was troubled by them, even at Bergen-Belsen.

I made plans for what I would do to be "more religious" once my residency was over. Realizing that I didn't know enough about my own faith, I determined to learn more about God through reading the Bible. At the same time, I began to plan a trip somewhere that would help me fit the pieces together. Surely, I would be inspired and would find answers in Israel. I had dear friends as well as family in the land and so I arranged for a long-awaited visit to take place within weeks of finishing my residency.

As I boarded the plane for Haifa, I remembered the days of the Zionist youth organization and how Marga and I had helped to collect money for planting trees in the land. It was thrilling to see the "bloom in the desert." The transformation we'd dreamed of had come to pass, and in our small way, we'd helped.

As I went from place to place in Israel, I was deeply moved to know that I was in the land where all I had read about in the Bible had actually happened thousands of years ago. This added to my hunger to know God and my eagerness to read the Bible.

At the same time, I was disillusioned by the secularism and what I perceived as irreverence on the part of many Israelis. It seemed as though people were either extremely Orthodox or not religious at all. The Orthodox were a definite minority.

I stayed in Israel for seven weeks, glad for the experience and especially for the opportunity to see friends from my old Zionist youth group in Holland. However, I had not found answers to my spiritual questions.

I returned to Southern California and began working with a group of doctors twice a week. Soon it was four times a week, and then much to my delight, in January 1960, they asked me to join their practice on a permanent full-time basis.

My urgent desire to do something meaningful with my life was met beautifully in my pediatrics career. It enabled me to care for children in a way that was much more suited to my abilities and temperament than teaching. I was truly thankful to God. The sense of destiny I'd felt since I was spared from death at the hands of the Nazis was finally fulfilled. What satisfaction!

My schedule was still hectic and unpredictable, for one never knows when a child will become ill or have an accident. Still, to a large extent, I was "my own boss" and able to devote more thought to pursuits from which I'd limited myself during my internship and residency. I took Friday nights off to usher in the Sabbath properly. We had Kiddush at my parents' house and then went together to the temple.

Now was the time to resolve questions about my religion and to decide what kind of a Jew God wanted me to be. My birthday (February 28) was approaching and my sister wanted to know what I would like for a gift. I asked her for a Bible, a "whole" one with what I then considered the "Jewish" and "Christian" parts. She and Eric had one and it hadn't made heretics of them, so I decided I would have one, too. After all, I was constantly in contact with people who I assumed were Christians (mainly because I knew they weren't Jews). I wanted to understand something about what they believed, just so I wouldn't be ignorant.

Marga gave me a King James Version. I began at Genesis,

Chapter 1, intent on reading the whole thing. Soon I began to feel frustrated—I couldn't even begin to keep all those laws! Nevertheless, I soaked up page after page—occasionally glancing at portions of "the other" Bible, the Christian one.

I wasn't taking these occasional looks at the New Testament because I had intentions of becoming a Christian. I was simply curious to understand what others believed. I felt a twinge of uneasiness at first, but I remembered what the chaplain of Trinity had once said: "You can't go wrong if you're searching for the truth," and that gave me courage.

God knew I only wanted to know more about him, to learn what he required of me. After everything he had brought me through, I didn't believe he would allow me to be tricked into believing something I shouldn't.

I finally came to the prophet Isaiah, where to my astonishment I found two verses that mention God's *son* (Isaiah 7:14 and 9:6). That was quite a surprise. When I came to the Chapter 53, it seemed so obvious that it was talking about Jesus that I thought, "Well, this is a Christian translation, and they have slanted the text to sound that way." So the following Friday night at Temple Emmanuel (which I attended regularly) I took the Scriptures from the pew and opened to the Chapter 53 of Isaiah. The wording was a little different—but it *still* sounded like Jesus! Furthermore, the sixth verse echoed what I had been thinking all these years—that we were all going our own way.

I was surprised that I had never heard this passage before, because I usually paid very close attention to the Scripture readings in Temple. So I checked the reading schedule for the year and found, to my great astonishment, that the passage had been omitted.

I knew I must continue to search until I found God's way.

In the meantime, I enjoyed my growing practice. I loved the children and I enjoyed working closely with the parents, to calm and comfort them and give them guidance on how to care for their children. To me, being in private practice was like seeing friends all the time. After meeting with the parents two or three times, a bond develops. However, one cannot become personally involved with every family with whom one comes in contact professionally. I therefore made it a personal policy not to socialize with the families outside of the professional relationship. I made an exception in the case of the Palmers.

On May 17, 1960, Tommy Palmer was born. His adoptive mother, Lisa, called to ask if I would be his pediatrician. I agreed to meet with her and thought as I hung up what a pleasant voice and manner she had.

Through our regular visits with Tommy, I soon discovered that Milton Palmer, Tommy's proud papa, was a minister at a local Baptist church. I was impressed that the Palmers spoke of God as though he had an important part in their life. They talked about answered prayer. They seemed confident relating to God. I'd never seen that kind of faith in any of the so-called Christian friends I had made. I admired this and felt a twinge of jealousy.

Lisa and Milton knew I believed in God, the Bible, and the coming of the Messiah. They told me they believed Jesus was the Messiah whom I awaited, but they did not pressure me to respond. They carefully explained their faith without ridiculing my beliefs. The fact that I was Jewish never seemed to enter into their thinking, except on those occasions when I mentioned it as a roadblock to believing in Jesus. Then they were interested and answered me gently, again without pressure.

Eighteen months after Tommy was born, and we had come to a mutual respect and fondness for one another, the Palmers invited me to spend a weekend with them at Lake Arrowhead, a resort area about two hours away from Los Angeles. It was the first time they had extended a social invitation, and because I felt a special fondness and respect for them, I accepted.

They did not speak about God during the weekend, except at brief prayers before meals. They listened as I told about the camps. I let them know of my Bible reading because I wanted them to understand that I, too, was religious—in my own way.

After that weekend, I continued to spend time with the Palmers. I invited them to my home for dinner and accepted invitations to go to theirs. The first time I came to their home, I asked Milton, "How can anyone know what is the right religion? You're born into a religion and you do the best with it that you can." I'd made that statement to some of my friends and had never gotten an answer. I didn't really expect one from him, either. Yet he responded without hesitation, "I knew when I accepted the Messiah as my personal Savior."

That introduced me to two new ideas: First, he used the word "Messiah." I knew Christians believed in Jesus, but I hadn't really thought about the fact that they believe in him as the Jewish Messiah. He brought that into focus for me.

The second idea which interested me was the fact that he said, "*when* I accepted Jesus." I had assumed he was born a Christian and was surprised to hear that it was a decision he'd made as an adult. Furthermore, at one time he had been a very heavy drinker. Jesus had changed him, he said. I could not imagine Milton Palmer drunk! He was a godly man.

Milton had answered my question and felt free to ask one of his own. "What happened to the sacrifices in the Jewish religion?" I didn't know. I offered to look into it.

One Sunday afternoon I was visiting the Palmers and we read together the First Psalm. Pastor Palmer told me he would be preaching from that text for their evening service—would I like to come? I knew the Book of Psalms was in the Jewish Bible. It should be safe enough—yes, why not? I considered myself "religious" and was curious as to what he would say about a passage of the Jewish Scriptures.

Still, as I walked into the church, I recited the Sh'ma. Like many Jewish people, I thought Christians worshiped three gods and I wanted God to know that I believed in him alone.

Milton's sermon was impressive. He expounded on the ungodly and the righteous from my Jewish Bible. He was teaching from the text so everything he said was true, according to God's Word. Then he quoted Jesus, from the Gospel of John: "I am the way, the truth, and the life. No one comes to the Father except through Me." His meaning was clear: No one could be truly godly without Jesus. I was very angry. Yet angry as I was, those words haunted me.

I'd been praying and trusting and wanting to obey God all my life with never a thought about Jesus. It occurred to me that if God was shedding new light on what it means to obey him, I was now responsible to act accordingly. I didn't want to believe in Jesus, but I didn't want to reject him if he really was God's way for me to be obedient. There was the matter of Isaiah 53. It had sounded like Jesus when I read it on my own, with no one to pressure me. Could it possibly be that we didn't make sacrifice for sin anymore because Jesus took care of the sacrifice once and for all? I began asking God to show me if it were true.

I didn't tell the Palmers how much I was thinking about all this or how the things they were saying impressed me. At one time Milton suggested, "You should read the Book of Luke and the Book of Romans. Luke was written by a doctor who wrote an accurate account, just as you write up a chart in your office. And the reasoning in the Book of Romans might appeal to you." I never let them know that I actually read those books. I was very careful because I did not want to be pushed in any way, shape or form. I wanted the issue to be strictly between God and me.

The more I explored the claims of Jesus, the more I tried to cling to traditional Judaism. After all, the people who persecuted me were Christians as far as I was concerned. I didn't want to be a Christian. I just wanted to be right with God.

I brought out my old Orthodox *siddur* and began reading the morning prayers and the Thirteen Articles of Faith. I knew that every Jew ought to believe these firmly and rehearse them daily, so I did. As I read, "I believe with a perfect faith that all the words of the prophets are true," I remembered Isaiah. Of course, the Articles of Faith affirmed the fact that the Messiah was an important aspect of Judaism as well. They even mentioned belief in resurrection, which I had never realized was a Jewish concept.

I continued going to Friday night services at Temple but even the sermons there seemed to be drawing me closer to Jesus. One message was taken from a passage in Exodus: "You shall not follow a crowd to do evil" (Exodus 23:2). To me, that verse meant I should not follow what the majority of people are doing; I should follow God. If I took the verse to its logical conclusion, I also had to do what is right, even if that meant being considered a traitor.

On June 30, 1962, I went to spend another weekend with the Palmers in Lake Arrowhead. We talked openly about Jesus. I asked question after question, including whether a Jew who believed in Jesus would be expected to give up his or her Jewishness. Milton said no; Jesus came as a Jew to Jewish people in fulfillment of Jewish prophecies. Believing in him would certainly put me at odds with rabbinic teaching, but then it was

God, and not any person, who'd made me Jewish.

When Milton asked if I wanted to accept Jesus as my Messiah that night, I said no. I did not want to make a rash decision. I prayed once again before I went to bed that God would show me if it was true. I slept soundly through the night.

At six o'clock the next morning I awoke with the realization that God was speaking to my heart. Jesus was the Messiah. I was responsible to believe and obey. My search was over.

My first test of faith was my family's reaction. At their urging (for no other reason than my faith in Jesus), I visited a psychiatrist and took psychological tests. The doctor pronounced that he had never seen anyone so balanced and content.

A more serious problem was my father's ill health. His cardiologist had informed me seven years earlier that, at most, my father would live another five years. Having seen his greatly enlarged heart on X-ray, I knew the cardiologist was correct, scientifically speaking. According to his prognosis, my father was already living on "borrowed time." His response to my belief in Jesus was "If you want me to die, go right ahead." I was afraid of losing my father, and I knew that my grief would be compounded by the fact that the whole family would consider it my fault.

In the midst of all this, the oral portion of my pediatric boards was approaching. Usually I did well on written exams and "froze" for the orals. Then my father suffered a severe heart failure and was at the point of death just before I had to leave for Chicago for the tests. I did the only thing I could do; I brought my fears to the Lord. He not only gave me peace, but I was the calmest of twelve doctors being tested. I passed the boards, and my father lived through the crisis. In fact, he lived another nine years till he, too, accepted the Messiah!

I always had believed in God and prayed regularly, but knowing the Lord in a personal way through the Messiah and trusting that he paid the penalty for my sins was a totally new experience. For the first time, I didn't worry about which laws to keep in order to please him. His standard is perfection and only Jesus has met that standard. The good things I would do then, I would do out of love, not because they could make me acceptable to God.

When I felt it appropriate, I would tell my patients of my faith in Jesus. I had a Jewish family referred to me by the rabbi in Glendale shortly after I came to believe in Jesus. (He did not know that!) I told them frankly about my faith. They knew I was a camp survivor, and I think they were somewhat impressed with that—but if they were impressed by my faith in Jesus, I never knew.

I learned from my patients' reactions when I told them that I had become a "Christian" that many who I assumed were Christians apparently were not. Those who had true faith in Jesus were excited, but many others looked at me strangely and didn't know how to respond.

I found it interesting that those who disagreed with or questioned my faith did not want me to use the Bible to explain my beliefs. People have preconceived ideas as to why a Jew would believe in Jesus, and many were not willing to hear anything to the contrary.

My right-hand helper and I prayed every morning before I started seeing patients. I had books and pamphlets in the waiting room telling about Jesus. The one that I kept replenishing was titled *None of These Diseases,* by S. I. McMillan, M.D. Even though I had my name stamped all over them, they kept disap-

pearing! I believe that some of my patients received more than physical care—because that book explained how God wants to heal us spiritually, through Jesus.

I am a small person who survived despite even smaller odds, but I have a big God, and nothing is too small for his notice. God knows you, and God knows your every disappointment and hurt. He wants to make a big difference in your life.

J. Vera Schlamm, MD, retired in 1995 after years of practicing Pediatrics in Glendale and Pasadena, California.

DANIEL M. GOLD

I felt a negative reaction begin to build. I did not know much about Jesus, but I knew that we Jews were not supposed to believe in him. Therefore, it came as a great surprise to me that these men invited me to pray with them—and I accepted. The prayer was simply to acknowledge that I was a sinner, asking God to forgive me and to reveal himself to me—to come into my life and prove his existence.

I was born in Santa Monica, California, in 1954 and raised in the nearby San Fernando Valley. My father, Ernest M. Gold, (now deceased) was a physician. My mother, Elaine Stepanovich, is a teacher and homemaker living in Hawaii. I have an older brother, as well as a younger brother and sister.

Both my parents are Jewish, as are my grandparents. Most of our family's observance revolved around the times we spent with them. For Passover my grandmother always prepared a nice *seder*, but I didn't appreciate its true significance. My favorite part of the evening was the search for the hidden *matzoh*, and the funny prize we'd receive for finding it.

My paternal grandmother came to the United States from Hungary to escape the pogroms. She always wore a simple dress tied at the waist—except maybe for the synagogue, when she might dress up just a little. It was impossible to visit her without eating a meal, which was no hardship because she was a good cook. I especially remember her beet *borscht, matzoh ball* soup, and the delicious *hamantashen* with poppy seeds that she made for *Purim*. I remember her very fondly.

Nevertheless, memories of my grandparents and our Jewish roots do not include God. I neither talked to nor expected to hear from him.

My childhood had ordinary joys, but also sadness. My father was busy with his research and there seemed very little of him left over for his family. Eventually my parents divorced. My brother and I continued to live with my father while my mother moved to Hawaii and eventually remarried.

I graduated high school in the early 1970's and enrolled in the University of California at Davis. It was then that I developed a bit of wanderlust. On weekends, some of us did a little "hoboing" on the train that ran through town. We'd jump on board and go wherever the train took us. (The summer after my freshman year, my cousin and I ended up in Michigan.)

After that summer, I did not return to school. Like many of my peers, I was disillusioned with the "establishment" and decided that college wasn't for me. I wanted a simple life that would enable me to go where I wanted and find or make whatever I needed along the way.

I'd visited my mom in Hawaii on a few occasions and always thought it would be a good place to live someday. With nothing to hold me in California, I packed a few things and moved. I was nineteen years old.

I got a job in a health food restaurant run by counterculture types similar to myself. We had a lot of local clientele and some tourists that came through as well. The "establishment" didn't much like us, and the board of health shut us down. There'd been an outbreak of hepatitis, and they blamed it on our restaurant. We were required to take blood tests and were told that two of us were positive. However, independent tests proved negative. Later, officials discovered that the outbreak had started at one of the hotels, but the damage was done and we were shut down.

At that point, I thought, "Hey, if this is what society is all about, I'll just get away from it all." I'd made frequent hiking trips out in the jungle, and figured sooner or later I'd build myself a tree house and live there. The incident with the restaurant simply made it sooner.

Robinson Crusoe I wasn't, but I managed to put together a few comforts in the jungle. My tree house was about ten feet off the ground and provided a place to sleep as well as shelter when it was wet outside. I made a floor from bamboo poles fastened together with rope. Then I split more bamboo and wove it into a mat to cover the poles. The walls were also bamboo, but the roof was plastic to keep out the rain. Down below I had a small woodburning fireplace set up against a rock. I had a little grill there and built myself kind of an oven to cook my meals.

I had a lucky break when an old oil drum floated up on the beach about a mile and a half away. I hauled it into the jungle and set it over some rocks so I could build a fire beneath it. That became my hot water heater, and a hookup with a garden hose provided hot showers. A fresh stream ran beneath the tree house, so water supply was no problem.

I was fairly self-sufficient and lived as a hermit for a year and a half. My house was a twelve-mile hike from the nearest road, and from that road it was another twelve or fifteen miles to the nearest town, where there were just a couple of hundred people. That's where I got my mail. Since I didn't have an address, they held my mail at the post office until I came to pick it up. That was about twice a month—I'd come out to buy rice and other staples, as well as candles, matches and the like.

I was living where I wanted, the way I wanted, but something happened to me in Hawaii—something that took me by surprise and eventually changed everything. Psalm 19 describes a kind of revelation that comes simply from observing creation. It's a general kind of revelation that just lets you know that God is real. That was my experience.

Surrounded by so much natural beauty, living primarily off the land, watching the sun coming up every morning—I knew that all these wonders were not accidental or random. I knew that some transcendent force existed in the universe. That was all I knew, but it was enough to lead me into a spiritual quest. I had to know more about Whoever had created so much beauty. I decided to explore the Bible—the Jewish Bible—and I read most of it over a six-month period.

On those occasions when I ventured out of my solitude, I picked up whatever "religious" information I could find in the little general store. Most of that input was Eastern, so I read about Tibetan philosophy as well as Hindu and some of the Chinese philosophies. I also read contemporary counterculture authors like Carlos Castaneda The common thread woven through these various religions seemed to be the idea that the devotee can ultimately ascend to Deity.

I learned a little about Jesus from my forays into New Age religions, but I always viewed Christianity as a perversion of the

Jewish faith. I don't really know exactly when or where I learned to feel that way. My assumptions were not based on study, or even experience. I had no animosity toward Christians; I simply avoided them when possible.

None of the Eastern religions were as compelling as what I found in the Bible. I read about the elaborate system of atonement God designed so that unholy people could come into his holy presence. "But surely I'm not one of those unholy people," I thought. "After all," I reasoned to myself, "I was no criminal. When I rebelled, it was against institutions tarnished by greed and corruption." However, God's Word tore away at my pretense of goodness.

His standard of righteousness, so succinctly stated in Deuteronomy 6:5, was overwhelming: "You shall love the LORD your God with all your heart, with all your soul, and with all your strength." Further, we were supposed to love our neighbor as we loved ourselves. No wonder Solomon, the wise king of Israel, declared, "For there is not a just man on earth who does good and does not sin" (Ecclesiastes 7:20). When I read the Psalms, I saw "The LORD looks down from heaven upon the children of men, to see if there are any who understand, who seek God. They have all turned aside" (Psalm 14:2–3). The prophet Isaiah echoed this sentiment with "All of us like sheep have gone astray, each to his own way."

It was easy to see that the world around me was evil and corrupt, but I began to realize that my own behavior was not what it should be. I was not capable—or at least not naturally inclined—to live up to my own expectations, much less God's.

For example, I felt that people should care for one another—even be self-sacrificing when necessary to meet one another's needs. Yet I was not always as kind to others as I'd hoped they'd be to me. In fact, I was downright selfish at times. That reality hit me particularly hard when a young girl came to me seeking help. She was quite distraught, but selfishly, I paid little attention to her. Soon after, she committed suicide. I knew I could have been more sensitive to her needs and wondered if perhaps I could have made a difference in her life. Her death haunted me and gave me much cause for reflection.

Another area where I knew I'd failed was my relationship with my father. True, I believed that he had failed me, but I hadn't done much to communicate any desire for reconciliation. I had a collection of letters that I'd written but never mailed—so, after years of separation, I mailed them all at once.

My father wrote back and said, "I'd like you to come home. I'll buy some land if you'll just come home and farm it." I couldn't pass up the opportunity to visit my father as well as have land of my own. So I headed back to Davis, California.

I was only in his home for a day or two when we started arguing again. I left and wandered around the university until I found a cooperative house in the middle of the campus. The eight people who lived there had a large organic garden. I asked if I could live in their garden in return for work, and they agreed. At night I'd sleep under the tree in the garden, and in the daytime I'd roll up my blanket and do some gardening. That was my housing situation until the end of August, when school started again.

Despite the conflict with my father, I really did want to be with him. One day I returned to his house to try to talk things out. While I was waiting for him to come home, it happened.

Two men knocked on the door. My younger brother was in the shower, so I was the only one available to answer the door.

My father's house was the last door they approached that day. "They" were a couple of Christians, going door-to-door in the neighborhood, telling people about Jesus. They asked me a simple question: "If you were to die today, are you certain you would go to heaven?" I was deeply troubled by the question, because I knew the answer was no.

As those two men stood on the doorstep, I had to admit what I already knew: My life, measured against God's righteous standard, would not be acceptable to him. As I pondered that, the question seemed to reverberate within me: Why should I think I was going to end up in the presence of a holy and righteous God?

I listened intently as these men told me how God had provided a way to heaven. They talked about the system of sacrifice; they talked about the children of Israel and the years of wandering in the desert. They talked about a tabernacle God ordained and the offerings he commanded. Later, when the nation became established, a permanent Temple was erected in Jerusalem for this purpose. I knew these things were true because I had read about them in the Bible. I also knew that for me, there was no Temple, no tabernacle, no Levites or priests.

These men told me that those were temporary solutions, shadows of the atonement that God had in store for his people. They said that God had always planned that his Messiah would come and give his life as a ransom for his people. His death, an amazing act of self-sacrifice, stood as the punishment for my sin. He had no sin and no need for atonement. His resurrection was proof that his sacrifice had satisfied the justice of God. Anyone who would trust him could be reconciled to God. Anyone— including me.

That was my first real exposure to Christianity.

Most religions I had read about require rigorous liturgical disciplines to attain "oneness" with God. I knew that I could never reach the pinnacle that so many of the religions teach are attainable by human effort. They say that we must keep working to perfect ourselves. I knew I was nowhere near perfect and would not become so through my own efforts.

In contrast, these men were describing something that matched what I had seen in the pages of the Jewish Bible: a Holy God descending to sinful humanity—a God who would accept me for what I was, asking only that I put my faith in him.

I did not know much about Jesus, but I knew that we Jews were not supposed to believe in him. Therefore, it came as a great surprise to me that these men invited me to pray with them—and I accepted. The prayer was simply to acknowledge that I was a sinner and to ask God to forgive me and reveal himself to me—to come into my life and prove his existence.

After the short prayer, I told those men that I would study the claims they made about this Jesus.

The whole conversation lasted about twenty minutes and took place on the doorstep. I never even invited them into the house— but I had invited God into my life.

They came back to follow up with me several days later. By then, I had read the Gospel of John and was convinced that Jesus was true. I felt God had answered my prayer, that he had revealed himself to me. Whatever prejudices I might have had concerning Christianity disappeared when I actually read the gospel. I received it with joy. I knew that Jesus was the Messiah I had longed for, and I felt drawn to him.

The most convincing aspect of the gospel was the fact that it dealt with my sin. I believe God helped me to understand my own unrighteousness before I ever heard about Jesus. Had the men stopped one house short of my father's, I would not have heard the message. Yet had I not been reading the Bible, had I not become so aware of the gap between God and myself, I probably would have responded differently. As it was, when I heard about the redemptive sacrifice Y'shua made, my heart was at peace with God. That was in July 1976. Over the next month, I read the rest of the New Testament. It confirmed my decision. I never turned back.

One of the first things that happened was I realized that God was not happy with my relationship with my father. I had broken the fifth commandment rather continuously. I had said terrible things to him in the course of our quarrels. At one point I told him, "I don't care if you live or die." My attempts to rectify the situation always seemed to end with more anger. I realized that the relationship would not be right until I was more concerned with how I had wronged my father than I was with how he had wronged me.

One of the first things I did after deciding to follow Jesus was to spend several hours confessing to my father that I had wronged him. I remember weeping, and telling him I had behaved like the Prodigal Son. Over the next four years, I spent quite a bit of time going to my father's house, looking for ways to honor him. I'd cut the grass or help out in the garage, or whatever I could do to let him know I was there to serve and honor him.

In time, we became best friends. When I got married (four years later), my father told the pastor he could not believe the difference that Jesus Christ had made in my life.

Now back to the summer of 1976. The pastor of the church I began attending encouraged me to go back to school. I explained that it was much too late for me to do anything (by then it was mid-August) and that I couldn't afford it anyhow. Well, he persuaded me to enroll and I was accepted two weeks later. So I began classes at U.C. Davis—the same school I'd dropped out of some three years earlier. I got a job washing dishes and another cleaning a restaurant. I held several jobs over the next three years and managed to graduate from college debt free. I never returned to my tree house in Hawaii.

I began studying agriculture, but the type of agriculture they do there is more of a business. I wanted to do something that would bring me into contact with people. Obviously, God had changed me quite a bit from the Hawaiian hermit who had to travel over twenty-five miles just to say hello to another human being!

Before I became a Christian, medicine was the last career I would have chosen because of the tension with my father. I also feared that as a doctor, I would be bound to neglect my (future) family. So when I first sensed that God was leading me to become a doctor, my response was, "Uh . . . are you sure about that?" However, I was willing to do whatever God wanted, so I began to take pre-med courses. God truly makes radical changes when we trust him with our life decisions!

I got married my senior year of college, and my wife Karen and I moved to Texas. I'd been accepted to medical school in California, but it was cheaper to go to the University of Texas. I enrolled in the medical branch in Galveston and graduated in 1984, finishing my residency in 1988.

Karen and I have five children. Yes, it is challenging to practice medicine and spend time with the family, but it's not impossible. And as unexpected a turn as it was for me to choose this profession, it was nothing compared to my sudden decision to follow Jesus.

Although that decision was sudden and totally unexpected, I've never regretted it nor felt that I acted hastily. It wasn't until later that I learned just how beautifully faith in Jesus fulfills the Jewish hope for the promised Messiah. For example,

The prophets said the Messiah would

1. Be born of a virgin—Isaiah 7:14
   Jesus was. (Matthew 1:18, 24–25)
2. Come from the family line of David—Jeremiah 23:5
   Jesus did. (Luke 3:23–31)

3. Be born in Bethlehem—Micah 5:2
   Jesus was. (Matthew 2:1)
4. Bear the sin of many—Isaiah 53:12
   Jesus did. (Romans 5:12–15)
5. Be crucified—Psalm 22:16, Zechariah 12:10
   Jesus was. (Luke 23:33)

Numerous other prophecies describe a multitude of details about the Messiah. Even such a minute event as the dividing of his garments at his death was foretold hundreds of years before the fulfillment of this event! I encourage you to search these things out for yourself.

Daniel Gold, MD, is a fellow of the American Academy of Ophthalmology and a Diplomat of the American Board of Ophthalmology. He practices in Palestine, Texas.

BERNIE COHEN

I was frustrated with my conclusions; I did not want to believe that this Y'shua was true. I was afraid of what my parents would think. I feared that they would label me as a traitor and cut me off forever from the family. I dug in my heels and refused to go further.

My father must have grinned when the exhausted nurse announced, "Congratulations, Mr. Cohen—you have a son!" I arrived with a lusty cry, and the news quickly spread from Miami Beach to all the relatives scattered throughout the Northeast. It's not that I was the first grandchild, but after my three girl cousins, finally there was a boy.

My grandparents immigrated from Russia and Poland, fugitives from political persecution and changing times. They came to America to make new homes, to dream of the future and to raise children who could look forward to something wonderful. Lou Cohen and Ann Rosenthal were two such children who grew up in transplanted east European neighborhoods: Lou in Brooklyn and Ann in Atlantic City.

They understood and respected their Jewish traditions, but they were a new generation, straining for independence. For example, although my mother came from an Orthodox family, she participated in many high school dramas. According to my mother, a well-known New York vaudeville actress approached her after one of the plays and offered to train her in New York. The family thought it over and decided that she was needed at home. I don't believe she ever resented the decision, but I could just tell by the way she spoke of it that she would have loved to have had such an adventure.

My father's father was a strict man, and Dad was ready to leave home just about as soon as the Navy would take him. He joined shortly after the bombing of Pearl Harbor. After the war, my parents met, married and rushed off to Miami to begin a new life. I never knew why they wanted to be so far from their families, but my arrival that warm July morning in 1951 began a healing process in the family.

They named me Bernard, but in the temple I was called Ben Tzion, meaning "son of Zion." When I was three years old, my brother, Barry, was born. His Hebrew name was "Baruch" or blessed. The doctor pronounced it a miracle that he was born alive—his identical twin was stillborn.

My father was raised Orthodox but had swung to Reform. He and my mother reached a compromise early in their marriage and raised us as Conservative Jews.

Holidays bring back mostly pleasant memories, although I admit I *kvetched* about fasting on Yom Kippur. I eagerly anticipated the final blast of the *shofar*—not for its religious significance, but for its gastronomic significance: the end of the fast!

Most holidays were fun: marching in the *Simchas Torah* parades, twirling groggers at *Purim,* and building the booths for *Sukkot.* My mother made the best *latkes* in the neighborhood for Chanukah—and when it came to playing dreidel, I always won the most pennies. And how can I forget the *Pesach* seders? They were long enough to try the patience of any child . . . except for the fact that my parents allowed me to drink the sweet wine!

I attended Hebrew school and Saturday school from the age of five. I enjoyed learning about Bible heroes and Jewish traditions. Then there were the Hebrew lessons—we had contests to see who could read the fastest. When I was ten, the temple moved about eight miles away and my "formal" Jewish education ended for a while.

My mother continued to teach us at home. She explained that God had especially chosen the Jewish people and that he always watched over us. Under her supervision, I prayed each night, thanking God for keeping us safe and healthy. I didn't understand what it meant to be chosen, but apparently it made it necessary for me to do good deeds and excel in school. My parents were especially insistent on the latter, and I usually tried to do my part.

Despite the prayers thanking God for good health, I developed asthma. Toward my eleventh birthday it became serious enough for my parents to send me to a drier climate. Off I went to the Children's Asthmatic Research Institute and Hospital in Denver. I lived in a dormitory with about eighteen other asthmatic boys for about two years.

Of course, my family came to visit me. My mother told me a story in conjunction with one of those visits that made a lasting impression. They were driving over a mountain pass when they found themselves facing another car and what should have been a head-on collision. My mother insisted that she saw an angel on our car that pushed the other vehicle away. I always remembered that story, and it reinforced my belief in God.

Even with visits from the family, I was still pretty much on my own. House parents aren't the same as real parents, and without the constant encouragement to excel, my grades took a back seat. On the other hand, my religious education flourished. A local Orthodox rabbi took me under his wing and thanks to his tutelage, I was probably ahead of most boys my age. In addition to teaching me to *dovven* and read Hebrew, he spent time instructing me in the areas of Jewish history and culture.

Like most Jewish boys, I looked forward to my *bar mitzvah.* The preparation was long and tedious, but in the end, I would be a man. I would wear a *tallis,* go to the front of the temple and be called to read from the *Torah.* Most importantly, I would be finished with Hebrew school!

My family *qvelled* as I led the service that summer day in Atlantic City. The rabbi presented me with a beautiful Bible (which I still have) but it was several years before I actually read it.

I felt the same as ever. Yet according to the Jewish religion, on this, the milestone of my thirteenth birthday, I had become a man. Thus my religious education ended.

It was time to focus on my secular education. By then I knew I wanted to be a doctor; according to my parents, I started announcing that intention when I was four years old. If I had to say what first attracted me to the profession, it would probably be my pediatrician. He was so kind and so knowing that I found myself wanting to help people like he did.

At any rate, I had to get serious about school. My hard work paid off, and four years of Tulane University in New Orleans was the prize. And what an eye opener it was. My protected lifestyle in a predominantly Jewish Miami neighborhood had left me unprepared for the temptations of "Sin City."

I lived with several other students and was impressed by their diverse lifestyles. Harry was the smiling, good-natured athlete who was always prepared to be everyone's friend. Lee was the typical 1960s hippie with his drug-oriented culture. We had two geniuses, Hunter and Jody, both of whom later became physicians. Then there was Phil, a minister's son who seemed to think he was perfect. I was the token Jew.

Phil routinely referred to me as a "Christ-killer." This was new to me, and I found it as confusing as it was degrading. How could Phil possibly imagine I was somehow connected to Jesus? Jesus had no part in my life or culture. I used his name as an expletive when things went wrong, but I'd heard gentiles do the same and hardly thought it merited a charge of murder. I thought Phil was a little crazy for believing this myth about Jesus. The strangest part was, Phil would accuse me of killing Jesus with one breath, and with the other he would tell me that this Jesus had died for my sins and that I needed to "accept" him.

By the end of my freshman year in college, the tension between Phil and me erupted into a fist fight. He had insulted my people one time too many, and I lost control. The fight only lasted a couple minutes and I lost, but my roommates applauded my efforts, especially since my antagonist was significantly larger than I.

Phil eventually apologized, but I didn't listen. He didn't return the following year either; he married his high school sweetheart and probably followed his father to the pulpit. Phil had made quite an impression, despite our short acquaintance.

I had learned to hate Christianity.

In fact, I hated the idea of being religious. Phil represented more than an anti-Semitic Christian to me. He was always talking about God, his religion was obviously important to him and yet he was mean spirited and prejudiced. His self-righteousness was so hypocritical that I told myself if being godly meant imitating Phil, I wanted no part of it.

I can't blame Phil for my declining belief in God. My belief in God had begun to deteriorate for reasons that had nothing to do with Phil. Tulane was an interesting college. About a third of the students were Catholic, a third Jewish, and a third "other."

Most of the Jews there were nominal in their beliefs. In college it's easy to intellectualize God's existence. I had gradually come to believe that God was "out there," and I never concerned myself with thoughts of him unless I was in trouble and needed his help. However, after the fist fight with Phil, I doubted God's very existence. Phil's hypocrisy led me to think that we were merely products of our upbringing. I became an agnostic.

Like many college-age guys, I began to think only of myself and the gratification of my needs and desires. My grades slipped, I experimented with various substances, and I renounced any religious beliefs. By my third year of college, I had abandoned my Jewish traditions. I was basically on a downward emotional spiral, barely motivated enough to maintain the grades necessary for medical school.

At the time, I didn't understand what depression was, but now I suspect that I was somewhat depressed. Perhaps it was a result of the drugs, or maybe just uncertainty about whether I wanted to continue toward a career in medicine.

Then I met Jim. Jim was recovering from a failed relationship with his girlfriend, Sandy. She was Jewish; he was not. I found myself very attracted to her, despite something very odd: she believed in Y'shua (Jesus) as the Messiah. I pretended to listen, to be interested in her beliefs, so that I could spend time with her. I secretly hoped to convert her back to Judaism—never mind that I was an agnostic at the time!

Sandy came from a family of several generations of rabbis. Her parents were very upset about her beliefs, and as a result, Sandy endured forced counseling sessions with religious leaders and psychologists. Yet she held firmly to her faith in Y'shua.

Sandy told me that the prophets of the Hebrew Scriptures pointed to Y'shua as the Messiah. She believed that God had forgiven her sins through Y'shua's sacrificial death, and she said that faith in Y'shua was necessary to receive eternal life. I replied that there was only one God, he didn't have a son, and there was no such thing as eternal life.

I challenged her to point out specific prophesies and she did. Over the next six months, I not only opened my bar mitzvah Bible, which had remained shut for so many years—I actually read much of it.

I discovered that the prophet Micah had predicted that the Messiah would be born in Bethlehem (Micah 5:2) and that Jeremiah stated the Messiah would be of the seed of David (Jeremiah 23:5). Isaiah prophesied the unusual circumstances of the Messiah's birth (Isaiah 7:14) and described his reign (Isaiah 9:1–8). And in one of the most poetic and wondrous passages I had ever seen, that same prophet described the sufferings of the servant Messiah and the revelation of what was to come in the days ahead (Isaiah 52:13–53:12).

Sandy also pointed me to Jeremiah and his prophesy of the new covenant, a covenant based on a change in mind and heart and a new closeness to God (Jeremiah 31:31–34). Ezekiel further elaborated upon the cleansing from sin and the new spirit God would place in our hearts (Ezekiel 36:26ff).

I was amazed by these prophesies, and became convinced that God planned to send a Messiah to accomplish these events.

As a child, I had always believed that the Bible was true. Through adolescence my belief wavered. But then, I hadn't read the Scriptures for myself. As I saw those Scriptures, I did not doubt that my Bible was true, and that the promise of a Messiah was real.

But was it Y'shua? Or was the Messiah still to come? Coming from a Jewish background, I understood that God had given the sacrificial system, that he had instructed Moses very specifically, and that following the system was an act of obedience to seek God's forgiveness. I also understood that when the Temple was destroyed, the sacrificial system was suspended, although I didn't know enough history at the time to understand why.

Sandy explained that God did not do away with the sacrificial system even though the Temple was destroyed. The Law and all its requirements remained. She also explained to me that God had provided his ultimate sacrifice through Jesus. She said that Jesus was the Lamb of God, the final sacrifice for forgiveness of sins, both then and in the future for all those who would accept that sacrifice. Faith in him, she said, satisfied God's requirements for atonement. Without him, we were accountable for our own sins, without the Temple, the sacrificial system, and all the things necessary to obtain atonement.

Sandy also explained that the destruction of the Temple in A.D. 70 precluded any future person from claiming they were the Messiah. The genealogical records that could link a person's ancestry to the tribe of Judah were destroyed. That made sense to me, but it did not prove Y'shua was the Messiah.

The biggest issue that Sandy and I discussed was whether or not accepting Jesus meant that I wouldn't be Jewish any longer. She explained to me that all the first Christians were Jews and that accepting Jesus would not diminish my Jewish identity.

Sandy suggested I read the Gospel of John in the "New Testament." I was alarmed by such a suggestion; Jews did not read the New Testament. That was "for gentiles only." Besides, I didn't have a copy. Still, I really wanted to prove that Sandy was wrong and establish a deeper friendship with her at the same time. So I agreed to borrow her copy of *Good News for Modern Man,* a modern paraphrase of the New Testament. I read the Gospel of John and then the other three Gospels: Luke, Mark, and Matthew. The texts were amazing, and I found much that I did not understand.

What type of man was this Y'shua? How did he perform all those miracles? Why did he have to die if he was God? Did he really rise from the dead? And what did this mean for Jews? Sandy helped answer my questions, but with every batch of answers I had a fresh crop of questions.

I was frustrated with my conclusions; I did not want to believe that this Y'shua was true. I was afraid of what my parents would think. I feared that they would label me as a traitor and cut me off forever from the family. I dug in my heels and refused to go further.

Before long, Jim and Sandy got back together. I could no longer cherish any hopes of a blossoming romance.

In the spring of 1971, Sandy invited me to go with her to a "Bible retreat" in Hattiesburg, Mississippi. It was sponsored by a group called InterVarsity, and it was a way to leave campus for the weekend. She promised some fun activities, and yes, there would be some speakers to listen to. I agreed to go, although to this day I don't know why I did.

The conference speaker chose a passage in the Book of Romans. It was a section I had not read, and I took many notes. Romans was written by a man named Paul. He had a way of writing that seemed to speak more clearly to me than any other portion of the New Testament I had read.

Paul explained how humanity had all sinned. He explained about righteousness and how all of us, including Jews, fell short of God's glory. However, God had provided a way for us to be reconciled to him, and that was through faith in his son, Y'shua.

God's provision was an example of his love toward us. "While we were still sinners, Christ died for us" (Romans 5:8). God's grace was a free gift, and asking Y'shua into my life would change my inner being and create a new relationship with God. I would receive the Holy Spirit from God and have power over my own sin and unrighteousness. I would share in Y'shua's glory and have eternal life with him.

For the first time, I understood God's holiness and my own sinfulness. I could see that the human race was at odds with God, that we were in rebellion, not even wanting to admit his existence despite all the evidence of creation that pointed to a Creator. I felt for the first time that the relationship I really wanted was not with Sandy but with the God who was such an important part of her life.

That night I asked Y'shua into my life and repented of my sins. I immediately felt changed; there was a lightness to my step and I felt I was floating when walking back to my cabin. I knew God had given me his Spirit and that Y'shua would be with me forever.

How does a changed person act when there is good news to share? I told everyone I knew. My roommates couldn't believe it; in time they convinced me to quit discussing my faith with them.

I went home for the summer and continued to tell people about my wonderful new life, including my mother. No one had prepared me for her response. She spent the entire summer attempting to dissuade me from my faith in Y'shua. I had no Christian friends in Miami, no support group to pray for me. I was on my own with God; he was faithful and sustained me.

I found a group of Jewish Christians in Miami and attended some of their meetings. It was a relief to find that I wasn't the only Jewish believer in Jesus. I realized with some sadness that this was the last summer I would spend at home with my parents. I couldn't blame them for not understanding my faith. Their refusal to accept my right—in fact my responsibility—to decide what I should believe convinced me that I no longer belonged under their roof, no matter how much we loved each other.

I wanted to incorporate my Jewish traditions and culture into the faith I now had in Y'shua, but it was difficult and I became frustrated. God would later provide some answers through a new evangelistic group called Jews for Jesus. My encounter with their singing group in 1974 made a lasting impact on my life. They demonstrated that it was possible to be Jewish, participate in the traditions I cherished, and express my beliefs in Y'shua at the same time.

My senior year in college was exciting. I met my future bride. We were quite different, but we both loved Jesus and together we grew in faith and knowledge of the Lord. I became a Bible study leader for InterVarsity and eventually assumed an associate staff position with them while in medical school.

Another Jewish believer and I organized an outreach book table in the Tulane University Center on weekends. The *Jewish Press* learned about us and warned the Jewish community of our presence. This thoroughly embarrassed my brother, who was also at Tulane, and thus began a long estrangement between us. Many years would pass before our relationship healed.

Martha and I decided to marry while I was in medical school. We had ceremonies in both the temple and the church; it was our attempt to heal some wounds and make a statement about our union and faith.

With renewed enthusiasm, I implemented several expressions of Jewish life into our new family. Martha (who is not Jewish) has been a jewel. Over the years she has become as excited about Jewish tradition as I am. My mother still has the edge on latkes, but Martha is getting close. One of the proudest days of our life was the day our son stood at the *bimah* and was bar mitzvah.

Much has happened over the last twenty years to strengthen my faith in Y'shua. Through his grace, I survived the rigors of medical school and residency, and I strove to bring him glory through the art and practice I learned. God gave me a gift, and I was able to recognize depression that others could not discern. I have prayed with people while they hurt, and I have celebrated with others as God's glory was revealed in healings.

My belief in God had a definite impact on my practice. I remember a young girl in Tennessee who was unmarried and pregnant. She was a Christian who had lapsed in her faith and wanted to have an abortion. I counseled her for several weeks, at least two or three times a week. She kept her baby, later saying that if it hadn't been for our discussions, she would have had an abortion.

I recall a couple in their mid-forties who had two teenage children. I had to present them with the news that the wife was pregnant. They were scared, and they didn't know what to do—the idea of raising another child from infancy did not fit in with their plans at all. God helped us work through the issues together and they elected to keep the baby.

There was a middle-aged teacher who had bouts with depression and questions about the reality of God. We discussed her questions over a period of months and she eventually made a profession of faith in Jesus. That released her from her depression.

I thank God for the decision that some mothers made to keep their babies after counseling and prayer. And I have mourned for those who chose otherwise.

One pitfall of the medical profession is that our patients can perceive us as godlike. Knowing Y'shua has taught me that it is not I who heals, but it is through the power of God that all things are possible. I am grateful to be an instrument through which he works.

I practiced family medicine for fifteen years. My partner for seven years was a kind and compassionate Jewish family physician named Roy. He knew my beliefs (I explained them to him on more than one occasion) and though we thought differently on matters of faith, it was a good partnership.

I have also practiced with a group of Christian physicians, and planned to create a large Christian multidisciplinary outreach in Florida. However, years of faith in Y'shua have taught me that God's plans for my life may differ from my own.

I gradually shifted away from practicing clinical medicine and into business. This process took several years, but it was a deliberate decision based on what I saw happening in the field of medicine.

The practice of medicine is becoming more and more influenced by large insurance companies without the input of community physicians. I felt that more physicians needed to involve themselves with administrative medicine in order to maintain the high level of quality care to which we are accustomed. I also believed that managed care was good for medicine. It can help us determine more cost-effective ways to treat people, eliminate ineffective procedures and allow us to care for a greater percentage of lower-income people.

I see managed care as the best vehicle for promoting preventive health initiatives. Many people with older indemnity type insurance do not seek medical care until illness leaves them no choice. In any case, I took several courses, decided I enjoyed administration, and got my MBA so that I would be prepared.

In 1993, I entered the world of business and health care. I now manage the medical operations of a health maintenance organization. Business is not the world of medicine as I knew it. In medicine, there are basic ethical standards by which physicians practice their art. Business ethics also exist, but many professionals conduct themselves with varying degrees of principle. I have much to learn and a long way to go in being more like Y'shua. I pray that I will be able to follow the exhortation the Apostle Paul gave in one of his epistles: "Only let your conduct be worthy of the gospel of Christ" (Philippians 1:27). "But indeed I also count all things loss for the excellence of the knowledge of Christ Jesus my Lord, for whom I have suffered the loss of all things" (Philippians 3:8).

Bernie Cohen, MD, is a board certified family physician. He received his MBA in 1993 and is currently a senior executive with a medical managed care organization in Florida.

ARTHUR BARLIS

One day we drove by a church. In fact, the building had once housed the Conservative synagogue of which I'd been president. Since then, I had driven by the church many times, but suddenly I noticed a sign that I had never seen before: Ohr Chadash, Messianic Congregation. I was surprised to see a Jewish name on the building again—even more surprised when I realized that these Jews believed in Jesus.

My father and mother were born in 1910—he in Eastern Poland near the Russian border, she in a little Jewish village near Kiev. Promises of a better life in "the new world" brought both their families to the United States. They were in their twenties when they met in New England, a "match" made by a distant relative.

I was born in 1939 in Providence, Rhode Island. My father owned a grocery store (at one point he owned interest in three) and my mother was a homemaker. Our neighborhood was almost totally Jewish, and our home "somewhat" traditional.

My maternal grandmother lived with us when I was small, and since she never spoke English, I grew up learning Yiddish along with English. It was out of respect for her that my parents kept a kosher home—we even had a separate set of dishes for Passover. Yet when we ate out, we didn't worry about kosher or non-kosher. At home, my mother lit candles every *Shabbat.* I used to watch her hands motioning as if to encircled the flames while she prayed. When my little sister was old enough, she followed along in the ritual. After the candles were lit, we shared our Sabbath dinner. Ironically, we did so without my father—who worked every Friday night!

We attended High Holiday services, first at an Orthodox synagogue and later at a Conservative synagogue. We attended Shabbat services occasionally. Most of the prayers were in Hebrew and had little meaning to me.

Being Jewish was a matter of fact in our home and in our neighborhood. I didn't feel the need to ask what it meant, nor did anyone offer to explain. I only recall one family member who spoke to me about God: my maternal grandmother. Often in moments of tenderness, she told me that God loved me and that I was special to him. Moreover, she said that God was watching over me, and that perhaps I'd grow up to be a rabbi. As a little boy of three, four, or five, I had no idea what it meant to be special in God's sight, but it sounded wonderful.

My father's parents lived nearby. I loved to visit them, as Dad's mother cooked delicious Old World dishes. Our visits there were rather infrequent, though; when we did go, my grandfather hardly spoke to me, or to anyone, as far as I could see. I still picture him sitting at the kitchen table, studying his holy books in Hebrew. The Jewish religion was obviously important to him, but whatever he thought or felt remained in his own mind and heart.

At age eleven, I was enrolled in Hebrew school in preparation for my *bar mitzvah*. There I learned Deuteronomy 6:4 (the *Sh'ma*, the Jewish confession of faith). The rabbi explained that by saying the Sh'ma, we could actually communicate with God. I took his words to heart and began a lifelong habit of reciting this verse every evening, for it was the only link to God that I knew. I spoke the words to a stranger—I did not know God—but I very much wanted to know him. I didn't even mind regularly attending Saturday morning worship services during this period.

After I became bar mitzvah, I wanted to observe Jewish traditions. I started to put on *tefillin* and, unlike some of the boys my age, I continued to attend services. I had my own copy of the Torah, the first five books of Moses, and I intended to read it cover to cover. However, I did not even get through Genesis. You see, my post-bar mitzvah fervor lasted only a couple of months.

My years at school were peaceful and uneventful. My two great desires were (1) to be a doctor and help people, and (2) to be a great tennis player and have fun. My tennis wasn't good enough to support the latter dream, so I opted for medicine.

Doctors learn to take charge and control situations, behaviors to which my personality seemed well suited. By all appearances I was doing well. Yet now and then, some inexplicable feelings of emptiness troubled me. Medical school and training left little time for introspection, but during rare moments when I stopped

to reflect, I was discomfited. I sensed that something was missing. I didn't know what it was, but it related to the question, "Is this all there is to life?" I quickly pushed aside that question because I feared the answer.

I feared that I might not really be able to help people. Constant contact with disease and death throughout medical school underscored the fact that doctors cannot fix everything. I chose to block out feelings of emptiness and I sidestepped questions of mortality because I feared God, and most of all, I feared dying. Pushing aside my vague discomfort, I made myself unaware of these troubling questions and enjoyed the fact that things were going wonderfully for me and I was doing exactly what I wanted with my life.

Although I was somewhat fearful of God, I also believed he was helping me accomplish my goals. I wanted to express gratitude for his blessings but didn't know how—and so I continued to recite the Sh'ma each night. That was my way of telling God that I knew he existed and somehow had a part in my life. Perhaps this was my grandmother's influence, for no one else had ever suggested that God would take a personal interest in me.

I chose the field of ophthalmology for several reasons. I was eager to do surgery and eager to see results, to know that I was making a difference. Even after medical school I had difficulty dealing with terminal illness. I was particularly frustrated with areas of medicine that offered poor odds of actually helping a patient. Ophthalmology was one of the few subspecialties where there were few malignancies, a low mortality rate and a high percentage of patients whom we could greatly benefit.

In the mid-1960's, I entered the field of ophthalmology, got married and had a son. Our little family moved to Clearwater in 1971 and had another son the same year—and another two years later.

We joined the Reform synagogue in town; I preferred the Reform services because they were mostly in English. My wife, who was from an Orthodox background, was unhappy there. We compromised and joined the Conservative synagogue. At first, ours were the only children in that congregation, so we were delighted when a core group of families, all with small children, decided to join. We became very active in synagogue life, and it wasn't long before there was a clash between the original members, who were mostly elderly, and the younger families that had joined. Disagreements arose over how to attract new members and especially how to attract new families. Finally, the board of directors of that synagogue basically said, "We quit; you take over." So a group of us did. In fact, I was elected the president of the congregation.

We hired a young rabbi, moved into a larger facility and grew into a fairly substantial synagogue with a membership of 300 people. As president, I was expected to attend either the Friday or the Saturday services. I hoped the rabbi would help me understand who God was and how I could relate to him. Each week I hoped for a spiritual breakthrough, and each week I left with no clearer understanding of God than I'd had when I came. The sermons were about being good and kind and observing God's laws. I wanted to understand how all that fit into my life. I thought that religion, my Jewish religion, would explain all this to me. It did not.

As the responsibilities of a family and a medical practice grew, my feelings of inexplicable emptiness also grew. I knew that I appeared to have a wonderful and successful life. I loved ophthalmology, but it was not the answer. My marriage was not the answer. The loving relationship with my children was not the answer. My involvement in synagogue (religion) was not the answer. When I was alone with my thoughts, I realized with dismay that nothing I had was giving me the joy and peace that I imagined should fill that empty spot.

I was committed to the synagogue, and I appreciated the linkage with Jewish history that it provided, but I found myself with no desire to continue attending services on a weekly basis. I began alternating Saturdays with the vice president and other officers. The synagogue remained an important part of my life even though I experienced no spiritual fulfillment there. I was president of that congregation for about four years and a member of the board of directors for another four.

With my marriage ending in 1984, I was definitely looking for answers. I was despondent because, although my wife was absolutely wonderful to our children, I never felt that she cared very deeply for me. Something important was lacking in our relationship and I did not know how to fix it. The failed marriage was very painful and caused me to reflect on that growing sense of emptiness.

An acquaintance of mine, having the same disappointments, soon became an important part of my life. I had known Bettye since 1971; her husband worked at the same hospital as I did. From the very beginning, I sensed a love, a peace, a radiance that I had never seen in anyone else. This was very impressive to me.

I was both attracted to, and jealous of, the qualities I saw in Bettye. She explained that she had "given her life to God" when she was eight years old. She grew up with a love for Jesus, the Bible, and the Jewish people. She had been very involved in church—not only on Sunday, but every Wednesday with youth groups—ever since she was a little girl. (And I had balked at going to services once a week!)

Soon Bettye was praying for me faithfully. She gave me a Bible (which I didn't read). And the stronger our relationship became, the more I could see something very wonderful about her. She patiently repeated that Jesus was the reason for the qualities I envied in her, but it was all rather confusing. I remember thinking that, although Jesus was wonderful for Bettye, he had nothing to do with me. I understood, and yet I really didn't understand it.

You see, this was the first time I'd heard about Jesus. No one in my family had ever mentioned him—good, bad or indifferent—nor did friends in elementary or high school. I grew up thinking that Jesus was somehow the non-Jewish version of our God. I assumed that all non-Jews in Providence, Rhode Island were Christians. I did not even know that Jesus was Jewish.

When I left the insulation of my Jewish neighborhood, no one ever provided a different perspective. Not one person in college, medical school, internship or residency ever told me of their faith in Jesus. All I ever knew or thought I knew about Jesus was that he had nothing to do with me because I was Jewish.

Through Bettye, I began to see that Jesus was not the gentile counterpart to the God in whom I believed. He seemed so central to her life and personality. God was certainly an element of my life, but I could not attribute my behavior or outlook to a relationship with him. I could appreciate that Bettye had what I was lacking. However, no matter what she said, it never dawned on me that Jesus might be the answer for me as well. In my world view, Jesus would never be an option simply because I was Jewish. If anything, I made more of an effort to demonstrate that I was not going to lose my Jewishness in this relationship.

I therefore insisted that we be married in a Conservative synagogue, and that meant that Bettye would have to convert. She and I met with the rabbi of the Conservative congregation in Tampa, who obviously knew much more about the situation than either of us. He commented that we came from diverse backgrounds and were likely to experience quite a clash of culture. Of course I didn't feel any of this. I only felt a great love for Bettye.

When the rabbi told Bettye that she would have to renounce her faith in Jesus in order to convert, she replied that she could never do that. I should add that Bettye's faith was not even at its strongest at that point. She had been disappointed in her life, even disappointed in God over the pain of her first marriage. Nor was she active in church at that time. Yet she would never turn her back on Jesus. She was quite forthright about that.

Looking back, I realize that the rabbi should have dismissed us from his study and refused to marry us. Instead he said, "Well, we'll deal with this later." We never did. We were married in a Conservative Jewish wedding ceremony despite the fact that my wife was a strong believer in Jesus.

I remember reassuring Betty that, although I did not understand the importance of Jesus in her life, I could accept and respect her personal decision. To me, God was merely a component of one's life. I wanted to keep my Jewish God and as long as Bettye understood that, we were fine. I had no spiritual understanding of her position, but I accepted it because I loved her.

Nevertheless, the "clashes" the rabbi foretold became apparent almost immediately. Our conflict was not so much that I was a Jew and she was a gentile (and a Southern Baptist to boot!) Differences in our culture and upbringing accounted for some of why we saw life differently, but there were other issues. I had developed a very controlling and self-centered nature. Medicine was demanding and sometimes very disappointing. Quite a few doctors become demanding (and disappointing) as well. Behavior that was accepted or at least tolerated in the hospital did not translate well at home.

Before we married, I felt that Bettye's and my love for each other was all that we needed. I soon realized that was not going to be the case. I really needed to change. I needed to stop trying to control everything, including my wife. I wanted to change. Yet somehow I either couldn't or wouldn't. I really could not fault Bettye. If the love that we shared was not creating as wonderful a relationship as I'd expected, it was not because she had misrepresented herself. It was me.

That was when I first allowed myself to wonder if Jesus might be more than Betty's answer—if he might be mine as well. It wasn't until that crisis of feeling that there was something radically wrong between Bettye and myself that I finally understood that the radically wrong part was me. Once I knew that, I cried out to God, asking him to show me what to do. I told God that I loved Bettye and did not want our marriage to fail. I did not want to disappoint my wife. I was not yet at a point where it occurred to me that I might be disappointing God, but I did realize that God, and not I, had the power to effect real and lasting changes.

We continued attending the Conservative synagogue on an occasional basis. I particularly remember the High Holiday services. Betty was there out of respect for me, not because she was gaining anything spiritual. To my dismay, my overall impression of that service was that there had been a total lack of anything spiritual in it. As we talked about it, I began to sense that the old inexplicable emptiness, the "something missing" was something spiritual, and very important. While it was not the first time I realized that I hadn't found anything spiritually profound in my synagogue, perhaps it was the first time I realized how very much I wanted to find something spiritually significant somewhere.

Bettye and I began reading book after book on personal relationships in an effort to reconcile some of our differences. One such book by John Powell stated that the best marriages involve a third party—God. We started watching TV programs like *Zola*

Levitt and *L'Chaim,* programs that presented a message that Jesus was the Jewish Messiah. Meanwhile, Bettye continued to simply, lovingly and patiently try to help me to understand my need for Jesus. She didn't harp at me or tell me, "I'm praying for you; you need Jesus in your life." (I found out later that she and her whole family had been praying for me.) She would simply point out where our lives and attitudes were different. If I would ask why we were seeing things so differently, she would tell me that she was trying to see things through Jesus' eyes.

One day we drove by a church. In fact, the building had once housed the Conservative synagogue of which I'd been president. I had driven by the church many times, but suddenly I noticed a sign which I had never seen before: *Ohr Chadash, Messianic Congregation.* I was surprised to see a Jewish name on the building again—even more surprised when I realized that these Jews believed in Jesus. I made a phone call and talked to John Fischer, who told me that he was the rabbi of the synagogue. He urged me to please come to a Friday night service.

Early in January 1988, I entered the once familiar door with trepidation and excitement. There was a spirit of joy, peace, love, reverence, praise, and worship in this congregation of Jewish and Gentile believers that I had never seen anywhere before. The message I heard was about Y'shua (Jesus). John Fischer seemed equally at home with Old and New Testaments.

I left that service touched in a way that I'd never been touched before. All night, in and out of sleep, my thoughts were filled with the question "God, is this *your* way for me to know you?" That night, I had either a dream or a vision about Y'shua. It was such a restless night that it's hard to say if I was awake or asleep, but I saw a pure white figure that I recognized as Jesus at the foot of my bed. He told me that I needed to read about him, that I needed to read the Gospels—the first four books of the "New Testament."

I felt compelled to follow that directive. With some trepidation I began to read the Gospel of Matthew. Then I went on to read Mark, Luke and John, and when I was finished, it was as though I had been spiritually opened up. I realized my controlling, proud nature was, in fact, a result of my rebellion and sin against God. This Jesus, whom I never knew and never thought I should know, seemed to be reaching out to me from the pages of this book with love, compassion, understanding, forgiveness and wisdom—and in a very Jewish way. It was clear to me that Jesus was who he claimed to be. He was the Messiah.

As I continued to pore over the Bible daily, I began to understand why the Bible is so unique and special. It reveals God's nature—God's grace and mercy and love. In addition to my own study, I looked forward to times when Bettye and I would read the Bible together.

I read many of the prophetic messianic passages of the Jewish Bible, including parts of Zechariah and Isaiah. Had I only read these texts when I was younger, I thought, I would have recognized the compelling evidence that Jesus was the Messiah. Wouldn't I? Perhaps I wouldn't have, because it was not the acceptable Jewish thing to do.

Somewhere in this time framework, I responded to a Jews for Jesus ad I saw in a secular publication. I don't remember if it was a newspaper or magazine, but the ad offered a book titled *Jesus for Jews,* about Jewish people who believed in Jesus.

As I read about other Jews and reflected on the decisions they made about Jesus, I began to see how God works in people's lives. I read how objections were overcome, and I understood the importance of knowing who Jesus was for myself, rather than accepting what others said about him.

I continued watching Christian television, particularly programs that featured Jewish believers in Jesus, like *Zola Levitt, The Jewish Voice* and *Love Song for the Messiah.* I continued to attend the messianic services on Friday nights and to enjoy the spiritual nurture I found there. John Fischer was a great help and encouragement.

I had a tremendous desire to understand more about "messianic Jews," so Bettye and I attended a convention of messianic congregations in Denver. Sid Roth, one of the speakers, gave a seminar titled "Sharing Y'shua." At the end of his seminar, he provided an opportunity for people publicly to confess their faith in Y'shua. I literally leapt out of my seat to do so. Later that summer I had my immersion (baptism) in the gulf of Mexico off

Clearwater, Florida.

We continued to attend the messianic synagogue for a couple of years, maybe a little longer. We attended a Bible study that John Fischer was holding and I participated in my first messianic Passover *seder.* What an awesome awakening to see how God had depicted his redemptive work through Y'shua in the Passover seder.

Bettye's prayers for me had been answered. She was very happy to attend the messianic congregation with me, yet there was much she could not understand there, because much of it was in Hebrew. We decided to concurrently attend a nondenominational church in Clearwater. The pastor of that church also happened to be Jewish, which was helpful to me.

You see, though I believed in Jesus, I still had a fear of going to a church, of losing my Jewish identity among the gentile majority. God eventually broke down that fear as I realized that the church was meant to be a group of people from diverse backgrounds. It took a while to see that my identity as a Jew was not going to cease because I was in the minority.

Eventually we settled into a church right in our own neighborhood. There is a small but definite number of Jewish members, and we have a fellowship meeting once a month. We also conduct Passover seders and do what we can to share the Jewishness of our Christian faith with the rest of the church.

Since I've become a believer in Jesus, I've undergone major, remarkable changes—changes that show a loving God has been at work in my life. He dealt with those areas in which I was perversely unwilling to change, while desperately wanting to improve the quality of my life. My self-centered outlook was replaced with a genuine desire to be used by God. Best of all, when I "turned the controls over" to the Almighty, I began to see that I could be strong without having to be in control. When my need to control turned to a consuming desire to please God and obey him, the "inexplicable emptiness" was filled. The peace and joy I'd envied were mine.

The changes have not only been personal, but professional as well. At times, God gives opportunities to treat "spiritual blindness" along with physical visual loss. I developed an appreciation of how to treat each patient with a servant spirit.

Bettye began working in my office three years after we were married. She did well as an ophthalmic technician and then proceeded to help in every aspect of the practice. She became the office administrator as God allowed our practice to grow. Her caring and joyous personality became a tremendous asset to an ophthalmology practice that is still growing.

We have a busy practice and I feel that each patient is in my office for a reason. I pray for God's wisdom in dealing with my patients, in diagnosing them, and in treating them with Christlike love and compassion.

There is enough reading material in the office to indicate my faith so that anyone who is interested can easily ask what it is all about. Consequently, not a day goes by that I don't have the opportunity to explain the Lord's involvement in my life to at lease one inquiring patient. I also ask all surgical patients if I can pray with them regarding their upcoming surgery. The ease with which I've had successful surgeries since 1988 has made the reality of answered prayer abundantly clear to me.

When telling fellow Jews about my faith, the reply often comes, "It's not for me. I wasn't brought up to believe any of this!" NEITHER WAS I. Many of us fear opening our minds to something we were taught that Jews should not believe. We don't want to be disloyal and we don't want to lose our Jewish identity. Having experienced these fears myself, I tell people that loyalty is good and right, but it is not a function of loyalty to curtail a search for truth. If anyone senses that Jesus might be true, I urge them to pray that God will show them the truth, and I urge them to examine Jesus' claims.

Jeremiah 29:13 says, "and you will seek me and find me when you shall search for me with all your heart." In John 5:39, Jesus said, "You search the Scriptures; for in them you think you have eternal life; and these are they which testify of Me." Indeed, passages like Deuteronomy 18:15 do seem to testify of him. In John 5:46, Jesus says, "For if you believed Moses, you would believe Me: for he wrote about Me." I think of verses like Genesis 3:15 and 12:3.

In John 8:58, Jesus says, "Most assuredly, I say to you, before Abraham was, I AM" (see Exodus 3:14). Who in the Old

Testament is "I AM?". In John 10:30, Jesus says, "I and My Father are One." In John 14:6, Jesus says, "I am the way, the truth, and the life. No one comes to the Father, except through Me."

These passages have earthshaking implications. No person can convince another of their truth. But God stands ready to reveal truth to those who want to know, regardless of what it may cost.

As a physician, I learned to seek knowledge because that knowledge can change people's lives. In medicine, one cannot be satisfied with the status quo on the basis that we learned it in medical school or because a beloved mentor taught us. The field of ophthalmology especially demonstrates how new information has enabled us to improve or restore the precious gift of sight. The Bible is certainly not new, but it contains information that is new to many people.

People can have their M.D.'s and Ph.D.'s, their practices and all that goes with them—but to be truly successful and fulfilled, we need to be reconciled with God. Anyone who comes to God with a repentant heart (*t'shuva*) and receives God's atonement through Messiah Jesus will have spiritual sight. It is the ability to see the reality of God working in our lives that brings true peace (*shalom*).

Dr. Arthur Barlis is a diplomat of the American Board of Ophthalmology in private practice of ophthalmology in Dunedin, Florida. He is also clinical assistant professor of ophthalmology at the University of South Florida School of Medicine in Tampa, Florida.

David Madenberg

I wanted answers! I had ridiculed, mocked, and attempted to belittle God to no avail—so I switched tactics and tried to test him instead. "If you are so all-powerful, heal me of these illnesses right now! I've never asked you for much, why not do this for me? How do you expect me to ease my patients' pain when my own suffering is consuming me?"

It was oppressively hot and humid, a typical July evening in the inner city of Chicago. Neighbors shouted, dogs barked and sirens wailed. The aroma of ethnic cooking seeped through cracks in the plastered green walls of the emergency department in the City General Hospital.

I stood at a small, rectangular window at the nurses' station and gazed down at the street. Two men were in a heated argument while a motorist narrowly missed a small child who ran across the intersection. Farther up the block, gang members spray-painted a storefront as a hooker negotiated with her client.

The sights and sounds inside proved even more unpleasant. We often referred to the emergency department as "the Cave" because of its poorly lit and gloomy atmosphere—and because of the way that sound carried. The screams of a young woman experiencing severe abdominal pain echoed throughout the department, while an alcoholic retched blood and half-digested spaghetti onto the floor in another room. (The emergency staff eventually got used to the nauseating odor of alcohol mixed with stomach contents.) Halfway down the hall, a youth lay bloodied from a gang fight, his face severely bruised and swollen, his arms and chest variegated with multiple superficial knife wounds. At least twenty other people waited impatiently to be examined as we worked feverishly to treat the sick and wounded on this sultry summer night.

With all sixteen examination rooms occupied, several patients were lying on stretchers in the hallway across from the nurses' station. Even more streamed into the already overcrowded waiting area. A few were enraged to hear that it would be three hours before a physician could attend to them. As always, patients who needed us the least complained the most about the wait. They were the ones who came to the emergency department mainly because they could see a doctor without an appointment.

Suddenly a nurse cried out to me from the corridor, "Dr. Madenberg, come to the trauma room! We have a gunshot wound to the abdomen that someone just dragged in."

I dropped the instruments I'd been using to suture a young boy's leg, I felt that surge of adrenaline I had come to know and despise. My heart was pounding inside my chest as I ran through that dingy, foul-smelling hallway, passing a suffering mass of humanity lying on gurneys. I could feel my stomach lining burn as gastric acids wreaked havoc with a newly acquired ulcer. When I reached the gunshot victim, I was absorbed in my own suffering. *Why do I have to be on duty tonight? Why do I always pull these busy shifts? Why couldn't another resident take some of this heat?*

But I knew why. As a senior resident in my final year of an emergency medicine training program, it was my dubious honor to serve as the attending or supervising physician to a junior resident, an intern, and two medical students. For the entire year, I was scheduled to work straight night shifts, five days a week, every other month, in addition to the required residency rotations.

My patient was a black teen lying in a pool of his own blood. He was barely conscious and exhibited almost no respiratory effort.

"Get two large-bore IVs in him *stat,* and I'll put in an arterial line," I yelled to the intern. At the same time, the junior resident was attempting to place a tube into the patient's windpipe in order to help him breathe. "Run the fluids wide open and get some O-negative blood into him fast!" I shouted to one of the nurses. "And call the surgical resident down here now!" I knew the patient would die unless we got him to the operating room immediately. "Tell the surgeon we may have to crack the patient's chest down here if we aren't able to raise his blood pressure with fluids very soon."

As we continued the resuscitation, I could hear cries of pain coming from the waiting area as even more people poured into the emergency department. My heart was racing and beads of perspiration formed on my forehead. *How is the woman with abdominal pain doing?* I wondered. *Is it her appendix, or does she have a tubal pregnancy? What if the alcoholic bleeds out before I can get back to reevaluate him? Did the medical student complete the suturing on the little boy's leg?*

My own abdominal pain intensified as a nurse informed me that the paramedics were en route with a possible heart attack victim. "Where in hell are we going to put him?" I shouted, as the sweat began to drip from my brow. "The corridor is already lined with patients on gurneys!" My concern froze into icy fear. "Some of these patients will die unless I do something!" I said, shuddering from the thought. "Call the medical resident and ask him to make room in the ICU for the paramedic patient!" I ordered the nurse. Could she hear the fear in my voice?

I literally trembled at the thought of more critically ill patients arriving, because the department was filled to capacity. I would not be able to examine the "walking wounded" (those who came with sore throats and earaches), for hours. I knew from experience that some people become belligerent if not seen by a physician within a certain period of time, regardless of how minor their complaints. One querulous patient had instigated a near riot in the waiting area—even punched a nurse—because of the wait.

What am I doing here? I asked myself. *Why am I putting myself through this abuse?* Just then, the surgical resident arrived and whisked the teen gunshot victim off to surgery.

By six o'clock the next morning, we had the emergency department under control. The moaning woman with abdominal pain was recovering from her emergency appendectomy, while the alcoholic vomiting blood was resting comfortably in the intensive care unit, his bleeding ulcer under control. The young boy with the leg laceration had been sutured by the medical student and sent home. The teen with multiple injuries from the gang fight was treated and admitted to the hospital for observation. The gunshot victim, however, had died in the operating room from massive internal injuries. Only two patients remained to be examined—a middle-aged man complaining of a sore throat and a young girl with an earache.

One more hour and I'm outta this cave, I promised myself as

I watched the seconds ticking away on the clock above the triage nurses' desk. My muscles were so racked with tension that I felt as though I had just been battered in a boxing ring. Taking several deep breaths, I slowly exhaled, imagining all the tension flowing from my body. After deep breathing for about fifteen minutes, I felt more in control as the nervous energy that had bombarded me throughout the entire shift disappeared. Unfortunately, the thought of having to return to the Cave that night sent waves of anxiety through my body, again causing my muscles to tense. I rose slowly from the chair and walked, zombielike, to the cafeteria. I needed a cup of coffee to prepare for my hour-long ride home.

The hour passed, and I went home and straight to bed. At this point in my life, sleep was my only refuge and source of peace. That night when I returned to the Cave, the shift was every bit as stressful as the previous night. It was Saturday night and the unrelenting summer heat continued, causing tempers to flare. A fight broke out in the waiting area, and a man pulled a handgun out from under his shirt. Fortunately, the weapon was not loaded, and security officers quickly subdued its owner.

In addition to the typical Saturday night crowd of drunkards and brawlers, I found myself confronted with two additional problems—lab and X-ray. Laboratory and radiology technicians who work quickly are crucial to the efficiency of an emergency department. Without their cooperation, a patient's stay may be prolonged for hours pending test results. As a senior resident, not only was I required to oversee the entire emergency staff and evaluate every patient, but it was incumbent upon me to serve as interdepartmental diplomat. I had learned that if a physician wanted X-rays or labs performed quickly, he had to be a politician. If a doctor was too demanding or pugnacious toward the technicians, test results would take forever to return.

Tyrone was on duty that night. He was extremely muscular and stood well over six feet tall. Well-versed in the martial arts, he held a black belt in karate. He also performed his duties at a snail's pace and had a talent for disappearing. When Tyrone was on duty, it was a sure bet that X-rays would take an inordinate length of time. This, of course, created chaos and overcrowding in our department.

In addition to the delays caused by Tyrone, weekends nearly always meant prolonged waits for lab test results. This was due to a dearth of technicians resulting from employee cutbacks. Even the best lab technicians were so inundated with work that they were frequently unable to perform tests in a timely fashion. It was not unusual for a critically ill patient to remain in the emergency department for hours prior to being transferred to the intensive care unit. This placed an almost unbearable pressure on me to "move the meat." I was often forced to make important medical decisions based on insufficient data.

The toll on my body increased. I developed a chronic sinus infection and sore throat. After three months of continuous penicillin therapy, I developed an allergic reaction to the antibiotic. This consisted of five weeks of giant hives all over my body, and a red, itchy rash. At the same time I developed pain in my muscles and joints, particularly in my hands, elbows and feet.

A simple handshake, let alone a complex procedure, made me grimace from pain. The prolonged time spent on my feet was causing severe discomfort.

I consulted three different rheumatologists as to the etiology of my condition, and they suggested that I might be developing an early form of a potentially crippling arthritis for which there was no cure—only treatment to relieve some of the pain. Unfortunately, I could not take the anti-inflammatories that could ameliorate the pain because they exacerbated my ulcer. By then the stomach ulcer also prevented me from eating most of the foods I enjoyed.

By the middle of the year, I felt I could no longer cope. The stresses of the Cave tormented me emotionally, and the persistent sinus drainage robbed me of my sleep. I could not eat. due to the ulcer pain, nor could I exercise or even walk for prolonged periods without pain in my muscles and joints.

God, what is happening to me? I screamed silently. I felt completely helpless and no longer in control of my life. I feared that I would never recover from my infirmities as I slowly succumbed to the multiple stressors in my life. I felt absolutely powerless and did not know where to go or to whom I could turn for help. My physician colleagues were not able to help me. I was becoming very angry, resentful and sometimes outright hostile toward my patients.

I could see no end to the madness of the Cave short of giving up and resigning from my residency, an unacceptable alternative. The only solution to my dilemma, it seemed, was permanent sleep.

No longer was I able to keep myself going with such thoughts as *Come on, only a few more months and I'll be out of this life of hell.* I felt as though my life were dangling by a delicate thread and that one more assault on my body or my emotions would sever that line. I felt trapped, cornered without a way of escape. Even if I managed to graduate, how would I practice medicine in such ill health? Having enjoyed so many years of physical well-being and success, I could not understand why this was happening to me now.

The Wrestling Match

I could not help but believe that it all had something to do with God. *Why is God tormenting me?* I asked myself. *What have I done to incur his wrath?* With only a few months left in my residency, why had God abandoned me? Why had he left me an orphan to fend for myself?

I had worked hard and knew I deserved better. I had always considered myself to be a good person. I tried to treat others as I would have them treat me. I had grown up "semi-religious" having attended Hebrew school until I became *bar mitzvah.* I always believed in an all-powerful Creator God whom I truly feared, and not in the biblical sense. Yet, in all my life, I never sat down to read the Bible with the intent of understanding what was written in it. Nor did I pray to God unless I desperately needed something from him. I could never understand grown men and women who got down on their knees to pray; it appeared so childish, self-demeaning and, frankly, unnecessary. Except now, everything had gone haywire. I had some things I wanted to say to God, but I didn't want to say them on my knees. My "prayer" took me by surprise.

It happened after a night shift in May, when the thread suspending me over the abyss nearly broke. During that shift, we treated a near record number of patients, including violent crime victims, heart attacks, minor traumas, and a multitude of seriously ill patients. It felt like our emergency department was the only one open for business in the entire city. By shift change the following morning, I silently asked God to take my life and end the suffering.

As I dragged myself to my car, I could not discern which part of my body hurt the most. I was beyond fatigue, feeling very angry and bitter about life. I was beginning to take my internalized anger and hostility out on my patients, "so dumb they don't even have the common sense to give their kids Tylenol for fever before seeking medical attention." I felt abused and mistreated, taken advantage of by patients, ancillary hospital personnel and my superiors. I was becoming judgmental, alienating myself from the emergency staff because of my bitterness and poor attitude.

I pulled out of the physicians' parking lot, overwhelming anger pervading my entire being as I contemplated how a good, merciful and so-called just God would allow these physical ailments to befall an innocent man. I had questioned myself over and over as to what reprehensible offense I might have committed against God to incur such a heavy dose of his wrath and judgment; I concluded that it was God, not I, who was grossly at fault.

As I merged onto the freeway I began to accuse him verbally. "God, why are you doing this to me?" I shouted. "I'm a good person and one of your chosen people! I'm not an evildoer who kills or steals or cheats others! How can you call yourself merciful and just when you are doing these things to me? I treat people fairly, so why don't you treat me the same way?"

I had always feared God's anger; I was certain he would never forgive me for talking to him in this manner. Yet at that point, I really didn't care. What could God do to me? If I incurred a death sentence from God it would be a welcome escape from my misery. I began cursing God, chiding myself for believing in him and his supposed perfection. "How can you be so cruel?" I screamed, as tears of anger and frustration began flowing down my cheeks. I felt the rage intensify beyond my control. Never had I felt such hatred or animosity as I did during that ride home from work.

As words of unchecked rage continued to spew from my mouth, I understood the extent of the bitterness and resentment I had felt toward God all these months. I felt cheated and scorned by him, sentenced to a life of permanent pain and suffering for no just cause. As I continued my tirade, I posed an age-old question to God. "Why is it you allow good people to suffer while the wicked and sinful people of the world go unscathed? Why are the bad people allowed to succeed and do well? Surely a merciful and just God can see the unfairness," I said mockingly. "So, why do you punish me for no reason?" I shouted angrily. "If you are such a just and loving God, why don't you take these illnesses from me and give them to someone who really deserves them?"

By this time, I was afraid I might lose control of the car. After a few minutes, I regained my composure and continued my argument with God. "I always believed you were merciful and kind! Why are you punishing me for no just cause?" I asked. "What have I done to so offend you? Tell me!" I demanded. "If you are putting an innocent man through such torment, yet allowing the real sinners to go unpunished, how can I possibly believe that you are fair in your judgments? How can I ever again believe you are an all-loving, all-knowing, and all-merciful God?"

I felt so betrayed. My frustration and sense of helplessness grew to the point where I began laughing through my tears. "I may just as well become a sinner if you are going to punish me anyway," I told God. "Perhaps if I do become sinful, you might treat me like a sinner and stop punishing me!" I mocked. My irreverence at this point surprised even me. *Yet, what more can God do to me?* I thought.

As a Jew, certain values had been instilled in me throughout my formative years. Fairness to others and accountability for one's own actions were of paramount importance. I had learned to demand it of myself, and I expected it from not only other people but also from God. I also believed in retribution for evil. "An eye for an eye," I had often hear my mom say, and I interpreted it as righteous revenge.

So, I was perfectly willing to accept God's punishment for any evil I might have committed, but in my estimation I had done no wrong! How could God fail to see this? Was it possible for God to make a mistake? If so, then either my parents and religious leaders had lied to me or they had been grossly misinformed! My anger gave way to moroseness and self-pity. I felt rejected by God and overwhelmed by the thought that he hated me for no reason.

Another belief instilled from my youth was that success is based on a person's own efforts. If a person worked or studied hard enough and expended sufficient energy to accomplish a goal, success was guaranteed. I had no reason to doubt this belief as my relatives and Jewish neighbors were successful professionals who preached this same "gospel" for success. A corollary to the "formula" that I'd heard my mother and grandmother repeat quite often was "God helps those who help themselves." I had always felt in complete control of my life because I thought I understood the rules for success. Rarely did I fail in any endeavor. I worked and studied hard so God would help me obtain good grades and attain the recognition I deserved. I grew up believing that God was watching over me with a rod, and I did not want to do anything to anger him. I lived a good life and felt that I had earned God's favor, not his wrath. I had held up my end of the deal and was furious that God had cheated me by withholding the blessings I felt were rightfully mine.

After all, I never smoked and only rarely drank an alcoholic beverage. I rarely gambled, and in all my life I had never been involved in an actual fist fight. I was well liked and never deliberately stepped on anyone's toes to grab the brass ring. I took care of my body, had always been a good athlete and was proud that I had earned a black belt in Korean karate in less than two years. I was also proud of the fact that I had been one of only a handful of students in my high school graduating class to have completed medical training. I was proud that I had endured thirteen years of advanced education, having performed admirably in medical school and graduating with honors. I was proud to have been so well respected by the attending physicians and medical students during my residency training. I was proud that I gave to charitable organizations and to those who were less fortunate when I did not need that extra dollar.

Yes, I was quite proud of myself, and why not? In fact, I rarely hesitated to boast quietly to others because I believed my recognition was hard earned and I deserved people's praise. Certainly my parents always praised me for my accomplishments, telling me how proud they were of me and how proud I should be of myself. I expected that God would be proud of me, too, and bless me accordingly. So, why did it feel like I was under some kind of curse?

I wanted answers! I had ridiculed, mocked, and attempted to belittle God to no avail—so I switched tactics and tried to test him instead. "If you are so all-powerful, heal me of these illnesses right now! I've never asked you for much, why not do this for me? How do you expect me to ease my patients' pain when my own suffering is consuming me? I know that you can rid me of this misery anytime, God!"

Then I entered the "bargaining phase." I promised God that if he healed me I would do more for him and his cause. I begged and pleaded for my health, but, once again, I felt totally helpless, with no control over my future.

I reached my apartment emotionally drained. I had nothing more to say to God. He had not heard me, or even if he had, my outburst of hate and disrespect had probably earned me everlasting wrath.

I experienced a curious calm that I had not known for a long time. I thought it might simply be my utter exhaustion, or perhaps it was the relief born of finally telling God exactly how I felt. However, along with that calm I felt something else. God was no longer on my side! Somehow we had become enemies. How could anyone speak to God in the way I did and not be severely punished? I had wrestled with God—and lost.

The Bible

I realized at that point that my life as I had known it was over. I was doomed to fail in every aspect of life: work, social life, marriage—all would be on a downward spiral. Perhaps one day God would forgive me, but I knew he would never forget. God's blessings would be cut off, just as a stream of water from a faucet—and who could blame him? By my standards, I had just given God every right to despise and punish me.

All I wanted at that moment was to crawl into bed and sleep

for a week. Yet as I walked toward the door of the apartment building, I sensed "something" telling me to go upstairs and read my wife's Bible. I was stunned! It made no sense. Where did that idea come from, I wondered. Reading was the last thing I wanted to do—and the Bible? After the hour-long argument I just had with God? Besides, when in all my life had I read the Bible, except as a child, in Hebrew school? Occasionally, I read for Saturday morning services at temple. I did not find reading the Bible at all enjoyable.

How could reading the Bible help me to overcome my current dilemma or get me through the remainder of my residency? I wondered silently. I trudged up the three flights of stairs to our apartment, totally exhausted.

My wife, Paula, greeted me at the door. She took one look at my face and asked what had happened. I described my hour-long one-sided "conversation" with God. Then I told her that something within me suggested that I should read the Bible. She was not surprised.

"That's a good idea," she said. "At least it will offer you some comfort." Paula had been raised Methodist and was accustomed to reading the Bible and praying each night before bed.

"Comfort?" I retorted. "How can reading a book written so long ago offer me comfort or ease my pain?" I had never known my Jewish friends or family members, except perhaps my Grandmother Gert, to resort to this kind of behavior when the going got rough. Paula had her religious upbringing and I had mine. "God helps those who help themselves," I told Paula. Even if I couldn't believe it anymore, it was what I thought I should believe if I was going to believe anything. I undressed and crawled into bed for a long sleep, my only true comfort.

Several weeks passed. Nothing changed with respect to my physical and emotional health. I did not cease to believe in God as Ruler and Creator of the universe. As a physician, I knew all too well that the human body is much too intricately designed to have come into existence randomly from vapors or to have evolved from primeval forms of life—but I absolutely refused to read the Bible. I would not waste what little spare time I had reading a book written thousands of years ago, a book describing a benevolent, merciful God. I would never read such a fictitious book! Not now, not ever!

With each day, with each hour I spent in the Cave, I became more bitter, resentful and pugnacious. I was sarcastic and short-tempered. My behavior was not confined to work or limited to patients.

More often than not, I would bring it home with me. Eventually our marriage fell into disarray. After alienating my wife, I had no support system and no one toward whom I could vent my anger. Throughout this time, the thought "go read the Bible" continued to haunt me, popping into my mind at the most unpredictable moments. I resisted, refusing to give in to such an inane idea. How could that ancient book possibly help me at work or at home? Then I hit rock bottom.

I was on duty late one evening when a young woman in her early twenties was carried into the emergency department by a male companion. He told the triage nurse that "Michelle" had been drinking heavily and was experiencing abdominal pain. He helped the nurse place her onto the gurney, then quickly disappeared.

She was dressed as if she had just come from a wedding. Her maroon velvet gown was trimmed with white French lace around the neckline and hem. The all-too-familiar odor of alcohol was on her breath and clothing. There was vomitus spattered on part of her face and in her beautifully braided hair.

Unbelievably filthy language flowed from her mouth as she abused each person who tried to help her. It turned out to be the insult that pushed me beyond my limit and over the edge. With no warning, all sense of reason departed. I grabbed Michelle by her collar and shook her several times. With each shake, her head lifted off the examination cart at least a foot and crashed back down onto the hard, metal frame. As I shook her, I screamed, "If you don't shut the _____ up, I'm going to throw your _____ out of here!" When I finished, the entire department was silent. Michelle was looking at me horror-stricken while the nurses and medical students watched in disbelief. How could a senior resident treat a patient like that?

I strode into my office and slammed the door behind me. I was dazed by my own actions, disgusted by what I had done and fearful of the consequences. Would I be terminated from my residency with only a few short weeks to go? Would all I had invested be for naught? I had entered the field of medicine with noble intentions—I wanted to save lives. It was a decision I'd made in 1970. I was in basic training when three of my platoon mates died of meningitis. When I got back to school, I dropped my original plans (pre-law) and went into pre-med.

Had I thrown away my career in one moment of anger? As I considered the horrendous possibilities, that "voice" from within me once again urged me to read the Bible. This time I did not brush it aside. I recognized the seriousness of what I had just done and somehow I knew I had to change. I felt my future as a physician was in jeopardy and I had nothing to lose. *Okay, I'll read that _____ book,* I said to myself. Then I put my head down on my desk and closed my eyes.

I was awakened by my replacement at 7 A.M. Incredibly, no more patients had come into the emergency department after the incident with Michelle.

I went home and slept until the afternoon. When I awoke, my thoughts turned to Michelle and I felt sick. She had not been injured, but the thought that I had grabbed a patient in anger repulsed me. As I got out of bed, I glanced over at my wife's night table. Her Bible seemed to draw me. Reluctantly, I picked it up and began thumbing through it. "So this is a Christian Bible," I thought. All the text was in English. I did not want to read it, could not imagine that it would help.

I was holding something totally foreign to me. The fact that it was written completely in English and read like any other book made it strange. Our holy books read from right to left. One had to read Hebrew. But this Bible was easy to read and, to my amazement, as I skimmed I actually understood its contents. It even contained the same verses and stories that were printed in my Hebrew Bible!

Yet I felt extremely uncomfortable holding this Christian Bible in my hand. Perhaps it was because I had been called such derogatory names as "kike" or "sheenie" by so-called Christian friends.

One such incident occurred while I was in high school. I was walking home from my Catholic girlfriend's house one afternoon when "Jake," a Polish-Catholic acquaintance of mine, greeted me and we began walking together. I could tell that he was disturbed by something, so I asked him what was wrong. "Our Jew land-lord raised the rent again and he just raised it a few months ago!" Jake yelled. "My dad is having a hard time paying it now because he was just laid off from the [steel] mill." Jake then began a tirade wherein he derided every "Jew bastard" who had ever lived. He commented on how the "rich Jews" owned every-thing and how it was too bad that Hitler couldn't "finish the job." After he concluded, Jake looked at me with his angry brown eyes and said, "Hey, you're Jewish." I stared at him perplexed, as he proceeded to shout obscenities at me until I became so angry that I retaliated with a few of my own.

We were on the verge of blows when I looked at him and said, "Jake, I thought you were my friend. Why are you acting this way?" Jake hesitated, looked at me scornfully, shouted, "You sheenie!" and then walked away. I was completely dumfounded. Why would a friend, a professed Christian, turn on me like that? Didn't his religion teach people to love or at least respect one another?

I was still holding Paula's Bible as I recalled another incident from high school. Tommie, another Christian friend of mine, came to my house each morning and we would walk to school together. One morning, for no apparent reason, Tommie asked me how it felt to know that I wouldn't go to heaven when I died. "How can you ask that?" I asked Tommie indignantly. "I'm a good person! Of course I'll go to heaven!"

"No you won't!" Tommie insisted. "You won't go to heaven unless you believe in Jesus as your Savior."

"I'll never do that!" I said with determination. "I'm Jewish and I'm proud of my heritage. Believing in your Christian god is against my religion! You can believe what you want, but don't tell me I'll never get to heaven unless I believe in Jesus!"

That ended our conversation. Oddly enough, I never forgot Tommie's words. Every so often over the years they flashed through my mind. Why I continued to recall such a trivial inci-dent was a mystery to me. Perhaps it was because my young friend seemed so sure of himself, and I knew that I could not even allow myself to consider whether what he said was true. After all,

I was Jewish, one of the chosen people. Never mind that I did not know what we were chosen for, besides not believing in Jesus.

My thoughts wandered as I continued to stare at the pages of Paula's Bible. *Why should I bother to read it? Wasn't it for hypo-critical Christians like Jake? Why try to discover anything about God when he torments me to the point of suicidal ideation?* Then I recalled once again the incident with Michelle. *What do I have to lose? I can't sink any lower than I am now.* I decided that I would read the Bible but not read the "New Testament" part. I recalled my religious training: "For you shall worship no other god, for the Lord, whose name *is* Jealous, *is* a jealous God" (Exodus 34:14). I would avoid anything that contradicted Jewish teachings or suggested that I worship another god.

I reluctantly turned to the pages of Genesis. Although I had never read Genesis in its entirety, I recognized many passages from my boyhood religious training.   Memories of Hebrew school returned as I reread the story of Cain and Abel and how Cain murdered his brother Abel out of jealousy.

I studied the life of Joseph: how he was thrown down a well by his angry brothers and left to die because of a prophetic dream in which his older brothers were required to bow down before him. I marveled at how Joseph, rather than avenging himself, began to cry when he saw his brothers and had great compassion on them. *Would I have shown the same mercy?* I wondered.

I found the Book of Genesis so fascinating that I couldn't put the Bible down. I read through the entire book in a matter of hours. Never before had I read the Bible for pure pleasure. Never had I found it so interesting or so revealing of human nature. I felt as though I were engrossed in a best-selling novel or exciting mystery.

I purchased my own copy of the Bible.

The Book of Exodus was just as fascinating as Genesis. I read of the many plagues God sent on the Egyptians and how, on the first Passover, firstborn Jews were spared from death by sprinkling the door posts of their homes with blood from a sacrificial lamb.

I continued to read the five books of Moses. Like Paula, I kept my Bible on the night stand beside the bed. I was amazed at how

I went from not wanting to read the Bible to looking forward to my daily ritual of immersing myself in Scripture before I went to sleep. I wondered what was happening to me. I had never been a particularly religious person. Yet I found that studying the Bible quenched a thirst in me that I could not comprehend. Whatever was happening to me, it felt very good.

Nevertheless, the Books of Leviticus and Deuteronomy contained portions of Scripture that disturbed me. A central theme was how frequently the people of Israel sinned before God and what they needed to do to receive forgiveness and cleansing. God was very specific as to the system he provided. There were even offerings to be made for those sins that people committed without knowing it!

These laws were disturbing to me because I simply could not comprehend why a merciful and compassionate God would punish a person who unintentionally commits a sin. What troubled me more was relating these ancient laws to our current world. I was a good person who tried not to sin, but did I do so unintentionally? Was God punishing me for some sin I might have committed inadvertently?

The fifth book of Moses, the Book of Deuteronomy, describes how many times the people of Israel rebelled against God and consequently wandered in the desert for forty years. Also in the Book of Deuteronomy, we read God's words of instruction to Moses for the Israelites prior to entering the Promised Land.

"Behold, I set before you today a blessing and a curse: the blessing, if you obey the commandments of the LORD your God which I command you today; and the curse, if you do not obey the commandments of the LORD your God, but turn aside from the way which I command you today, to go after other gods which you have not known" (Deuteronomy 11:26–28).

Among the many other commands, I read: "That which has gone from your lips you shall keep and perform, for you voluntarily vowed to the LORD your God what you have promised with your mouth" (Deuteronomy 23:23).

How many times in my life had I promised God I would do this for him if he would to that for me, yet failed to keep my end of the bargain, though God answered my prayers? How many times had I taken God for granted? How many times had I failed God? As I pondered these questions, a greater question loomed in my mind: *Could I be a sinner in the eyes of God?*

Many other portions of the Book of Deuteronomy bothered me, but none more than Chapter 28, wherein God described what he would do to those who disobey his commands.

"But it shall come to pass, if you do not obey the voice of the LORD your God, to observe carefully all His commandments and His statutes I command you today, that all these curses will come upon you and overtake you" (Deuteronomy 28:15).

"The LORD will strike you with consumption, with fever, with inflammation, with severe burning fever, with the sword, with scorching, and with mildew; they shall pursue you until you perish" (Deuteronomy 28:22).

"The LORD will strike you with the boils of Egypt, with tumors, with the scab, and with the itch, from which you cannot be healed. The LORD will strike you with madness and . . . confusion of heart" (Deuteronomy 28:27–28).

"Moreover all these curses shall come upon you and pursue and overtake you . . . because you did not obey the voice of the LORD your God, to keep His commandments and His statutes which He commanded you" (Deuteronomy 28:45).

"If you do not carefully observe all the words of this law that are written in this book . . . then the LORD will bring upon you . . . great and prolonged plagues—and serious and prolonged sicknesses" (Deuteronomy 28:58–59).

"Your life shall hang in doubt before you; you shall fear day and night, and have no assurance of life. In the morning you shall say, 'Oh, that it were evening!' And at evening you shall say, 'Oh, that it were morning!' because of the fear which terrifies your heart" (Deuteronomy 28:66–67).

These verses struck a chord as they seemed to describe many of my symptoms so well. Once again I wondered: *Could I really be a sinner in the eyes of God? Am I being punished for some sin that I have committed before God? Does God really hold our generation accountable to these ancient laws?*

As a physician, if I didn't have the answer to a particular problem, I would look it up in a textbook. The answers to these questions, however, could not be found in any medical text.

Perhaps I could call Rabbi Kaufman and he would enlighten me regarding the series of questions that popped into my head. How could a person realize all of the sins he might have committed if they were done unknowingly? How could a person possibly remember all of the laws and rules imposed upon him by God? Why did God require the intercessory prayers and the sacrificing of animals by a priest on behalf of a sinner to make atonement for his sins? Why were animal sacrifices and the shedding of blood so important to God for the atonement of sin?

I attempted to analyze these questions and put them into perspective, as I was accustomed to doing from my medical training. Unfortunately, my analysis simply brought up more questions. How do we cleanse ourselves today? Although the Temple was destroyed thousands of years ago, where in the Bible is it written that because of its destruction, God canceled his commandments for the atoning of sin? Where is it written that just by attending High Holiday services during Rosh Hashanah and Yom Kippur a person could expect God to forgive his sins of the previous year? I hoped that as I read through the Old Testament I would find answers to these mind-boggling questions.

Weeks passed and May arrived, bringing spring weather to Chicago. Little had changed with respect to my ailing body or my workload. I was relieved, however, that nothing adverse arose from the Michelle incident. For whatever reason, she didn't report her experience to my superiors, for which I was truly grateful. I continued to suffer from the pain of arthritis, ulcers, and esophageal irritation, yet my mental attitude and general outlook on life began to improve at home and at work. No longer did I view patients as the enemy. I became far less antagonistic.

I attributed the improvement to the fact that in two short months my residency would be completed and I would never again have to set foot in the Cave! Furthermore, I had just received notification from a large hospital in Milwaukee to which I had applied, offering me a position in their emergency department as a full-time staff physician. I was elated because this particular hospital had been my first choice of employment. Paula was overjoyed because we would be moving back to her hometown. She longed for the companionship of her friends and family. She was all of twenty-one years of age, and this was the first time that she had ever been away from them for any length of time.

Paula and I had met four years earlier in a small, community hospital in a western suburb of Milwaukee. I was a fourth-year medical student, and I commuted there once a week from Chicago to take medical histories and perform physical exams on hospitalized patients. Paula worked as a dietary aide in order to pay her tuition for cosmetology school. I was recently divorced and dating several women. I was very attracted to Paula. During breaks we managed to talk over coffee and, during one of our conversations, I learned that she had just turned eighteen. I proceeded to inform her that I was nearly ten years her senior. I inquired as to how she would feel about going out with an older, divorced, Jewish man. Paula told me that none of those things posed a problem for her, so we began to see each other as often as our schedules would permit. Eventually, the other women faded from my life because of my love for Paula. After two years of commuter dating and after I completed medical school and internship, Paula and I were married.

Paula made a number of new friends during the two years spent in Chicago, but she was homesick. As a result of our constant bickering, my horrendous call schedule, and my self-pity, I had been ignoring Paula and was oblivious to her needs. I hoped the upcoming changes would improve our situation. I would soon be gone from the Cave, and Paula would be reunited with her friends and family. Would our marriage survive? Would I end up going through a second divorce? *Only time will tell,* I thought to myself.

I read the entire Hebrew Scriptures from cover to cover in a period of four months. I never felt more Jewish or more proud of my Jewish heritage. However, I also discovered that our ancestors were a proud, stubborn and rebellious people. Although God had chosen the Jews through his covenant with Abraham, and charged the Jewish people to teach all nations about him and his laws, obstinacy, pride, and hardened hearts often precluded obedience. Much of the time, the prevailing attitude was "I'll do it my way." This, of course, got our people in trouble with God on many occasions.

As I continued reading the Scriptures, two central themes seemed to predominate, especially in the books of the Prophets. The first was that of pride and stubbornness demonstrated by the Jewish people in their persistent obedience-disobedience relationship with God. The second was that of Israel's need for a Messiah who would save my people from God's wrath and the coming Day of Judgment.

Prophet after prophet, prophecy upon prophecy, God kept warning the people of Israel through his messengers to forsake other gods. Time after time, God cautioned them against disobedience. Instance after instance, God implored the people of Israel to return to him.

And just as God warned his people Israel to repent before the coming day of wrath, he also promised to send a Messiah who would save them from that awful day and bring peace and prosperity.

"For unto us a Child is born, unto us a Son is given: and the government will be upon His shoulder. And His name will be called Wonderful, Counselor, Mighty God, Everlasting Father, Prince of Peace. Of the increase of His government and peace there will be no end. Upon the throne of David and over His kingdom, to order it and establish it with judgment and justice from that time forward, even forever. The zeal of the Lord of hosts will perform this" (Isaiah 9:6–7).

And, again, God states through his prophet, Jeremiah: "Behold *the* days are coming," says the LORD, "that I will raise to David a Branch of righteousness; a King shall reign and prosper, and execute judgment and righteousness in earth.

"In His days Judah will be saved, and Israel will dwell safely; now this *is* His name by which He will be called: THE LORD OUR RIGHTEOUSNESS" (Jeremiah 23:5–6).

It seemed like God was telling his people that although terrible, bone-chilling times were ahead, he planned to send a Messiah, a King who would save Israel from sin and govern the people justly and with righteousness. But I did not recall anywhere that the Messiah actually arrived.

Does God still intend to send our Messiah? I wondered. *And if so, when?*

The Turning Point

Fast forward to mid-autumn. The clean, crisp Wisconsin air blew gently across my face as I walked down the country road, enjoying a day off from work. While crossing the old creek bridge, I glanced at a small school of fish swimming in the slowly moving brook, creating tiny ripples in the crystal clear water.

I had eagerly accepted the offer to work at the Milwaukee hospital. Being a staff physician in the busy emergency department of a large, urban hospital was a demanding job that still carried a certain amount of stress. Yet it did not even come close to the pressures I'd experienced as a senior resident in Chicago. It was as though a 500-pound boulder had been lifted from my shoulders. I enjoyed my new job and established good rapport with both colleagues and patients.

It seemed likely that all my physical maladies had been catalyzed by multiple stressors that had converged on me. I knew that chronic anxiety could lead to depression and that depression could, in turn, manifest itself as any number of physical disabilities. Heartburn, ulcers, and arthritic symptoms are all common among those suffering from depression. With the reduction of stress in my life, I expected my afflictions to dissipate. Likewise, reducing the stress would help to improve our strained marriage. I noticed that Paula seemed to feel the strain beginning to ease.

I was still concerned, though, as to what God's involvement might be in this scenario. Was it God, or was it simply the turmoil in my life that had caused all of this physical and emotional suffering? Or could it have been a combination of both? From time to time I recalled God's words to the people of Israel from the Book of Deuteronomy and wondered.

As the months passed, I became comfortable in my new environment. I regained my "sick" sense of humor, performing practical jokes on various members of the emergency staff. They grew accustomed to my antics and sometimes attempted to get even with me. These shenanigans served as stress reducers for all of us. One nurse who had worked in the emergency department for years told me that the atmosphere in the department was much less tense since I began working there and that I was "a breath of fresh air." How things had changed since I left Chicago!

I was the first physician hired by the hospital with formal training in the specialty of emergency medicine. In addition to the mischief I brought to Milwaukee, I brought organizational skills and my fondness for teaching.

Almost anything can happen at any time in an emergency department (abbreviated "E.D."). It is often likened to a powder keg waiting to explode. Thus, E.D. docs do not have the luxury of time, as do physicians in other specialties. We cannot schedule patient visits because appointments are not required in the E.D. Nor do E.D. docs have control over how many or what types of patients are seen in a specified period of time. We must be quick, efficient, thorough and aggressive in diagnosing and treating patients. These are skills I learned in emergency medicine residency training, and the staff noticed those skills.

My nickname of "Maddog" lived on in Milwaukee! It was a name bestowed upon me by a resident while I was in my third year of medical school because of my aggressive approach in treating patients. As the months passed, my reputation grew, and I gained the trust of the doctors and nurses in the department. I felt at home and very much at ease with life in Milwaukee.

Therefore, it came as a surprise that I was no better physically. Arthritis continued to plague me, and profuse sinus drainage caused my throat to swell. The heartburn was unrelenting and tormented me day and night. At least the physical afflictions were more bearable with the easing of the emotional stress.

There was one notable exception to the decrease of stress in my life, and that was the strife between Paula and me. Rather than lessening, the discord crescendoed. We consulted various marriage counselors in an attempt to understand and, hopefully, solve our problems. Such efforts, however, seemed futile. The first counselor stated in no uncertain terms that, in his professional opinion, our relationship was on the edge of the abyss. He recommended that we divorce.

Paula and I were taken aback, having both been under the illusion that marital counselors are supposed to prevent divorce. We were shaken by his advice but reluctant to follow it. We still cared for each other but had difficulty expressing ourselves or openly communicating our needs except for the all too frequent disparaging remarks we flung at each other. Yet we became frightened enough of divorce to attempt to converse nightly, utilizing techniques we learned during our counseling sessions. After a few nights of "communicating," we discovered the best solution to our bickering was to avoid each other as much as possible.

Neither Paula nor I resorted to romantic interludes outside of the marriage. For reasons neither of us could understand, we knew in our hearts that adultery and divorce were not the answer to our problems. So we continued living together despite the attendant misery.

Although we bickered, Paula did offer words of encouragement with respect to my Bible study. We began to read Scripture together daily. She continually suggested that I read the New Testament, but each time I declined. The New Testament was for Christians and, as a Jew, I had no desire to read about "their god."

I had been brought up to believe that Jesus was a learned rabbi and great prophet, such as Buddha or Mohammed. I knew, however, that he could not possibly be God or the "Son of God" as Christians claimed. I also knew from reading my Bible that *my* God, the God of Abraham, Isaac, and Jacob, the God of Israel, was a jealous God who warned our people not to worship any other gods! I had resolved not to waste my time reading the "New Testament," which I knew was about Jesus, the god of the *goyim.*

However, my resolve began to weaken as I continued to feel that God had abandoned me to my physical and marital problems. What did I have to lose by reading the New Testament? What would God do to me that he hadn't already done? After ruminating for weeks I decided to explore the Christian version of the Bible. My caveat was that if I felt too uncomfortable, I would immediately stop. Paula was delighted that I had decided to forge ahead. For the first time in months, we spoke civilly to one another and actually smiled when we conversed.

At that moment, a couple of questions flashed through my mind. *How could Paula, a Bible-reading Christian, treat me so badly? Aren't Christians supposed to love others, especially their spouses?* Judaism certainly teaches us to respect people and their views, though we may disagree. I just did not understand how Christians thought. Then I thought somewhat sarcastically,

Perhaps reading the New Testament will enlighten me!

I opened my Bible to the first book of the New Testament, the Gospel according to Matthew. The first chapter described the genealogy of Jesus, beginning with Abraham, Isaac, and Jacob through Jesse, the father of King David, then through David and Solomon all the way to Joseph, "the husband of Mary, of whom was born Jesus, who is called Christ" (Matthew 1:16).

So far, so good, I thought. This confirms what I already know: Jesus was Jewish.

The following chapter described how Mary, after she was betrothed to Joseph (but they had not consummated their relationship) "was found with child of the Holy Spirit" (Matthew 1:18). This was disturbing to me because I was well aware of how a woman becomes pregnant. I wasn't quite sure what was meant by the "Holy Spirit," but if it was not human, how could Mary be impregnated? I knew Christians believed and accepted this as truth.

I continued to read of how upset Joseph became when he discovered Mary was pregnant, though he never had slept with her.

> But while he thought about these things, behold, an angel of the Lord appeared to him in a dream saying, "Joseph, son of David, do not be afraid to take to you Mary for your wife, for that which is conceived in her is of the Holy Spirit. And she will bring forth a Son, and you shall call His name JESUS, for He will save His people from their sins." Now all this was done that it might be fulfilled which was spoken by the Lord through the prophet, saying: *"Behold, a virgin shall be with child, and bear a Son, and they shall call His name Immanuel,"* which is translated "God with us" (Matthew 1:20–24).

I was intrigued by this because I remembered coming across something very similar in the Book of Isaiah. I turned to Isaiah and in the seventh chapter I found the following: "Therefore the Lord Himself will give you a sign: Behold, the virgin shall conceive and bear a Son, and shall call His name Immanuel" (Isaiah 7:14).

I noted with interest the Old Testament Immanuel prophecy

might have been fulfilled by the birth of Jesus. But one fulfilled prophecy doesn't necessarily confirm Jesus as the Messiah! "Immanuel" must refer to the coming, future Messiah of Israel, I concluded. However, my curiosity was aroused. I continued reading. When Herod the king heard that wise men were seeking this baby as "the King of the Jews" he called all the chief priests and scribes of the people together and inquired of them where the Christ (Messiah) was to be born. They answered, "In Bethlehem of Judea, for thus it is written by the prophet:

> *'But you, Bethlehem, in the land of Judah, are not the least among the rulers of Judah; for out of you shall come a Ruler who will shepherd My people Israel'"* (Matthew 2:5–6).

Again, I recalled a similar passage in one of the books of the prophets. I turned back to the Jewish portion of my Bible, and in the Book of Micah I found the following passage:

> But you, Bethlehem Ephrathah, *though* you are little among the thousands of Judah, *yet* out of you shall come forth to Me the One to be ruler in Israel . . . . And He shall stand and feed *His flock* in the strength of the LORD, in the majesty of the name of the LORD His God; and they shall abide, for now He shall be great to the ends of the earth; and this One shall be peace. (Micah 5:2,4-5)

So the Messiah of Israel was to come from Bethlehem and reign as ruler of Israel. *It's merely coincidence that Jesus was born in Bethlehem,* I thought. *How many thousands of other people were born there?* Still, I pondered over Isaiah 7:14.

As I continued reading, I learned how Herod felt threatened and extremely angry because of the rumors of the Messiah's birth. He ordered his soldiers to slay all male babies two years of age and under living in Bethlehem and its districts.

I continued to find references to the Hebrew prophets as I read through the gospel. *I was never taught any of this in Hebrew school!* I thought to myself. *Could it be possible that Jesus is the Messiah after all?* I was determined to read the New Testament in its entirety to find the answer.

I found it uncanny how the Hebrew prophecies so closely paralleled the events described in the Gospel of Matthew relating to Jesus and John the Baptist. I remained unconvinced that Jesus was the Messiah of Israel, but I found myself flipping back and forth to read the messianic prophecies.

Again, out of curiosity, I turned to the Book of Isaiah. "The people who walked in darkness have seen a great light; Those who dwelt in the land of the shadow of death, upon them a light has shined" (Isaiah 9:2).

Were these words literal or figurative? Was this "land" where Jesus preached literally darkened by constant fighting and its resultant shadow of death? Or, was Jesus, figuratively speaking, a "light" to the people who sat in darkness under the shadow of spiritual death because they lacked knowledge of God and his ways?

All my life I'd been taught that the Messiah of Israel had not yet come. *If my Jewish friends, relatives and religious leaders don't believe he is the Messiah, why should I?* I asked myself. Then a thought crossed my mind: how many of my Jewish friends and relatives have ever read their own Bibles for themselves, let alone the New Testament? How many know anything about the Bible, other than what they've been told by others? For the first time in my life, I understood the importance of reading the Bible for myself.

I completed reading Matthew and then tackled the Gospels of Mark, Luke and John. These first four books are based on the life and teachings of Jesus, each from a different perspective.

I was impressed by the words of Jesus and his love for people. I also noticed that Jesus taught with wisdom and authority. Some of the things he said pierced my heart like an arrow. I discovered that I had sinned against God by doing and saying things I had never before considered sinful.

Jesus said, "You have heard that it was said to those of old, *'You shall not commit adultery.'* But I say to you that whoever looks at a woman to lust for her has already committed adultery with her in her heart" (Matthew 5:27–28).

How many times had I committed that sin?

Jesus also taught that swearing by an oath is a sinful act.

But I say to you, do not swear at all: neither by heaven, for it is God's throne; nor by the earth, for it is His footstool; nor by Jerusalem, for it is the city of the great King. Nor shall you swear by your head, because you cannot make one hair white or black. But let your "Yes" be "Yes," and your "No," "No." For whatever is more than these is from the evil one [Satan]. (Matthew 5:34–37)

How many times had I sinned without knowing by saying, "I swear to God," or "I swear on my mother's grave"?

Jesus also spoke against seeking revenge: "Love your enemies, bless those who curse you, do good to those who hate you, and pray for those who spitefully use you and persecute you" (Matthew 5:44).

How many times had I told people that my middle initial "R" stood for "Revenge"? How many times had I commented that "revenge is sweet," and that "I don't get mad, I get even"? The sad part was that these were not merely clichés to me—I meant every word! I rarely acted on my desire for revenge in a socially unacceptable fashion, but I felt the desire so strongly at times that I worked myself up to a near frenzy.

Jesus taught that we should forgive those who commit injustices against us, and he spoke of the consequences of unforgiveness: "For if you forgive men their trespasses, your heavenly Father will also forgive you. But if you do not forgive men their trespasses, neither will your Father forgive your trespasses" (Matthew 6:14–15).

How often had I refused to forgive people for perceived injustices perpetrated against me? How many years had I held grudges against people for minor offenses? *Could my physical infirmities be due to the fact that I had not forgiven people?* I wondered, *Is it God punishing me, or am I bringing this suffering on myself because of an unforgiving heart?*

Jesus taught that we should not judge others because only God had the right.

Judge not, that you not be judged. For with what judgment you judge, you will be judged; and with the same measure you use, it will be measured back to you. And why do you look at the speck in your brother's eye, but do not consider the plank in your own eye? . . . Hypocrite! First remove the plank from your own eye, and then you will see clearly to remove the speck out of your brother's eye. (Matthew 7:1–3, 5)

I committed this offense perhaps twenty times a day. Criticizing and demeaning medical students while they were on my service was an art I had mastered by the end of my residency!

Jesus also spoke of giving to those who ask without making it public knowledge when performing acts of charity.

Therefore, when you do a charitable deed, do not sound a trumpet before you as the hypocrites do in the synagogues and in the streets, that they may have glory from men. Assuredly, I say to you, they have their reward. But when you do a charitable deed, do not let your left hand know what your right hand is doing, that your charitable deed may be in secret; and your Father who sees in secret will Himself reward you openly. (Matthew 6:2–4)

How frequently had I performed charitable deeds without expecting something in return? When I did manage to do something charitable, how often did I brag about my selflessness?

The teachings of Jesus made me very uncomfortable. Nevertheless, I had no desire to stop reading. In fact, I felt compelled to press on.

Jesus often framed his teachings in parables. In Matthew 13, he offered his disciples an explanation:

Therefore I speak to them in parables, because seeing they do not see, and hearing they do not hear, nor do they understand. And in them the prophecy of Isaiah is fulfilled, which says: *"Hearing you will hear and not understand, and seeing you will see and not perceive; for the heart of this people has grown dull. Their ears are hard of hearing, and their eyes they have closed, lest they should see with their eyes and hear with their ears, lest they should understand with their hearts and turn, so that I should heal them."* (Matthew 13:13–15)

I turned to Isaiah for confirmation and found a passage in Chapter 6 where God was instructing his prophet Isaiah to tell the people of Israel:

Keep on hearing, but do not understand; keep on seeing, but do not perceive. Make the heart of this people dull, and their ears heavy, and shut their eyes; lest they see with their eyes, and hear with their ears, and understand with their heart, and return and be healed." (Isaiah 6:9–10)

What was Jesus trying to tell his disciples? Was he saying that the Jewish people to whom he brought the message of God had closed their eyes, ears, minds and hearts to God and his message? Was Jesus telling them that Isaiah had prophesied that rejection? Dozens of questions began to flood my mind: *Do we Jews reject Jesus and His message without even comprehending it?* I felt extremely uncomfortable after having reread that verse in Isaiah—because I had reached a turning point.

I had questioned whether my people's rejection of Jesus as Messiah was justified.

I began asking myself if what others had taught me about the coming Messiah was convincing enough for me to state unequivocally that Jesus is not the Messiah. Did I have evidence other than word of mouth from one generation to the next that Jesus was not the Messiah of Israel? As a physician, would I accept as dogma the treatment of a life-threatening medical condition—on the sole basis that it was passed down from resident to resident? Would I act on that without first consulting my medical textbooks?!

Had I never been misinformed by others (albeit unintentionally) about important issues?

I remembered what I'd been taught: the Messiah hasn't yet come. If he had, the world would be filled with peace and harmony. Somehow, I didn't find that argument entirely satisfactory any more. I decided that I would keep an open mind regarding the Messiahship of Jesus as I continued to read through the New Testament.

Not only did Jesus teach with great wisdom; he performed miracles, many of which were healings.

The books of the Gospel described how Jesus' acts of mercy

angered some of the religious leaders. I was amazed and even angered by those who objected to his acts of mercy because he performed some of them on the Sabbath. I surmised they were either totally devoid of compassion or tremendously jealous of Jesus. Why else would they feel such animosity toward Jesus, when he preached about love and holiness while healing the sick?

As I continued reading through the Gospel chapters, I realized for the first time that Jesus openly claimed to be the Son of God. On one occasion, Jesus healed a paralytic by telling him, "Son, be of good cheer; your sins are forgiven you" (Matthew 9:2). In essence, Jesus himself was forgiving the man of his sins, something only God could do! Either Jesus was much more than I'd been taught he was, or else he was a blasphemer, as some of the Pharisees claimed. In neither case could I continue to think he was just a good man or a very special prophet.

Which other Jewish prophet ever referred to God as "Father?" Which one taught with such power and authority?

Despite the many miracles Jesus performed, he was despised by the Jewish religious establishment. Jesus was not easy on them, either. He used strong language as he accused them of hypocrisy, as written in the Book of Matthew, Chapter 23. "Serpents, brood of vipers! How can you escape the condemnation of hell?" (Matthew 23:33).

Jesus was telling the Jewish people that their religious leaders had failed them. They preached one thing yet did another. They performed charitable deeds in order to be recognized and revered by people. They were careful to give ten percent of their income for religion yet they lacked compassion and mercy.

As I read these words of accusation, I felt as though Jesus had directed them at me. I felt naked, my secret sins exposed, and I had nowhere to hide. I stood accused and convicted. I thought about all the things I'd said to God that morning as I drove home from the Cave in Chicago—how I'd ranted and raved about my innocence and God's unfairness—that he should go punish the sinners, not me—not righteous, innocent me. As I read Jesus' accusations to the Pharisees, all I could think was how wrong I was! How could I have said such things to God, the Creator of the Universe? How could I have believed that I was innocent, and

God the guilty one?

I wondered how those leaders must have felt when they heard the accusations I had just read—directly from Jesus!

I continued reading about Jesus' life, death and resurrection. I continued referring back to the Jewish prophets, who were quoted so often in the New Testament.

I was trained to make decisions based on evidence. As far as I was concerned, the evidence was overwhelming that Jesus was the Messiah. I felt I could no longer deny what so many Christians knew all their lives as truth. Yet I still struggled with the question of how all my family members, Jewish friends and religious teachers could be wrong. Would it not be logical to assume the majority was correct and I was wrong?

I had reached the point where I had to make two decisions. The first was whether or not to believe what was written in the New Testament. The second pretty much depended on the first: whether or not to believe Jesus is the Messiah.

The Decision

Could the New Testament authors have erred regarding their accounts of Jesus? I mused. Then I thought, *if we Jews believe what is written in the Bible by such patriarchs as Moses, why are we reluctant to believe what is in the New Testament, when it was written by such Jewish men as Matthew, Peter and Paul—especially when so much of it is quoting from the Hebrew Scriptures?*

I found that in my mind there was not a distinction between the "Old" and "New" Testaments. I did not feel I could believe what is written in the Old Testament portion of the Bible and reject that which is written in the New Testament. How could I ignore the many Old Testament prophecies fulfilled by Jesus?

In my mind, either the Old and New Testaments were both accurate accounts or they were both fables. I could no longer accept the dogma that Jews are to believe the "Old Testament" and ignore or reject the "Christian section," which was also written by Jews about largely Jewish concerns.

During this time of decision, Paula and I began attending church regularly in addition to our daily reading of Scripture. In the following two months, I completed reading the New

Testament. Somehow, there didn't seem to be much of a decision left. I believed that what I'd read was true.

My second decision was reached in March 1983 when I accepted that Jesus is indeed the Messiah. I publicly proclaimed my faith in him as Messiah and Lord in front of the church congregation and was baptized. This was not the end of my search, but rather the beginning of a wonderful, personal relationship with my Messiah.

A Lamp unto My Feet

Since 1983, there have been many positive changes in my life for which I am truly grateful. God promises to send his Spirit to every person who trusts in the atoning power of Jesus and accepts his free gift of salvation. It is through the power of his Spirit that God makes changes in a believer's life. This is how God has always worked: "'Not by might, nor by power, but by My Spirit,' says the LORD of Hosts" (Zechariah 4:6).

Through his Holy Spirit, God has been teaching me to look at life from an entirely different perspective. I have gone through an awakening, a spiritual rebirth, which some people refer to as the born-again experience. For me, this spiritual awakening was not some explosive event but rather a gradual process that began with recognizing Jesus as Savior and has continued to this day.

I look at things differently now, no longer guided through life by worldly wisdom and the so-called enlightenment I once craved. Nor do I follow the dazzling light of materialism or the popular glow of political correctness that the world reveres. The light that illuminates my path shines forth from Jesus, the Messiah.

Does that mean I gave up all that I enjoy? Absolutely not!

I still tease and laugh. I still attend social gatherings. I purchase nice clothing and drive a sports car. What has changed, however, is that these things do not signify meaning or purpose in my life. What has changed is that I have a standard on which to base my actions. If Jesus would not have said or done something, I do my best to avoid saying or doing it. If the word of God tells me that something is bad or to be avoided, I do my best to obey. I'm not influenced by popular opinion, especially if it conflicts with what God has revealed in the Bible.

God has gradually reshaped me and continues to do so day by day. I am slowly but surely learning the ways of God through reading of Scripture and daily prayer. Becoming the person God wants me to be is a process, and I don't claim to be "there" yet. However, God has changed me from a proud, self-centered, all-knowing physician who cared little for his patients into a spiritually thirsty, more compassionate servant who seeks to do God's will rather than his own.

We are not commanded by God to act as robots, to be unthinking or unfeeling, but we are exhorted to abstain from such things as he does not approve.

Indeed, my life has been transformed during these twelve years that I have been walking with Jesus. My relationship with Paula was irreparable in the eyes of several marital counselors. Yet nothing is impossible for God. He took our broken marriage, softened our hardened hearts and restored our relationship to health. He blessed Paula and me with three beautiful children who have brought us great joy.

I have been healed of my physical infirmities to the point where I exercise vigorously four to five times per week. For the most part, I eat anything I desire with little or no problem. I no longer require antibiotics for postnasal drainage because it has been completely healed. The deep depression has disappeared, and my outlook on life is largely positive.

Many people who witnessed the change in my behavior and attitude are bewildered. Some find it hard to believe I am the same person. How is it possible that an invisible God has so visibly altered my thoughts, attitudes and feelings? How can God change the heart of a Jewish man not only to accept Jesus, but to love him so much? My answer to them is that God is able to do all things, and that if he did it for me, he will do it for anyone. "Behold I am the LORD, the God of all flesh. Is there anything too hard for Me?" (Jeremiah 32:27).

The only explanation as to why I have been transformed so dramatically is that God has changed me. Out of his infinite love and mercy, God has changed me, and I am confident that he will continue to do so until the day he takes me to heaven.

I've seen God work in ways that I never would have believed.

My mother had breast cancer in 1977 and underwent a mastectomy. In 1993, she had a mass in the other breast, and the doctor ordered a needle biopsy. Many people were praying for her. When she went for the biopsy, the mass was gone. Following that experience, my mother came to faith in Jesus at the age of 65.

I grew up believing that God helps those who help themselves. However, having actually read the Bible for myself, I learned that God delights in helping those who not only love and fear him, but who desire to obey him and trust him to provide for their needs. God is truly loving and gracious. He takes a great interest in us and longs to have a personal relationship with each of us.

Another mistaken notion I had regarding God was that if a person lived a relatively moral life and performed good deeds, God would allow that person into heaven. Of all my erroneous conceptions, this was the most flawed and eternally dangerous.

Neither the Old nor the New Testament provides a basis for that notion. Both Testaments make it clear that no human being is righteous enough to come before God based on his or her merit.

It is human to want to control one's own destiny. We feel more in control of our eternal destiny when we believe we can earn a place in heaven with our own good deeds. Yet whether we like it or not, there is a "Higher Authority" to whom we must answer and whose laws we must obey. The only things that we can control are temporary and fast fleeting. God alone controls eternal things.

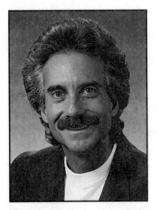

The preceding account was adapted from a book titled Jesus, Israel's Messiah, *by Dr. David R. Madenberg, with William J. Nelson. For information on ordering the book, write to:*

Vantage Press, Inc.
516 West 34th
New York, NY 10001

David Madenberg, MD, is a board certified Emergency Medicine physician, currently practicing in Southeast Wisconsin.

Part Four
Continuations of the Case

"IF YOU WANT LIFE, EXPECT PAIN."
(THE MIDRASH TEHILLIM)

by Susan Perlman

Doctors witness more suffering than most people. True, they don't all see the same amount; an oncologist will witness far more suffering than an ophthalmologist, and the doctor who works in the inner-city emergency room will face more crises per week than the one who has a rural family practice. Nevertheless, it is impossible to complete one's medical education without seeing a great deal of pain and suffering, and chances are, a doctor in nearly any field will deal with more suffering than the average professional. After all, people don't usually come to a physician because they are feeling good.

How many doctors have been called on to answer the age-old question "Why? Why do I have to suffer like this?" What text book, what medical journal, what case history can provide the answer to pain? In all probability, the question causes as much frustration and turmoil for the doctor as it does for the patient, because the physician hears the question raised time and time again, in one scenario after another. Oh, the doctor can explain about nerve endings and impulses to the brain and what causes sensations that hurt. But that's not what most people want to know, is it?

People usually become interested in the power of God when no other power is sufficient to help them. A person caught in a vortex of suffering might well ask, "If God exists and he is loving, why does everything hurt so much?" The physician has no easy answers because the "so much" is something known only by the patient. Nobody can sense the meaning or degree of another person's anguish. The pleadings of those in agony are not merely for answers or understanding; people want relief from their anguish.

If there is anything real in life, it is pain. If there is any feeling that all people seem to experience at some time, it is pain. If there is anything that begs we explain it, it is pain. Yet attempts to explain pain without bringing relief inevitably fail. Answers that cannot ease the distress merely exacerbate pain. One of the great benefits of being a physician is the ability to ease pain under certain circumstances—but doctors realize that life holds far more pain than even they can address.

The Problems, Pressures and Pains of Life

The pains of life press in around us. The desire to escape the pain, the pressures and the problems is only human. It is also impossible! Some dream of escaping life's problems and pains, but few want the escape of an untimely death.

Instead, we express our consternation with statements like "An all-powerful God should free us from pain. If he can and won't, then he is not a God of love; if he would remove pain but can't, then he is weak and ineffectual—just like us."

The Bible also outlines the problem of pain, which after all is as old as Adam and Eve. In fact, the above statement is rather like their son Cain's outcry to the Almighty:

> My punishment is greater than I can bear! [Which is better translated from the original Hebrew, "Is my iniquity too much for Thee to bear?"] Surely You have driven me out this day from the face of the ground; I shall be hidden from Your face; I shall be a fugitive and a vagabond on the earth, and it will happen *that* anyone who finds me will kill me. (Genesis 4:13–14)

It was, however, Isaiah the prophet who pleaded most eloquently when he turned to God and said,

> Oh, that You would rend the heavens! That You would come down! That the mountains might shake at Your presence . . . When You did awesome things *for which* we did not look, You came down, the mountains shook at Your presence. (Isaiah 64:1, 3; in Hebrews 63:19, 64:1)

Isaiah's plea seems to express the pain of the ages, from Cain to Job, from the Holocaust to the dying child with AIDS whose mother cries out to God, "If You would but tear open the heavens and come down" and stop it.

Then there are those who feel the Almighty is unable to answer the question of pain, so they have ceased asking. Rabbi Harold Kushner says,

> I believe in God . . . [but] I recognize His limitations. He is limited in what He can do by laws of nature and by the evolution of human nature and human moral freedom. I no longer hold God responsible for illnesses, accidents and natural disasters, because I realize that I gain little and lose so much when I blame God for those things. I can worship a God who hates suffering but cannot eliminate it, more easily than I can worship a God who chooses to make children suffer and die, for whatever exalted reason.[1]

Are Kushner's two options—that God is either powerless or loveless—the only possible answers to the problem of pain? No, indeed they are not.

Sometimes, God actually does tear the heavens open and come down. The prophet Isaiah saw God's power to tear the heavens and descend to rescue his people when Sennacherib brought siege against Jerusalem. At that time, Rabshakeh, the Assyrian commander, taunted Hezekiah, king of Judah, with these words:

> . . . Do not let your God in whom you trust deceive you, saying, "Jerusalem shall not be given into the hand of the king of Assyria." (Isaiah 37:10)

Rabshakeh was mistaken! God did act by the instrumentality of the "angel of the LORD" who "went out, and killed in the camp of the Assyrians one hundred and eighty-five thousand. . . . So Sennacherib king of Assyria departed and went away, returned home, and remained at Nineveh" (Isaiah 37:36,37).

For another 120 years Judah dwelt safely in its land. Judah and her king saw the might of Assyria defeated and destroyed while she enjoyed security under the protection of her Lord.

---

[1] *When Bad Things Happen to Good People* (New York: Avon Books, 1981), p. 134.

A different, but equally dramatic, example of God "tearing the heavens to come down" predates Isaiah. Job, in pain and convulsions, cried out,

> *Is* my strength the strength of stones? Or is my flesh bronze?. . . Oh, that I knew where I might find Him, *that* I might come to His seat . . . . I cry out to You, but You do not answer me; I stand up, and You regard me. *But* You have become cruel to me; with the strength of Your hand You oppose me. (Job 6:12; 23:3; 30:20–21)

God does answer Job, and out of the whirlwind he speaks personally to the angry, embittered man:

> Now prepare yourself like a man;
> I will question you, and you shall answer Me.
> Where were you when I laid the foundations of the earth?
> Tell *Me,* if you have understanding.
> Who determined its measurements?
> Surely you know!
> Or who stretched the line upon it?
> To what were its foundations fastened?
> Or who laid its cornerstone . . . ? (Job 38:3–6)

God was not giving Job a nature lesson. Job didn't only have a pain problem; he also had an identity problem. That was knowing who God was and where God was at this time of great distress.

Yet in the face of this challenge and in the midst of Job's despair, God spoke to remind Job whom he was addressing. Once he realigned his thinking to see the identity of the Almighty, Job's response was repentance, trust and belief in God, who is without limitations:

> "I know that You can do **everything,** [bold supplied] and that no purpose of *Yours* can be withheld from You. You asked, 'Who is this who hides counsel without knowledge?' Therefore I have uttered what I did not understand." (Job 42:2, 3)

One of the Hebrew verbs for pain, *parpar,* expresses the idea of "moving convulsively, struggling, twitching, jerking," such as is found in Job's description of his pain: "I was at ease, but He has *shattered* me" [*vai-pharpereni*]. (Job 16:12)

In modern Hebrew, however, the same word is transformed into a noun to denote a "butterfly." The reason is as follows: The beautiful, soaring butterfly was first an ugly, earth-bound grub. Then came the time for its transformation, and by extreme convulsions, pain and struggle, the ugly grub became a wondrous winged creature. Hence the words *convulsions* and *butterfly* are the same in Hebrew. And yet there are pains and convulsions that we cannot imagine could possibly be used in any kind of positive transformation.

What About the Holocaust?

A whole generation has passed, yet we are still standing dazed and amazed at this greatest tragedy in Jewish history. Despite thousands of books, many historic court transcripts, TV specials, and films and video testimonies of thousands of surviving eye witnesses—anyone who did not suffer through it first hand is absolutely unable to grasp the horror and pain.

No one has tried so hard to give us a glimpse into the pain and utter despair of the victims of the Holocaust as Elie Wiesel. He writes in *Night* of his first night at Birkenau:

> Never shall I forget that night, seven times cursed and seven times sealed. Never shall I forget that smoke. Never shall I forget the little faces of the children whose bodies I saw turned into wreaths of smoke beneath a silent blue sky. Never shall I forget that nocturnal silence which deprived me, for all eternity, of the desire to live. Never shall I forget those moments which murdered my God and my soul and turned my dreams to dust.[2]

As a result of the Holocaust, Wiesel abandoned all hope in a loving God. Belief in God no longer had significance for this sensitive, serious humanitarian. Yet some survivors responded differently to the horror of the Holocaust. After Auschwitz, one wrote,

> It never occurred to me to associate the calamity we were experiencing with God, to blame Him, or to believe in Him

---

[2]Elie Wiesel, *Night* (New York: Avon Books, 1969), p. 9.

less or cease believing in Him at all because He didn't
come to our aid. God doesn't owe us that, or anything. We
owe our lives to Him. If someone believes God is responsible for the death of six million because He didn't somehow do something to save them, he's got his thinking
reversed. We owe God our lives for the few or many years
we live.[3]

Ultimately, in this person's view, God tore the heavens open
and came down to the rescue of his people Israel. Deafening
defeat and discomfiture came to the Nazi powers.

Some have even seen good rise from the ashes of the evil con-
flagration. Survivors were welcomed into many countries. And
it is said that the nations were conditioned to realize that the
Jewish people could no longer be secure in Europe. The horror
of the Holocaust provided the emotional impetus, and the modern state of Israel was born—a Jewish homeland with doors
opened wide for those who had been stripped and laid bare, the
scattered exiles of her people. God is not absent in the presence
of suffering.

Messiah, Pain and Relief

For seekers who believe the word of God, an even greater
historical event confirms God's presence with his people. At the
juncture of history—when B.C.E. ended and C.E. began—a new
era was announced, heralded with an angelic song. It was
chanted by a special choir for the benefit of a few Jewish
shepherds who had to stay with their flock by night.

The reason for the song was the birth of the promised Messiah
of Israel in Bethlehem, the city of David. Most people were too
busy to notice it; they were wrapped up in their own concerns.
Others, crushed under the burden of pain, persecution and suffering, did not expect relief to come from such a humble source.
They reasoned that should relief come, it would be in the shape
of a sword, sharpened by God to destroy Israel's oppressors.

But the heavenly angels knew another and better way, and

[3]Reeve Robert Brenner, *The Faith and Doubt of Holocaust Survivors* (New
York: Free Press, 1980).

simple shepherds saw and believed:

> And behold, an angel of the Lord stood before them, and the glory of the Lord shone around them. . . . Then the angel said to them [the shepherds in Bethlehem's fields], "Do not be afraid; for behold, I bring you tidings of great joy which will be to all people. For there is born to you this day in the city of David a Savior, who is Christ [Messiah] the Lord." (Luke 2:9–11)

So began a career of pain and suffering for our Messiah—a lifetime of jerking, twisting, convulsions. First there was the persecution and flight from the cruel Herods; later he would know homelessness and human hunger; and before long there would be beatings and lashes, the painful plucking out of his beard and a crown of thorns pressed into his head by cruel Roman soldiers. Finally, those soldiers nailed his hands and feet to a tree as our prophets foretold, "They pierced My hands and My feet" (Psalm 22:16) and "they will look on Me whom they have pierced" (Zechariah 12:10).

Rabbi Kushner says he doesn't know what it means for God to suffer because "I don't believe that God is a person like me, with real eyes and real tear ducts to cry, and real nerve endings to feel pain."[4]

Yet the life and death of Y'shua is a gripping drama that declares God did identify with us, did in fact suffer with us, his creation. God became a man and lived and died as a human, enduring the cruelty and pain of the cross, so that the way of salvation could be achieved.

The prophet Isaiah spoke of how "by his [the Messiah's] stripes we are healed" and how he took upon himself "the iniquity of all of us." (Isaiah 53:5, 6)

The fulfillment of that prophecy revealed more of God's love and his power to transform pain to glory than the human race had ever known. The convulsions of the cross created a crown of conquest for the Messiah when he rose from the dead. His victory was accomplished by the spirit, not by the sword, and his

---

[4]Kushner, p. 85.

power over death has empowered countless others.

From time to time we hear of martyrs, people who are murdered because of their convictions. The widow of one such martyr, a missionary slain in Quito, Ecuador, wrote a poem to be read at her husband's memorial service. It offers a glimpse of what that transformation from pain to glory means—a look at pain from the other side of the grave:

The Other Side

This is not death—it's glory;
It isn't dark—it's light;
It isn't stumbling, groping, or even faith—it's sight;
This isn't grief—it's having my last tear wiped away;
It is sunrise—the morning of my eternal day;
This isn't praying—it's speaking face to face, and it's
    glimpsing at all the wonders of his grace;
This is the end of all pleading for strength to bear my pain;
    not even pain's dark memory will ever live again;
How did I bear the earth life before I came up higher?
    before my soul was granted its every deep desire? before
    I knew this rapture of meeting face to face with that one
    who sought me, saved me, and kept me by His grace?
This is not death—it's glory![5]

Coping with Pain Today

A tragedy is a lapse, a hole in the way things ought to be. Sickness is the absence of health. Death is the absence of life. Chaos is the absence of order. Accidents are the absence of proper performance. Our world is riddled with intermittent lapses in the way that things ought to be. Sometimes God intervenes to avert a tragedy, but not always. Nor does he intervene because of our insistence. God gave us the moral capacity to choose between good and evil. We have the freedom to act on God's will or our own.

Our first ancestors chose to act on their will, and we live with the consequences of their choice, as well as our own choices

---

[5]Richard A. Fowler, *Winning by Losing* (Chicago: Moody Press, 1986), p. 148.

today. Evil, pain, cruelty, injustice, hatred, strife, and sickness as well as death exist because of people's choices to exclude God. Some will say, however, that a good and loving God would not allow the choices of evil people to cause pain to the innocent, as, for example, has been the case in the orphanages of Romania. God has allowed people the freedom to make what they will of the world, and we must not blame him when the innocent suffer for it. Why should God continually impose his powerful presence? Why shouldn't he absent himself in response to the human desire to do without him?

Few people are satisfied with such an answer. But willful dissatisfaction with God and his rightful place as the standard of all that is good and worthy is part of the problem of pain. We cannot behave as though God has no right to disturb us with his expectations while we justify our own expectations for God to intervene and repair the continuum of the universe so that we can avert the disruptions. Those disruptions are natural in a world that has basically rebelled against its creator. Yet sometimes it is those very disruptions that make us aware of our need for God.

One might ask, "Why do we need pain? Couldn't we accomplish the same things with pleasure?" The answer is no, because pleasure tends to focus us on ourselves, our feelings and our perceptions. Pleasure gratifies ourselves and our will to be pleased, whereas pain can help us to focus outside of ourselves, to reach beyond ourselves, to find out what's there. Pleasure tends to make one self-centered, whereas a constructive response to pain can make a person more noble, other-centered and, hopefully, God-centered.

A crisis becomes an occasion for decline or advance. A self-centered person in a crisis can become more self-centered and wallow in self-pity. God-centered or God-seeking persons can be tempted to become self-centered in a crisis, but if they resist the temptation, they can be propelled forward in their quest for meaning.

It is important to know that we are not helpless and we are not hopeless. We cannot choose whether or not we will have pain, but we can choose how we will deal with pain and how we will allow problems to affect us.

That we will feel pain is inevitable. The Midrash Tehillim, commenting on Psalm 16:11, says, "If you want life, expect pain." To live is to endure the pressures of life. This is not a comforting thought! Nor is it a motto one would expect to see cross-stitched and hanging in a doctor's office. Nevertheless, it is comforting to know that we can decide if we are going to let life's pains press us down or if we are going to let them lift us up.

What that pain will mean to us, what it will accomplish in our lives, and what, if any, use it has depends on what we believe about God and people and how the two interact. If there is no God, then pain is the occasional and accidental absurdity, a prelude to death so that we can drag our bodies and beings off the scene to make room for another who in due season will suffer and die like us.

But if there is a God who cares, as the doctors in this book have testified, then pain becomes the occasion for us to look up and see God beckoning to us from beyond, letting us know that he does care. And if, as these physicians also believe, God has willingly entered into our suffering through his son, the Messiah Jesus, then the suffering we endure can lead us past the experience of this life and into eternal joy.

JEWISHNESS AND THE TRIUNITY OF GOD?
A SECOND OPINION

by Richard Harvey

"Hear, O Israel, Adonai Eloheinu Adonai is one. These three are one. How can the three Names be one? Only through the perception of faith; in the vision of the Holy Spirit, in the beholding of the hidden eye alone. . . . So it is with the mystery of the three-fold Divine manifestations designated by Adonai Eloheinu Adonai—three modes which yet form one unity."[1]

A Christian quote? Hardly. The above is taken from the *Zohar,* an ancient book of Jewish mysticism. The *Zohar* is somewhat esoteric and most contemporary Jews don't study it, but there are other Jewish books that refer to God's plurality as well.

Why then won't Jews discuss these things? Could it be that to do so might lead a person to consider Y'shua (Jesus)—to wonder if he might be who and what he claimed to be?[2] Rabbis denounce the idea that God would come to us in human flesh as utterly pagan and contrary to what "Judaism teaches." Whatever other points of theology on which they may disagree, on this issue they speak with one accord.

If it is the consensus of all the rabbis that belief in one God precludes the idea of a triune God, how is it possible that any self-respecting Jew could have written the opening quote? Wouldn't it fly in the face of all that Judaism teaches? To answer that question, we must ask another.

What Can We Actually Say that Judaism Teaches?

Some people see Judaism as a monolith of religion, with all its teachings resting on the narrow foundation of the *Sh'ma.* The Sh'ma certainly is a point of unity that all Jews must affirm. But

---

[1]Zohar II:43b (vol. 3, p. 134 in the Soncino Press edition).
[2]John 10:30.

it does not state, imply or even support many interpretations and opinions that are labeled "what Judaism teaches." Judaism is neither static nor monolithic! Therefore, phrases such as "Judaism teaches" or "according to our tradition" are relative. They do not mean "this was, is and always will be the one and only Jewish viewpoint."

Is there a basis for seeking a "second opinion" on the all-important question of the unity of God? If we were to find that God's oneness is not as simple as contemporary Judaism teaches, it would signal the necessity of exploring some rather crucial and complex issues.

If there is any possibility that Jesus is the cure for what ails the world, and more particularly, for what perhaps ails the reader, please consider this. That possible cure has been dismissed because of what we are told Judaism teaches: that to believe that God could be one yet more than one is nonsense. The insistence that there is no plurality within God precludes the hope that Jesus offers, because that insistence renders him a fake. He did, after all, claim to be one with the Father (God).

On the other hand, if the possibility of plurality within the Almighty exists, then belief in Jesus would not be heretical at all. Isn't it worth a "second opinion?" Isn't it worthwhile to see what the experts have said in the past? Are you willing to examine their teachings, even if they raise questions that most Jews feel it is wrong to ask?

There is no doubt that ancient sages struggled with several portions of the Hebrew Scriptures and their implications vis-à-vis God's plurality. Deuteronomy 6:4 (the Sh'ma) is but one such passage. Isaiah 6:8 is another: "Also I heard the voice of the Lord, saying, Whom shall I send, and who will go for Us?" However, the first "proof" passage on God as more than one appears in the first chapter of the Hebrew Scriptures: "And God said: Let us make man in our image, after our likeness" (Genesis 1:26).[3]

Rabbis who believed that each word, even each letter, of the Hebrew Scriptures is God's revelation had to admit that God

---

[3]Jewish Publication Society of America (Philadelphia, 1917). All quotations from Hebrew Scriptures are from this translation, unless otherwise stated.

spoke to himself and referred to himself in the plural. How can that be, when we know there is only one God?

Much in Genesis 1:26 seems to confirm the idea that there is one God whose oneness is complex. The idea of God's nature being triune (three in one) is mind-boggling. Contemplation of the infinite is always confusing to finite beings. Nevertheless, certain illustrations can help people grapple with the issue of a complex unity. C. S. Lewis, talented philologist, writer and debater, put it this way:

> We must remind ourselves that Christian theology does not believe God to be a person. It believes Him to be such that in Him a trinity of persons is consistent with a unity of Deity. In that sense it believes Him to be something very different from a person, just as a cube, in which six squares are consistent with unity of the body, is different from a square. (Flatlanders, attempting to imagine a cube, would either imagine the six squares coinciding, and thus destroy their distinctness, or else imagine them set out side by side, and thus destroy the unity. Our difficulties about the Trinity are of much the same kind.)[4]

Christians consider themselves monotheists, while Jewish tradition maintains that believers in a triunity of God reject monotheism. Yet the Hebrew Scriptures do imply some kind of plurality in the Divinity. Why else would Jewish sages offer various alternatives to explain passages such as Genesis 1:26? Evaluate the following methods our forebears used to deal with the text.

1. Change the text or translate it differently

According to Jewish tradition, scholars who worked on the Septuagint[5] translation of the Hebrew Scriptures for King Ptolemy were embarrassed by the plural pronouns in Genesis 1:26. They took the liberty of changing the text from "let us" to "let me."[6]

---

[4] Wayne Martindale and Jerry Root, eds., The Quotable Lewis (Tyndale House Publishers, Wheaton, IL: 1989), p. 587.

[5] A Greek translation of the Hebrew Scriptures written some two hundred years before Y'shua.

[6] As stated in "The Image of God in Man," D. J. A. Clines, *Tyndale Bulletin* (1968), p. 62, referring to J. Jervell, "Imago Dei . . . ," Göttingen (1960), p. 75.

Other rabbinical commentators also took liberties with the text. They attempted to translate the active "let us make" *(na'a'seh)* into a passive "there is made" *(niphal)*. These commentators also claimed that the phrase "in our image, after our likeness" was not said by God, but added as a postscript by Moses.[7] Such "liberties" violate the sacredness of Scripture.

The medieval rabbi Ibn Ezra described those commentators as "absurd."

2. The text describes God speaking to creation

Medieval commentators David Kimchi and Moses Maimonides accepted the talmudic interpretation of Rabbi Joshua b. Levi. Rabbi Levi explained that God was speaking to creation.

> AND GOD SAID: LET US MAKE MAN, ETC. With whom did He take counsel? R. Joshua b. Levi said: He took counsel with the works of heaven and earth, like a king who had two advisers without whose knowledge he did nothing whatsoever.[8]

Levi knew that the plural implied that God was speaking to someone and concluded that the Lord was seeking advice and approval from other beings. According to Rabbi Nachmanides, the plural reference denotes God speaking to the earth because "man's body would come from the earth and his spirit (soul) from God."[9] But the separation of a person into distinct parts owes more to the Greek influence of Aristotle's philosophy than to a careful and accurate reading of the text. The biblical view of humankind indicates that physical, spiritual and psychic aspects are held together in a composite and indivisible unity.

Rabbi Abarbanel explained that God was capable of making all the lesser works of creation but needed assistance when it came to human beings. That position denies God's omnipotence.

---

[7]Ibn Ezra's *Commentary on the Pentateuch: Genesis (Bereshit),* H. Norman Strickman and Arthur M. Silver, trans. (New York: Menorah Publishing, 1988), p. 43.

[8]Genesis Rabbah VIII.3 (Soncino Midrash Rabbah, p. 56).

[9]Referred to in Soncino Chumash (Soncino Press: London, 1956), p. 6.

3. God is addressing the angels around his throne

Rashi explains that God chose to demonstrate humility by consulting his inferiors:

> The meekness of the Holy One, blessed be He, they [the rabbis] learned from here: because man is in the likeness of the angels and they might envy him, therefore he took counsel with them . . . . Although they did not assist Him in forming him [the man] and although this use of the plural may give the heretics an occasion to rebel [i.e., to argue in favor of their own views], yet the verse does not refrain from teaching proper conduct and the virtue of humbleness, namely, that the greater should consult, and take permission from the smaller; for had it been written, "I shall make man," we could not, then, have learned that He spoke to His judicial council but to Himself.[10]

According to Rashi, if God had used the singular ("I" and "my") we could not have known he was addressing the angels. True—we would never have guessed that God was addressing angels, since there is no mention of angels in the text. But even with the plural, there is still no mention of angels in the text!

The text does not support the concept of God consulting angels in creation, and Rashi's argument became a source of confusion and disagreement among various rabbis.

4. God was speaking to the souls of the righteous unborn

One Jewish tradition states that the souls of the righteous existed before God created the world (and were present at Mount Sinai for the receiving of the law). Those who believe this tradition link Genesis 1:26 with the phrase "there they dwelt with the king in his work" from 1 Chronicles 4:23.

R. Joshua of Siknin said in Rabbi Levi's name: "With the supreme King of kings, the Holy One, blessed be He, sat the souls of the righteous with whom He took counsel before the creation of the world."[11]

---

[10]*Pentateuch with the commentary of Rashi*, Silberman edition, Jerusalem 5733, pp. 6–7.

[11]Genesis Rabbah, VIII.7, p. 59.

A later commentator rebutted the suggestion that God had partners in creation. He insisted that since no other beings are mentioned in the passage, it is not valid to invent them; in fact, it is best to maintain the solitude of God in creation: "Why was man created last? So that the heretics might not say there was a companion [i.e., Jesus] with Him in the work."[12]

5. God was keeping his own counsel

Some Jewish scholars believe that the mystery of Genesis 1:26 can be solved grammatically. They suggest a "plural of deliberation," whereby the plural expresses God's pondering within himself, concentrating his thoughts and meditating over his decision.

> Rabbi Ammi said: "He took counsel with His own heart. It may be compared to a king who had a palace built by an architect, but when he saw it, it did not please him: with whom is he to be indignant? Surely with the architect! Similarly, 'And it grieved Him at His heart.'" (Genesis 6:6)[13]

Several passages in Scripture describe a person deliberating by "consulting" some part of himself. In Psalm 42:6, the psalmist addresses his soul: "Why art thou cast down, O my soul? And why moanest thou within me?" Yet unlike Genesis 1:26, the psalmist uses the words "O my soul," and it is clear that he is deliberating within himself.

6. The royal "we"—plural of majesty

Just as Queen Victoria referred to herself in the plural ("We are not amused"), some say that God, as a majestic being, referred to himself the same way. This is a popular contemporary explanation. It does not raise the question of other beings. It rules out the possibility of God having a plural nature. It seems to be based on good linguistic evidence and analysis.

The Hertz Commentary on Genesis sees this explanation as one of two possibilities and points out that the first person plural is used for royalty in the Book of Ezra.[14] "The letter which ye

---

[12] Tosephta on Sanhedrin 8:7.

[13] Genesis Rabbah, VIII.3, p. 57.

[14] J. H. Hertz, ed., *The Pentateuch and Haftorahs,* (Oxford Univ. Press, 1940), p. 11.

sent unto us hath been plainly read before me" (Ezra 4:18) is the sole example of a "plural of majesty" construction in Scripture. It also happens to be one of the few portions of Scripture in Aramaic, a language similar to Hebrew.

It would be poor scholarship to build a case for a grammatical construction in Hebrew on the grounds of this Aramaic text. Even so, the Ezra passage does not necessarily contain a singular royal subject linked to a plural verb-form. If the plural of majesty were a regular Hebrew idiom, why is the singular "me" in the same line?

Rabbinical commentators and linguists recognize that the Hebrew language provides no real basis for such an explanation.[15] Ibn Ezra quotes the Gaon, . . . who suggests that the plural of Genesis 1:26 is the plural of majesty. He refuted that view in favor of God having consulted the angels.[16] However, we have already mentioned the difficulties of using angels to solve the mystery.

7. There are different aspects within God's being

Some rabbis acknowledge different aspects within God's nature. There is no consensus as to what these aspects are or how to distinguish one from another. For example, the Zohar describes God as being both male and female.[17]

8. The Word: Wisdom or messenger of God

Another way to explain Genesis 1:26 is to use the Memra, or "Word" of God. The Targum Neofiti (an early Aramaic paraphrase of the Hebrew text) translates verse 27: "And the Memra of the Lord created the man in his (own) likeness."[18]

---

[15]Gesenius's *Hebrew Grammar* (A. E. Cowley, ed., Oxford, 1976) says on the "plural of majesty": "Jewish grammarians call such plurals מֻרַף מֵמְרָמ plur. *virium or virtutum;* later grammarians call them *plur. excellentiae, magnltudinis, or plur. maiestaticus.* This last name may have been suggested by the *we* used by kings when speaking of themselves (cf. already I Macc. 10:19, 11:31); and the plural used by God in Genesis 1:26, and 11:7, Isaiah 6:8 has been incorrectly explained in this way. . . . It is best explained as a plural of *self-deliberation.* The use of the plural as a form of respectful address is quite foreign to Hebrew," p. 398.

[16]lbid., Soncino Chumash, p. 6.

[17]Zohar 22a–b (vol. 1, pp. 91–93 in the Soncino Press edition).

[18] Targum Neofiti 1: Genesis, Martin McNamara, trans. The Aramaic Bible, vol. 1A; (Collegeville, MN: The Liturgical Press, 1992), p. 55.

The Targum Onkelos on Deuteronomy 33:27 translates the Hebrew "underneath are the everlasting arms" as "And by His 'Memra' was the world created."

Like the personification of wisdom in Proverbs 8:22–31, the Word is often personified and assigned divine attributes, implying divine status.[19] Memra is used to describe God himself, especially when he is revealing himself to human beings. Rabbinical thought also links the Memra to the Messiah. The New Covenant portion of the Bible reveals a similar understanding of the role of the Word in creation.

The Book of Genesis records that God's dynamic act of creation was through his spoken word: "And God said, Let there be light . . . ," etc.[20] The New Covenant Gospel of John begins this way:

> In the beginning was the Word, and the Word was with God, and the Word was God. He was in the beginning with God. All things were made through Him and without Him nothing was made that was made. In Him was life, and the life was the light of men.[21]

Jewish believers in Jesus believe in the Word of creation in Genesis. Therefore he is not only the Messiah, but God in human form.

Why the Rabbis Won't Regard the Plurality of God with Credibility

Some rabbis agreed that the Genesis 1:26 passage gives weight to the case for God's plurality. Their position has not shaped the current position or practice of Jewish religious leaders:

> Rabbi Samuel ben Nahman said in Rabbi Jonathan's name: "When Moses was engaged in writing the Torah, he had to write the work of each. When he came to the verse, AND GOD SAID: LET US MAKE MAN, etc., he said:

---

[19]Compare Colossians 1:5, Hebrews 1:3, Revelation 3:14 with Proverbs 30:2-6. "By His Memra was the world created" corresponds to John 1:10.

[20]See Genesis 1:3, 6, 9, 11, 14, 20, 24, 26.

[21]John 1:1–4.

'Sovereign of the Universe! Why dost Thou furnish an excuse to heretics?' [for maintaining a plurality of deity]. 'Write,' replied He; 'whoever wishes to err may err.'"[22]

Some rabbis believe that to take the Scriptures at face value is to err. And yes, some out of concern to protect those who are deemed susceptible to such error, have set aside normative interpretations of various Scriptures. Rashi provided a clear example of this with the "suffering servant" passages of Isaiah 52 and 53.

The contemporary interpretation of Israel as the suffering servant was held by few of the early Jewish authorities. Nearly all believed it pointed to an individual and personal Messiah who would suffer and die for Israel's sin. But Rashi popularized the "national view" in the Middle Ages to refute the obvious messianic interpretation. Neither grammar, context nor logic supports this view, yet it is considered superior to the previously held (Jewish) view.

Similarly, in discussion of the Genesis 1 passage, various cases are presented in order to refute Jewish belief in Y'shua. Rabbis understood that a passage wherein God speaks and acts in the plural is significant evidence of diversity within his nature. They also knew that the New Covenant describes Y'shua as the eternal Word of God, the instrument of creation and the fullness of God in human form. They realized that people might make a connection between the two, and they designed their interpretations to counter "the heretics."[23]

> Rabbi Simlai said: "Wherever you find a point supporting the heretics, you find the refutation at its side. They [the heretics] asked him again: 'What is meant by, AND GOD SAID: LET US MAKE MAN?' 'Read what follows,' replied he: 'not, "And gods created [Hebrew: wa-yibre'u—the plural of the verb] man" is written here, but "And God created [Hebrew: wa-yibra—in the singular]"' (Genesis 1:27). When they [the heretics] went out

---

[22]Genesis Rabbah, VIII.8, p. 59.

[23]Hebrew *minim* literally "sectarians" but generally assumed to be a reference to Jewish Christians. See R. T. Herford, *Christianity in Talmud and Midrash* (London, 1903), p. 361ff.

his disciples said to him: 'Them you have dismissed with
a mere makeshift, but how will you answer us?'"[24]

Rabbi Simlai dealt with Jewish believers in Jesus by sidestep-
ping the question. His own disciples recognized that he had done
so and expressed the need for a more satisfying reply.

Some of the ancients admitted that certain Scriptures seemed
to pose a threat to their understanding of God. They sought ways
to direct others away from such disturbing conclusions, and, in
the case of Rashi, they openly explained that they made choices
based on the need to refute Christians.

A Warning and a Challenge

Reverence for the text prevented the ancient rabbis from
ignoring or altering the text. Nevertheless, for all their creative
solutions to the mystery of this passage, they could not agree on
an answer that would satisfy them all.

Today, however, Jewish thinkers are in danger of simply
excising from Scripture and from history clues that the rabbis
were hard pressed to explain. Such clues point to ideas most
Jewish people wish to avoid.

How many contemporary rabbis will say that some of their
interpretations and translations are strongly weighted to help people
avoid "unacceptable" beliefs? How many would admit that their
answers to these complex issues might even direct people away
from the Bible?

The ever evolving traditions of Judaism do not always empha-
size the fact that they have evolved, or that certain teachings have
been obscured for the purpose of shielding the Jewish people.
Without that shield, certain questions might arise . . . and the
traditional answers might not be sufficient to answer them.

Sherlock Holmes once observed that when you have elimi-
nated all possible explanations, the only remaining solution is the
truth, no matter how impossible it seems.

---

[24]Genesis Rabbah, VIII.9, p. 60.

BOTTOM LINE:
CAN JEWS BE FOR JESUS?

by Ruth Rosen

They were intelligent enough to complete medical school, focused enough to survive the rigors of residency. They had the means to be what most would call successful. How could they fail to realize one simple fact: that a person who accepts Jesus Christ as the Messiah can no longer be considered Jewish? If you have found yourself asking that question after reading the accounts in this book, we have a question for you as well. Are you willing to consider that being Jewish and believing in Jesus are not mutually exclusive? Is it possible that many believe they are mutually exclusive because of miscommunication and misunderstanding?

When a physician diagnoses a patient's condition, that physician does not base his or her diagnosis on what others have said about the patient. Nor does a good doctor base a diagnosis solely on what the patient says about his or her own condition. There is a whole body of knowledge, including books, journals, medical histories and experience, against which the doctor will measure the patient to draw objective conclusions.

We recognize the need for objectivity when it comes to the physical sciences. Yet when it comes to spiritual matters, many people rely on presupposed opinions—their own or someone else's—and the conclusions are not necessarily objective.

Many Jews (and gentiles) have only a partial understanding of Christianity. Most know that Christians believe Jesus died to atone for the sins of all who believe in him, and that Christians say he rose from the dead. Many do not understand how one becomes a Christian or what that "becoming" does or does not entail.

And what shall we say about the understanding of what it means to be Jewish? For every four Jews there are five opinions of what it means to be Jewish!

How can a person be certain that Jews who believe in Jesus

are no longer Jews when there is confusion over what it means to be a Jew, to be a Gentile, and to be a Christian? Would you be willing to examine the basis of a viewpoint that might differ radically from your own?

To Be a Jew

Some say that being Jewish is merely a matter of religion. If that were true, it would certainly mean that a person who accepts Jesus is not a Jew, since the religion of Judaism teaches that Jesus is not the Messiah. However, that definition would also mean that the majority of people now known as Jews are not. The definition excludes atheistic Jews, agnostic Jews and all other non-observant Jews.

Some have said that a real Jew is one who settles in the Land and raises a family there. While it is admirable to make *aliyah,* most Jews would object to a definition that depends on Israeli citizenship alone—once again, it excludes a majority of our people. Others argue that Jewish identity is determined by cultural and sociological rather than religious factors. The interesting thing about those who use this argument is that they often add a caveat: that Jews who believe in "other religions" should be excluded. The caveat undercuts the whole concept, since one cannot use a non-religious definition to include oneself, then turn and use religion to exclude others. Definitions must be consistent.

There is a way to circumvent the confusion and controversy over what it means to be a Jew. The Hebrew Scriptures pinpoint who is a Jew and why the Jewish people exist. Jews who believe in Jesus accept the Scriptures as the authoritative source of Jewishness. Genesis 12:1–3 narrates the birth of the Jewish people:

> Now the LORD had said to Abram; "Get out of your country, from your kindred and from your father's house, to a land that I will show you. I will make you a great nation; I will bless you and make your name great; and you shall be a blessing. I will bless those who bless you, and I will curse him who curses you; and in you all the families of the earth shall be blessed."

God's promise to Abraham is described further in Genesis 13:15–16 and Genesis 15:4–5. The Lord reiterates that promise through Isaac (Genesis 26:2–5, 24) and again through Jacob (Genesis 28:13–15). Biblically, a Jew is a Jew because of God's promise.

The promise concerns the descendants of those to whom it was made. That means the promise of God to the Jewish people belongs to descendants of Abraham and Sarah, Isaac and Rebekah, Jacob and Leah and Rachel. No human being can revoke God's promise. But although that is how one becomes a Jew, being Jewish should be more than a matter of race, religion or nationhood. We were meant to be not only a people of promise but also a people of purpose. That purpose was first outlined in Exodus 19:5–6: "Now, therefore, if you will indeed obey My voice and keep My covenant, then you shall be a special treasure to me above all people; for all the earth *is* Mine. And you shall be to Me a kingdom of priests and a holy nation."

God describes what will be but allows people to decide if they want to participate in the purpose. A Jew is part of the people of Israel in any case, but some do not know or care what it means. Nevertheless, neither apathy nor even apostasy makes one cease to be a Jew. The Jewish Bible cites case after case where the nation of Israel was characterized by one or the other. God dealt with his people—sometimes harshly—for straying but never withdrew the promise or the peoplehood from the descendants of Jacob. We see the same thing in Jewish Law:

Even though a Jew undergoes the rites of admission to another religious faith and formally renounces the Jewish religion, he remains—as far as the *halakhah* [law] is concerned—a Jew, albeit a sinner (Sanh. 44a). According to Nahmanides this attitude derives from the fact that the covenant between God and Israel was made "with him that standeth here with us today before the Lord our God and also with him that is not with us here today" (Deuteronomy 29:14; Nahmanides ad loc.).[1]

Even those who choose to hide their Jewishness are still Jews to God. No person can bestow or revoke that Jewishness.

---

[1]*Encyclopaedia Judaica*, Vol. 3, pp. 211, 212. Copyright 1972 by Keter Publishing House, Jerusalem, Israel.

What Is a Gentile?

The word *goy* means "nation," and it usually refers to non-Jewish nations. A goy, or gentile, is simply anyone who is not a Jew. To say that a Jew who believes in Jesus is no longer a Jew is the same as saying he or she became a gentile, which is impossible. There are no formerly Jewish gentiles. A person must be born a gentile.

What Is a Christian?

Would it surprise you to know that someone who goes to a church all his or her life is not necessarily a Christian? Jews and gentiles are what they are because of how they were born, but people become Christians because of what they believe. One cannot be born a Christian since people aren't born believing in anything, except maybe the importance of a full stomach and a clean diaper. Who, then, are Christians?

The first Christians were Jewish followers of Jesus, and they were not known as Christians. They described their belief in Jesus and his teachings as "the Way."[2] Believing in Jesus is more than a religious idea; it is a personal relationship that affects the manner in which one lives.

The first people to be called "Christians" were probably mostly gentiles who lived in Antioch. It was not an appellation they chose for themselves. They were called Christians (probably by gentiles) because they were always talking about and trying to be like Christ, which is simply the Greek translation for Messiah. The name might well have been meant to mock them, but it has become a badge of honor for people who love Jesus and want to obey his teachings.

Christians were and are Jews and gentiles who, of their own free will, chose to trust in Jesus, the Jewish Messiah, as the one who offered himself as a sacrifice for the sins of the world. John 3:16 has often been described as the gospel in a nutshell. It reads: "For God so loved the world that He gave His only begotten Son, that whoever believes in Him should not perish but have everlasting life." Note the words *world* and *whoever.* These universal terms include Jews and gentiles.

---

[2]See Acts 9:2; 19:9, 23; 24:14, 22.

Everyone who chooses Jesus is a convert, whether gentile or Jew. To convert means to turn, not from being a Jew or gentile, not from history or heritage, but from sin. Gentile converts of the first century didn't become Jews, even though the majority of believers in Jesus then were Jewish. Jewish converts today don't become gentiles, even though the majority of believers now are gentiles. At the point of turning to God, or conversion, everyone must experience the same thing according to Jesus:

> Jesus answered and said to him, "Most assuredly, I say to you, unless one is born again, he cannot see the kingdom of God."

> Nicodemus said to Him, "How can a man be born when he is old? Can he enter a second time into his mother's womb and be born?"

> Jesus answered, "Most assuredly, I say to you, unless one is born of water and the Spirit he cannot enter the kingdom of God. That which is born of the flesh is flesh, and that which is born of the Spirit is spirit." (John 3:3–6)

The reconciliation with God that Jesus offered cannot be conferred by birth, but only by rebirth. Therefore, being born Jewish or gentile has no bearing on whether one is a Christian.

Clarifying the Issue of Belief

Confusion over why some of us Jews believe in Jesus causes confusion over why we insist on maintaining our Jewish identity. Many people assume our belief in Jesus constitutes a decision to disassociate from our history, our Jewish people and our God because we like someone else's history, people and God better. The accusation of self-hatred stems from the idea that we want to identify with those who have persecuted us.

Our choice is to identify with Y'shua, not with people who persecuted us in his name. Jewish believers in Jesus feel it is a mistake to evaluate him on the basis of those who profess him as Savior but practice hatred in opposition to his teachings. The ability to think objectively and make logical comparisons is crucial here.

Besides, why would a self-hating Jew accept Jesus and then insist on calling himself or herself a Jew? Why not call ourselves former Jews or forget being Jewish altogether if we converted because we hated being Jewish?

Others have suggested that we chose Jesus to avoid persecution. A person once said, "If there would be another Hitler, don't think that you would escape the ovens just because you believe in Jesus." That's true! People who don't like Jews generally don't care if they believe in Jesus, and those of us who do believe in him know that firsthand. If we wanted to be treated like gentiles, wouldn't it suit our purpose more to change our names and hide our identity?

When Jewish believers in Y'shua are excluded from the larger Jewish community, they are often told that they have excluded themselves. This is not exactly true, because many if not most would still like to be included. Jews are not generally expected to conform to certain beliefs or non-beliefs in order to be considered Jews—except when it come to Jesus.

The assumption that we chose to believe in Jesus because we didn't want to be Jews is entirely wrong. It was never our intention to be cut off from Jewish family, friends or heritage. Most of us didn't choose to believe in Jesus because we found non-Jewish culture more pleasant or admirable. Most of us didn't choose to believe at all. We chose to be open to discover. And it happened.

When it happened, we admitted and committed based on the discovery that Jesus is the Jewish Messiah foretold in the Jewish Bible.

Further, we value our Jewishness. It is exciting to be a part of the people whom God promised would bring blessing to the whole world! It is awesome to read the Jewish Bible and know that these are our ancestors. Yet our tie to our people is not simply a matter of ancient history. We believe that God continues to have a purpose and a plan for the Jewish people. Jews who believe in the Messiah Jesus feel we have found our destiny. We feel a connection to the past, a purpose for the present and a great hope for the future.

There have been some who are not interested in hearing from us why we believe in Jesus, why we haven't stopped identifying ourselves as Jews. They publicly accuse Jews who believe in Jesus of employing a false (Jewish) identity to lure people into believing in Jesus. That is an untrue, unfair and illogical accusation that should not go unchallenged.

The accusation implies that some Jews might believe in Jesus if they thought they could do so without giving up their Jewish identity. Would you stop and think about what that means for a moment? Now here's a question: In a time when assimilation is rampant and all too many people don't bother to identify themselves as Jews, why the pressure to regard Jewish believers in Jesus as non-Jews? Why is the party line in one Jewish newspaper after another that people pretending to be Jews want to lure you into Christianity?

The answer is in the accusation itself. Which is more probable: To "lure" Jews into becoming Christians by assuring them that they will still be Jews? Or to deter Jews from considering Jesus by assuring them that they will not be Jews if they accept him?

The latter is far more likely. First, people cannot be motivated to believe in Jesus on the basis of something they already possess: namely, Jewish identity. Second, in order to honestly consider Jesus, a person must be willing to stop thinking about who he or she is and concentrate on who Jesus is. And third, any potential Jewish believers in Jesus ought to be warned that if they do allow themselves to consider him, they may be regarded as traitors by many who don't understand. Jesus gave fair warning to his followers of the rejection they would encounter, and those who want to be like him must do the same. In light of these things, it is difficult to see how the statement that "Jewish believers in Jesus are still Jews" is a lure.

If denying the Jewish identity of those who believe in Jesus is to serve as a deterrent, a question arises: Why? Why deter Jews from considering Jesus? Perhaps because those who believe in him accept his authority above any other. Jesus was and is always a threat to the status quo. Most Jews know that belief in Jesus would make them objects of disappointment, displeasure and perhaps disenfranchisement. Seekers don't know with the same certainty the reality of God's promises to those who trust him. That is why they are seeking.

Many think Jesus might be true but are unwilling to risk finding out because, whereas they don't quite know what to expect from God, they do know what to expect from people. When God seems remote, people tend to look to one another for acceptance and guidance. And God does seem remote—until that moment when we decide to know him, whatever the cost. The moment we risk everything to know God is the moment of faith.

What Is Faith?

People use the word *faith* to mean different things. Some speak of "the Jewish faith" or "the Christian faith" when they mean "religion." Others say "I have my own faith" meaning they have a religious opinion that is private and ought not to be challenged. Still others say "I'm a member of the _____ faith because I could never believe in a God who _____." Such people are expressing personal preference, using the concept of faith to reinforce their own sense of right and wrong.

Faith is not a matter of taste, opinion or affiliation. Faith is not casting a vote for what we think God is or ought to be like. Nor is it a profession made for the purpose of being with others who profess likewise.

The Book of Hebrews in the "New Testament" describes faith as the "substance" of things hoped for, the "evidence" of things not seen, and then goes on to illustrate by pointing out great heroes of faith from the Hebrew Scriptures.[3]

Substance and evidence are difficult words to understand in the context of faith. We think of substance as physical matter, but that is only one meaning. The primary meaning according to the New World Dictionary is "the real or essential part or element of anything." And while people tend to think of evidence as something visible, it has to do with grounds for belief.

Many people are accustomed to thinking that whatever we cannot perceive with our five senses somehow exists in a different way, a way that enables us to shape it according to our imagination, our preference or our sincerity. Yet this is no more true in the spiritual realm than it is in the physical. Micro-organisms

---

[3] See Hebrews 11:1. The words *substance* and *evidence* are used in the King James and New King James versions.

that are invisible to the naked eye are all around us. Those of us who haven't the equipment or the desire to view them can imagine how they look and behave. It takes the proper lens to know if our opinions are right or wrong.

Unlike a micro-organism, God is too big for us to see. We are limited in what we can perceive with our senses, as wonderful as those senses are. Nevertheless, the fact that we can't fully apprehend God with our senses does not mean that God is whatever we decide he should be, or that faith in God is whatever religious opinion we happen to hold.

Faith is the real or essential part of what we hope for; it is grounds for believing what we cannot see. In other words, faith is not a guess at what might be. It is not wishful thinking. It is trusting what is, even when what is can only be perceived through a nonphysical "lens." Faith is based on perception and rooted in reality. There are many religions and many ideas, but in order to qualify as faith in the biblical sense, a person's belief about God must be true.

Faith is belief, trust and commitment, not to a religion, but to a reality: The Reality, which is the object of faith. There's not one Reality for Jews and another Reality for Buddhists or Baptists; therefore, there is not one faith for Jews and another, different faith for everyone else. People cannot choose "a faith" any more than they can choose "a reality." If there is one God, there is one faith.

What Is Our Choice?

People can choose to keep their eyes closed if there is something they do not wish to see. Once people choose to open their eyes, what they see is not a matter of choice. It is the same with faith. Once we choose to open our minds and hearts, we may find ourselves "seeing" with eyes of faith something other than our own preference or choice.

For the person who chooses to know and act on the truth, there are not many roads to God. Truth is objective and singular by nature. It can be perceived, misperceived, ignored or acted upon, but there are no personal versions of truth. The choice to seek truth despite the consequences is a difficult and personal one. At the same time, the choice to know and act on truth opens the door to a way people will not otherwise see. When that way presents itself, and one sees where it leads, there is such joy and wonder that to turn away from that way is unthinkable.

For us, the choice was not whether to be Jewish. The Almighty decided that for us. The choice is not whether to believe or not believe in Jesus. People believe what they see, whether through eyes of flesh or eyes of faith. Rather, the choice is whether to open the eyes of faith, regardless of what one might see.

CONCLUSION: MEET THE GREAT PHYSICIAN

by David Brickner

I've got to reach him, she thought, *or I'll die.* It didn't seem likely that she would make it. She was pressed between too many people. She couldn't see past anyone's shoulders, but she could feel. Everyone was demanding, pushing and shoving. It was hot. Dust from many roads choked her constantly parched throat. The stench of sweat, filth and her own blood filled her nostrils. Perhaps because she felt that death was so near, a dizzying patchwork of memories seemed to swirl around her mind.

It began with the birth of her first and only child. The birth itself was not unusual, but long after the time when a woman could be pronounced clean, she was still ritually impure. The hemorrhaging simply could not be stopped. Sometimes the oozing would subside but never for long. She could never gain enough strength.

Her husband was a decent man. He worked hard, gave all that he had to buy the best remedies possible. The physician in her small village recommended a series of poultices, bandages, herbs and other medications. None of them brought relief—but all of them cost money. The money for treatments dwindled down to nothing, and so did her husband's hope. He tried not to let her see how disappointed and upset he was that she could not fulfill her motherly duties, let alone her wifely duties. He was just as troubled by the whispers that she must have done something terrible for God to allow her to suffer this way. The divorce was simple; he declared that she was perpetually unavailable and ritually unclean. For twelve years she had no friends, no family. Even lepers had one another for company but this woman had no one. Loneliness and dejection were her constant companions. Pain and weakness were all she could feel.

She was unclean, a castaway, abandoned by all. She knew she

was too fragile to live much longer. The fluttering in her head must surely have been the wings of the angel of death. Only a miracle could save her, but there had been no miracle till now. Even so, she knew miracles were not impossible. Some said that the Holy One of Israel was visiting his people once again. There was gossip that miracles even greater than those in the days of Moses or Elijah were happening every day—and not just for the wealthy, but mostly for poor and ordinary people like her. There were some, she knew, who doubted whether God cared enough to bother himself with ordinary events, either in days of old or now. They said that God was too big to deal with the ordinary pain, needs, and deaths of little people. Nevertheless, somehow she believed that God cared.

That belief energized her in a peculiar way to press through the gauntlet of wanting people, so she twisted through that crowd. And just when she was about to faint from the pressure of so many bodies and the heat and her own ill health, she found herself being pushed toward the one that all were pursuing. There he was—but his back was to her, and he was walking away. Everyone was shouting his name. She hadn't the strength to raise her voice over the din. She couldn't shout out her plea. In an instant she staggered and realized it had been a mistake to stand still while the crowd was still pressing ahead.

Whoever shoved her probably did not mean to; nevertheless, as she lurched forward, she realized this might be her only opportunity. Perhaps just by clutching his clothing she might receive his attention and ask for some of his healing power. Even as she thought of that power, she reached out her hand and touched the *tzit-tzit,* the fringes of his prayer shawl.

She didn't see the people on the edge of the crowd stop nor did she notice the awed, stark silence that fell on them. She didn't see the beatific glow on his face as he turned toward the crowd. She was oblivious to everything but the slow warmth that began in the tips of the fingers that had touched his garment. That warmth quickly spread until she felt it throughout her entire body. She knew the oozing blood had ceased. She felt strength for the first time in twelve years. Suddenly she realized how wrong, dreadfully wrong it was to touch him. A bleeding woman must never defile another by touching him. Then the understanding came to her. Her touch had not defiled him! Rather, his touch had made her holy, healthy and happier than she had ever been. Tears streamed down her cheeks, past her radiant smile, mixing with dust to muddy her face. But she didn't care. She had never known such joy and relief. In one instant he had accomplished what no physician had in those twelve tortured years.

Then she heard his voice. "Who touched me?" His tone was not angry yet she trembled as she stood before him, in awe of his power and his holiness. "Daughter," he said, beaming a smile of blessing (he couldn't have been much older than her), "your faith has healed you. Go in peace and be freed from your suffering."

She knew that this young man was the one that Isaiah had called "The Everlasting Father." Her suffering truly was at an end for she had encountered the only physician who can heal body, mind and soul with a touch. That physician was Y'shua, Jesus.[1]

The Gospels are filled with accounts of his miracles, many of which were healings. People responded in different ways to those miracles. Those who recognized their deficiencies sought Jesus. Others who considered themselves self-sufficient, physically and spiritually, resented him.

Jesus was compassionate to those who could admit their deficiencies. He was not as compassionate toward those who were proud and self-satisfied. He did not seem to regard them as any better than the common people who came to him with their sicknesses and their sorrows and their sins. Some people were infuriated to be regarded as no better than those they considered lowly. They did not realize that in God's eyes the difference between them and the common people was not significant.

Jesus is still touching people's lives. He is still showing compassion to those who recognize their need. Some who feel they don't need him resent what his message implies—that everyone is spiritually needy in God's eyes. Others know of their needs but do not feel free to seek spiritual solutions in Jesus. What about you? Do you know that you need the touch that heals, or are you content that God is satisfied with you just as you are?

---

[1]This was based on a true narrative of a healing recorded in the Gospel of John. The extra details supplied here are speculation.

Every account that you've read in this very book tells of a real and personal encounter with the Great Physician. These true stories are about men and women like you. Unlike that desperate woman who touched Y'shua's fringes, they were not forced by society to face the reality of their uncleanness. They are not weak individuals as the world measures strength and weakness. They are skilled in the practice of the healing arts, yet they recognized their own need to be healed.

If you are successful by the world's standards, many people will accept and admire you. Some will even encourage you to play God. Perhaps as intelligence and success are measured, you are in the "99th percentile." Nevertheless, Y'shua did not come to tell us that we don't measure up to other people's standards. He came to tell us we don't measure up to *God's* standards—and to offer himself as the solution to the gravest of all illnesses.

You see, there is a sickness far more dangerous than cancer or AIDS or any other disease that plagues the human race. It is a sickness of the soul called sin. We see its effects reported daily in newspapers and television but more personally in the life of every human being. Sin is worse than any physical illness. While physical disease has the power to separate one's body and soul, the spiritual disease of sin separates the soul from a holy and righteous God.

Everyone on this planet is spiritually quarantined—not because God is in any danger of being infected by our sin. Yet, because of the nature of his righteousness, his holiness would be defiled by our touch, our gaze, our linking ourselves to him.

Only Y'shua the Messiah can heal that terminal condition that requires the quarantine and separation of human beings from God. Through his remedy we can stand before a holy God during our lifetime and forever after.

Jesus doesn't pronounce a magic incantation or provide some kind of spiritual penicillin. He is a unique physician. He doesn't merely *provide* a cure for our disease—he *is* the cure. He became the cure by taking on himself all the sickness, all the disease, all the pain, all the suffering. When he died, the power of that disease called sin died with him. "Surely our diseases he did bear, and our pains he carried." When Jesus died on the cross, all the suffering and pain that sin causes in this world and in our lives was laid upon him, died with him and was buried with him even as the prophet Isaiah predicted: "Yet it pleased the LORD to bruise Him; He has put *Him* to grief. When you make His soul an offering for sin, He shall see *His* seed, He shall prolong *His* days, and the pleasure of the LORD shall prosper in His hand" (Isaiah 53:10).

However, that is only half of the account verified by the Bible. The tomb could not hold the Messiah Jesus. Neither disease nor the sins of others nor death could defeat him. The fact that Jesus rose from the dead makes the cure complete. He offers healing to all those who come to him. He'll bring healing to your soul for now and eternity. Then he'll bring the hope of a new body, an eternal body that will never be corrupted or sick again. "And God will wipe away every tear from their eyes; there shall be no more death, nor sorrow, nor crying. There shall be no more pain, for the former things have passed away" (Revelation 21:4).

All the physicians in this book have given a prescription for spiritual healing. In their personal and professional opinions, Jesus is the only cure that lasts forever.

Scientists may find treatments for many diseases, and the field of medicine is continually advancing to improve the quality of life and health. Nevertheless, eventually we will all die. Only one can give eternal life. We don't need to press through a crowd of people to touch him, but we must press through the barrier of public relations and public opinion if we would receive his healing touch.

Whether you are "down on your luck" or the envy of most, perhaps you know that deep down within yourself there is a bleeding of your own soul and a debilitation of your spirit. Maybe you've come to realize that you need something but don't know what. Maybe you've tried all the prescriptions and pleasures that this world has to offer but they've failed to give you hope. Y'shua can provide that unknown remedy. Perhaps now is the time to recognize there's only one Great Physician who can heal body, mind and soul.

The doctor will see you right now. You don't need to make an appointment. If you know it is time, God has an appointment with you—and you have an appointment with Destiny.

His question is not "Who touched me," but "Who will allow me to touch them?"

Will you let yourself say yes to him? Will you invite his healing touch? He is as close to you now as a believing, trusting word uttered in prayer. You don't have to be a doctor to join the ranks of those whose stories fill the pages of this book. All you need is the Great Physician to make you clean and spotless—whole, in his sight. Once he has healed your soul, he invites you to concern yourself with others who need his touch. He has a new life for you—a life filled with caring for others and serving him.

We want to help you in this new life of joy and service. To begin, please consider the invitation on page 229.

David Brickner,
Executive Director
Jews for Jesus

WHAT WILL YOU DO?

If you believe that true well-being comes from God, and if you want that peace and well-being, please consider the following:

1. God is concerned with every aspect of your life.

"Yet I will not forget you. See, I have inscribed you on the palms of My hands." (Isaiah 49:15–16)

2. You can't truly experience God's love because of sin.

"But your iniquities have separated you from your God, and your sins have hidden His face from you, so that He will not hear." (Isaiah 59:2)

3. Trust in God's provision of Y'shua (Jesus) to be your sin-bearer and Savior.

"But He was wounded for our transgressions, He was bruised for our iniquities; the chastisement for peace was upon Him, and by His stripes we are healed." (Isaiah 53:5)

4. Receive forgiveness of sins and a personal relationship with God by asking Y'shua to reign in your heart.

"If you confess with your mouth the Lord [Y'shua] and believe in your heart that God has raised Him from the dead, you will be saved. For with the heart one believes unto righteousness, and with the mouth confession is made unto salvation." (Romans 10:9, 10)

If you believe these verses and want to follow Y'shua, the doctor who can heal your soul, this is a prayer that will help you begin a new life: "Dear God, I know that I have sinned against you and I want to turn from my sin. I believe you provided Y'shua, Jesus, as an atonement for me. With this prayer I receive Jesus as my Savior and my Lord. Thank you God for cleansing me of sin, for healing my soul and for sealing my name in your Book of Life forever. Please help me live the life you have for me through Messiah. Amen."

If you just prayed this prayer or if you are considering doing so, please let us hear from you by filling out and returning this coupon:

(Please print)

Name _____

Street _____

City _____ State _____ Zip _____

Phone (___)_____ E-mail _____

❏ I read the texts from the Bible and prayed the prayer. I sign my name as a commitment to Y'shua as my savior and Lord.

Signed _____

Date _____

❏ I really don't understand or believe these texts yet but I am seriously willing to consider them and seek what God has for me.

❏ I already believe in Y'shua and want to know more about Jews for Jesus.

I am ❏ Jewish ❏ Gentile

Please return to Jews for Jesus, 60 Haight Street, San Francisco, CA 94102-5895

E-mail: jfj@jewsforjesus.org

Web: www.jewsforjesus.org

GLOSSARY

Note: Many Jewish words have variant spellings. Keep in mind that most of these words are not English, but Hebrew or Yiddish. The spellings you see are merely transliterations to help you pronounce them; there is no officially correct way to spell them.

The "ch" sound should be pronounced as a soft sound, as if you were trying to make a sound that is half "k" and half "h" at the same time. If you can't get the hang of it, just pronounce it as a simple "h."

aliyah — To go up—commonly used to refer to the immigration of a Jew to the land of Israel.

bar mitzvah — "Son of commandment." In the Jewish religion, thirteen is the age of accountability. This "rite of passage" is marked by a public reading from the Torah, often followed by a big celebration.

bimah — The synagogue pulpit or place of judgment.

borscht — An Old-World soup; if it's made with cabbage, it's sweet and sour and served hot. If it's made with beets, it can be served hot or cold with a dollop of sour cream.

chaluptzahs — (Also called *holishkes.*) Cabbage leaves stuffed with a mixture of ground beef, onions, tomatoes and rice. [ed: Recipes vary, but I like the sweet and sour recipe best. This is what my mother makes for me when she wants I should feel special.]

Chanukah — (Also spelled Hannukah.) There are even more ways to spell it, but however you spell it, it literally means "dedication" and is also known as the Festival of Lights. This eight-day holiday commemorates the ancient victory of a small group of Jews who, against all odds, overcame the Syrian tyrant who defiled the Temple and demanded to be worshiped as a god.

chazon
(Also spelled hazzan; plural hazzanut.) Cantor who leads worship in the synagogue services through the chanting of prayers. This "chanting" is melodic and in a minor key.

to dovven
(Also davening.) To recite liturgical prayers, often with a rocking motion.

dreidel
A spinning top with which children play games as part of the Hannukah celebration.

goyim
Literally "nations," it is a term that means one who belongs to another nation (i.e., a non-Jew).

goyishe
A sometimes derogatory adjective that describes something as non-Jewish or alien to Jewish culture.

Hadassah
This was Queen Esther's Hebrew name. The Hadassah organization, a Jewish women's group that started as a Zionist organization in 1912, was named for her. Today the Hadassah organization is known chiefly for promoting educational activities to aid in developing Jewish consciousness.

Haftorah
The prophetic portion of the weekly Bible reading in the synagogue.

Haggadah
Literally "the narrative" or "story." This is the book (or in some cases, condensed booklet) that gives the order of service for the Passover celebration. The Haggadah tells the story of how God brought Israel out from slavery in Egypt. Included are narratives, songs, psalms, and other prayers to commemorate freedom and praise the Almighty for his powerful acts of redemption.

hamantashen
High-calorie reminders of how our people were rescued from wicked Haman's plot on Purim. These three-cornered pastries or cookies are made with prune, poppy seed or apricot filling and represent the three-cornered hat of Haman, whose

defeat in destroying our people is cause for celebration. They also represent the diet many of us will have to go on after Purim.

Kaddish   Taken from the Hebrew word for holy or sacred, it refers to the "mourner's prayer," which is said in memory of departed loved ones. However, the prayer does not mention death but magnifies the supremacy and holiness of God.

kiddush   "Sanctification," a benediction that is said over a cup of wine to sanctify Sabbaths and holidays.

kreplach   Old-World Jewish dumplings—just the thing to serve in a bowl of chicken soup. They are usually filled with a mixture of ground meat and onions, but cabbage is also acceptable. Kreplach are a lot like Chinese potstickers or Polish pirogen, but ours are not fried.

Kristalnacht (Literally "Night of Glass.") It recalls the event in 1938 when Nazis encouraged the destruction of synagogues as well as the vandalism and looting of all Jewish businesses. The glass refers to the smashed windows of the pillaged buildings.

kvetch   To complain or to whine, but with style. "Oy" is a good expression when you want to kvetch, and it's helpful to roll your eyes as you say it.

latkes   Deep-fried potato pancakes; these you can really clog up your arteries with. Most Jews only indulge once a year, at Hannukah. The cooking oil reminds us of the legend of the oil that miraculously burned for eight days in the newly rededicated temple until a fresh supply could be obtained.

machers   VIPs, big shots—as in "So, now that you're a big macher at the office, you don't have time to come visit your mother?"

matzoh   Unleavened bread.

matzoh balls   Dumplings made of matzoh meal; unlike kre-plach, they are not stuffed with anything. The ideal matzoh ball is fluffy and light; it floats beautifully in chicken soup. Bad matzoh balls are more like matzoh bombs!

megilah   The scroll; often used to refer to the Scroll of Esther, which is traditionally read in the synagogue on the eve of Purim.

mikvah   A Jewish cleansing ritual that requires total emersion in water.

mishegoss   What your mother tells you if you say you don't want to get married—or worse yet, if you're married and you tell her you don't want to have children—craziness!

mishuganners   Crazy people, or those who involve themselves in *mishegoss.*

Mitlshule   Jewish middle school.

moyl   (Also spelled *mohel.*) Person who performs the ritual of circumcision on the eighth day after birth.

Pesach   Passover.

pogroms   Government-inspired raids on Jewish villages in Russia between 1881 and 1921. These attacks included looting, rape and bloodshed. Similar events occurred in Germany, Austria, Rumania and the Balkan countries. There were also pogroms in Poland after the country regained its independence in 1918.

Purim   Jewish holiday to commemorate God's preservation of our people, and the heroic foiling of a plan to destroy us. The origins of this holiday are found in the Book of Esther.

qvelled	(Past tense of *qvell*.) What a Jewish person does when he or she is about to burst with happiness and pride over the accomplishments of a loved one, as in, "You should have seen her qvell when her son graduated; you would have thought he was collecting a Nobel prize and not just a diploma."
Rosh Hashanah	Literally "head of the year," it has come to be known as the Jewish new year. In Scripture, it is referred to as the Day of Trumpets, or in Hebrew, Yom Truah (see Leviticus 23:24).
Ruach Ha Kodesh	The Holy Spirit.
seder	Literally "order," this refers to the Passover service, which includes several rituals, traditions, prayers and songs as well as a *gazunta* (big) meal.
Sh'ma	Passage of Scripture from Deuteronomy (6:4–11). Chanted as one of the most important of all Jewish prayers. it affirms the sovereignty and oneness of God. Sh'ma means "Hear" and the prayer begins, "Hear O Israel."
Shabbat	(Also called Shabbos.) Sabbath (see Leviticus 23:3).
shalom	A Jewish greeting that means peace and is used interchangeably for hello or good-bye.
shofar	Ram's horn that is sounded as a trumpet.
shul	Usually refers to the synagogue. A variant spelling, *shule,* could also refer to Hebrew school.
siddur	Prayer book. The *siddur* contains prayers arranged in a traditional order for daily worship as well as specified occasions, both public and private.
Simchas	(Also Simchat Torah) the joy of Torah, a celebration Torah when the cycle of reading the Bible is complete for the year and it's time to begin again in Genesis.

sukkah	Boothlike structure used to commemorate the holiday of Sukkot.
Sukkot	(Also sukkoth) literally, "tabernacles." This is an eight-day holiday of thanksgiving for the harvest.
t'shuva	To turn, to repent.
tallis	Prayer shawl worn over the outer garment by Jewish men for morning prayer, excepting certain holidays when it is worn in the afternoon or, as in the case of Yom Kippur, throughout services all day.
Talmud	Literally "research." Ancient writings that are a compilation of Jewish oral law, legend and interpretation of Scriptures. They are considered divinely inspired as the "perpetuation" of Torah by religious Jews. The compilation of the Talmud had ended by the sixth century, but the commentaries and addenda have continued.
tefillin	(Also spelled t'fillin.) Scriptures inscribed on parchment and encased in small leather boxes to be strapped on the arm and head for prayer. Two of the Scriptures on the parchment are from Exodus 13:1–10 and 13:11–16) and the other two are from Deuteronomy 6:4–9 and 11:13–20. The ritual of strapping the tefillin on for prayer is referred to as "laying tefillin" or "putting on tefillin." It is done in accordance with Exodus 13:9, "It shall be as a sign to you on your hand and as a memorial between your eyes." The ritual is to be performed each morning, excepting Sabbaths and holidays.
Torah	The Law, the first five books of Moses; can also refer to the Jewish Bible as a whole.
tzedacka	The obligation to do righteousness; charitable gifts are a form of *tzedacka*.

Y'shua   (Also spelled Yeshua.) The Jewish way to say
              Jesus.

Yiddish   A language spoken by Jews from Eastern Europe,
              which is a mixture of (mostly) German and
              Hebrew; Yiddishe is also an adjective to indicate
              the general Jewish nature of a person or thing, as
              in "My Yiddishe mama."

Yom Kippur   The Day of Atonement, the most sacred of all
              days on the Jewish calendar (see Leviticus 23:27).

SUGGESTED MATERIALS

If you do not yet believe in Jesus but want more information, the following might be helpful:

Benhayim, Menahem. *Jews, Gentiles and the New Testament.* Jerusalem: Yanetz Press, 1985. An examination of many charges leveled by critics of the New Testament, both Jewish and Gentile, against its alleged anti-Semitism.

Fruchtenbaum, Arnold G. *Jesus Was a Jew.* Nashville: Broadman Press, 1974. (Now published by Ariel Ministries). Written to show the relationship of Jesus to the Jewish people; how Jesus fit into his own Jewish society and how Jesus is still for Jewish people today.

Frydland, Rachmiel. *When Being Jewish Was a Crime.* Nashville: Thomas Nelson Publishers, 1978. This story of a Polish Jew who came to faith in Y'shua during the Nazi occupation dispels the myth that Jews become Christians to avoid persecution.

Frydland, Rachmiel. *What the Rabbis Know About the Messiah.* Cincinnati: Messianic Literature Outreach, 1993. A rabbinical scholar who came to know Y'shua as his savior shows that Jesus' life and message is not at all foreign to Jewish thinking.

Habermans, Gary R. *Ancient Evidence for the Life of Jesus.* Nashville: Thomas Nelson Publishers, 1984. A concise presentation of the evidence for the resurrection of Jesus.

The Jewish Case for Jesus. This audio cassette from Jews for Jesus uses a classic radio show format to explain through drama, music and testimony why some Jewish people believe that Jesus is the Messiah. (See address on p. 244.)

Kac, Arthur. *The Messiahship of Jesus.* Chicago: Moody Press, 1963. A compilation of quotes and excerpts from books, pamphlets and articles by Jews, past and present—some believers, some not—to authenticate the claims that Jesus is the Messiah of Israel.

Katz, Arthur. *Ben Israel.* Plainfield, NJ: Logos International, 1970. A candid presentation of a secular agnostic American-Jewish radical's odyssey to faith in Israel's Messiah.

Lewis, C. S. *Mere Christianity.* New York: Macmillan Publishing, 1964. An articulate and erudite apologetic for Christianity.

Lockyer, Herbert. *All the Messianic Prophecies of the Bible.* Rapids: Zondervan, 1973. Lists passages pointing to the Messiah.

McDowell, Josh. *Evidence That Demands a Verdict,* Vol. 1. San Bernardino, CA: Campus Crusade for Christ, 1972. A study of the reliability of Scriptures and their implications as regard Jesus.

McDowell, Josh. *The Resurrection Factor.* San Bernardino, CA: Here's Life Publishers, 1981. A scholarly and readable presentation of evidence from nonbiblical sources that Jesus lived a sinless life, died on a Roman cross and was resurrected.

McDowell, Josh, and Stewart, Don. *Answers to Tough Questions.* Nashville: Thomas Nelson Publishers. Answers to sixty-five commonly asked questions for the skeptic who is seeking.

Morrison, Frank. *Who Moved the Stone?* Downers Grove, IL: Inter-Varsity Press, 1958 (originally published 1930). An examination of the resurrection of Jesus by a lawyer who started out to disprove it and became convinced that it happened.

Riggans, Walter. *Jesus Ben Joseph.* Monarch Publications, 1993. This book established Jesus' thoroughly Jewish identity and the significance of that identity for Jewish people today.

Rosen, Moishe. *Y'shua.* Chicago: Moody Press, 1982. An argument for the messiahship of Jesus for Jewish people who are interested in examining the claims of the New Testament against the background of the Hebrew Scriptures and rabbinical writings.

Rosen, Moishe. *The Universe Is Broken: Who on Earth Can Fix It?* San Francisco: Purple Pomegranate Productions, 1991. This forty-eight-page booklet explores the source of life's problems and suggests how solutions can be found in Jesus.

Rosen, Ruth, ed. *Testimonies of Jews Who Believe in Jesus.* San Francisco, CA: Purple Pomegranate Productions, 1987. Fifteen Jewish people from all walks of life tell how they became convinced that Jesus is the Messiah.

Roth, Sid. *There Must Be Something More.* Brunswick, GA: Messianic Vision Press, 1994. Sid Roth thought the power of wealth and the occult could satisfy, but he paid a high price to experience their destructive power, until he met Jesus.

Schaeffer, Edith. *Christianity is Jewish.* Wheaton, IL: Tyndale House, 1977. Traces the continuity of faith from the Old Covenant to the New.

Telchin, Stan. *Betrayed!* Lincoln, VA: Chosen Books, 1981. The dramatic story of a Jewish father who set out to prove to his daughter that Jesus is not the Messiah, and proved to himself the exact opposite.

The Y'shua Challenge. San Francisco: Purple Pomegranate Productions, 1993. This forty-page booklet challenges some commonly held presuppositions about Jews believing in Jesus in a logical, thought-provoking way.

Also if you are Jewish, do not believe in Jesus and would like to read the perspectives of other Jews who do believe, a free subscription to an eight-page, bimonthly publication titled *ISSUES* is available by request through contacting:

ISSUES
P.O. Box 424885
San Francisco, CA 94142-4885

If you are Jewish and have become a believer in Y'shua, the following helps are available:

Brickner, David. *Mishpochah Matters: Speaking Frankly to God's Family.* San Francisco, CA: Purple Pomegranate Productions, 1996. An anthology of pastoral essays dealing with a wide range of topics of concern for any believer in Jesus, but particularly for

Jewish believers in Jesus. Among other issues, includes insights pertaining to marriage, miracles and dealing with death.

Bruce, F. F. *New Testament History.* Garden City, NY: Anchor Books, Doubleday, 1972. Helps the reader of the New Testament to see the books in the historical setting in which the events took place and the books themselves were written.

Buksbazen, Victor. *The Gospel in the Feasts of Israel.* Philadelphia: Spearhead Press, 1954. Explains how the Jewish festivals pointed to the coming of Jesus and his ministry as Messiah.

Douglas, J. D., ed. *The New Bible Dictionary.* Grand Rapids: Eerdmans, 1962. A thorough one-volume reference book about the people, places and subjects found in the Bible.

Edersheim, Alfred. *Old Testament Bible History.* Grand Rapids: Eerdmans, 1972. An excellent work on the history of Israel in the Old Testament by a Jewish-Christian scholar.

Fruchtenbaum, Arnold G. *Hebrew Christianity—Its Theology, History and Philosophy.* Washington, DC: Canon Press, 1974. An introduction to the modern Hebrew-Christian movement.

Glaser, Mitch and Zhava. *The Fall Feasts of Israel.* Chicago: Moody Press, 1987. An in-depth study of the origins, traditions and messianic implications of Rosh Hashanah, Yom Kippur, and Sukkot.

Growth Book. San Francisco: Jews for Jesus, 1983. A thirty-four-page booklet to help new Jewish believers in Jesus become oriented in their faith as well as understand how family and friends might respond to their belief in Jesus.

Juster, Daniel C. *Jewishness and Jesus.* Downers Grove, IL: InterVarsity Press, 1977. Dan Juster, leader of the Union of the Messianic Jewish Congregations in the United States, has given the perspective of Jesus in his Jewish setting.

Little, Paul. *Know Why You Believe.* Wheaton, IL: Scripture Press, 1970. Helps the layperson understand the reasonableness of our faith in Jesus.

Mears, Henrietta C. *What the Bible Is All About.* Glendale, CA: Regal Books/Gospel Light Publishers, 1974. An excellent "book-by-book" introduction to the Bible for beginners.

Rosen, Moishe and Ceil. *Christ in the Passover.* Chicago: Press, 1978. An explanation of the Jewish Passover feast as it was celebrated and fulfilled by Jesus at the Last Supper.

Schaeffer, Edith. *Christianity Is Jewish.* Wheaton, IL: Tyndale House, 1977.

Sire, James W. *Scripture Twisting.* Downers Grove, IL: Inter-Varsity Press, 1980. A look at how "cult" groups misuse the Scriptures, what we can learn from this, and how we can keep from going astray ourselves.

If you are not Jewish but are a believer in Jesus who wants to find out more about how Jesus is for Jews, the following might help:

DeRidder, Richard R. *God Has Not Rejected His People.* Grand Rapids: Baker Book House, 1977. Affirms God's continuing covenant relationship with Israel, and the need for Jews to be introduced to Jesus.

Edersheim, Alfred. *The Life and Times of Jesus the Messiah.* Grand Rapids: Eerdmans, 1971. An excellent, detailed study of the Jewish background of the life and ministry of Jesus.

Hagner, Donald A. *The Jewish Reclamation of Jesus.* Grand Rapids: Zondervan, 1984. An analysis and critique of the modern Jewish study of Jesus. Also includes a historical survey of the Jewish views of Jesus.

Jocz, Jakob. *The Jewish People and Jesus Christ.* London: SPCK, 1962. Scholarly and intriguing study of the relationship between Christians, the gospel message, and the Jewish people.

Jocz, Jakob. *The Jewish People and Jesus Christ after Auschwitz.* Grand Rapids: Baker Book House, 1981. An updated continuation of the previous book.

Kac, Arthur. *The Messianic Hope.* Grand Rapids: Baker Book House, 1975. An analytical look at the mission of Jesus of Nazareth in the light of the messianic expectations of the Old Testament and postbiblical Jewish teaching about Messiah, resurrection and life after death.

Kac, Arthur. *The Spiritual Dilemma of the Jewish People.* Chicago: Moody Press, 1963. An excellent analysis by a Jewish Christian of the factors at the heart of the present Jewish spiritual plight.

Whether or not you are Jewish, if you are seeking spiritual help to cope with a crisis, the following might help:

Bauman, Harold. *Living Through Grief.* Bromley, Kent England: Operation Mobilisation in association with Lion Publishing, 1960. A forty-six-page booklet that offers strength and hope in times of loss.

Ford, Leighton. *Sandy: A Heart for God.* Downers Grove: InterVarsity Press: 1985. A father tells a story of pain and victory in facing the tragic loss of his son.

Swindoll, Charles. *Hope.* Portland: Multnomah Press, 1983. How hope serves as an anchor for the soul, and how knowing Jesus can bring you through dangerous waters.

Yancy, Philip. *Where Is God When It Hurts?* Grand Rapids: Zondervan, 1977. In dealing with the issues of pain and evil, this book asks and answers the questions of why pain exists and how we can cope with it.

For more information, write to

Jews for Jesus
60 Haight Street
San Francisco, CA 94102-5895
E-mail: *jfj@jewsforjesus.org*
Web: *www.jewsforjesus.org*